AND THEN CAME
THE BLUES

AND THEN CAME THE BLUES

MY STORY OF SURVIVAL ON BOTH SIDES OF THE BADGE

A MEMOIR

Katrina Brownlee

OPEN LENS

All rights reserved. No part of this book may be reproduced, stored in a retrieval system, or transmitted in any form, by any means, including mechanical, electronic, photocopying, recording, or otherwise, without the prior written consent of the publisher. Some people's names have been changed in this volume to respect the privacy of those individuals.

This memoir is a work of nonfiction, but certain names, identifying details, and specific events have been altered or fictionalized to protect the privacy and confidentiality of individuals. While the narrative is based on the author's personal experiences, any resemblance to real people, living or dead, is purely coincidental unless otherwise stated. This work is intended to reflect the author's perspective and experiences, and not to infringe upon the privacy or reputation of others.

Published by Akashic Books
©2025 Katrina Brownlee and Annie Tucker
All photographs inside the book courtesy of Katrina Brownlee

ISBN: 978-1-63614-236-4
Library of Congress Control Number: 2024949342

All rights reserved
First printing

EU Authorized Representative details:
Easy Access System Europe
Mustamäe tee 50, 10621 Tallinn, Estonia
gpsr.request@easproject.com

Open Lens
c/o Akashic Books
Brooklyn, New York
Instagram, X, Facebook: AkashicBooks
info@akashicbooks.com
www.akashicbooks.com

Also available from Open Lens

Climb: Taking Every Step with Conviction, Courage, and Calculated Risk to Achieve a Thriving Career and a Successful Life
by Michelle Gadsden-Williams
with Carolyn M. Brown

*Pressure Makes Diamonds:
Becoming the Woman I Pretended to Be*
by Valerie Graves

*And Then I Danced:
Traveling the Road to LGBT Equality*
by Mark Segal

The Roving Tree
by Elsie Augustave

Makeda
by Randall Robinson

I am an ambassador for the broken. This book is dedicated to anyone who has experienced hopelessness, homelessness, domestic violence, violation or neglect by law enforcement, suicidal thoughts, sexual abuse, addiction, teenage pregnancy, loss of faith in God, or heartbreak. You can find healing and turn your brokenness into wholeness. I have been carrying this torch of hope for a long time, and now I am ready to pass it on to you.

Table of Contents

Prologue: Scream All You Want   9
Chapter 1: What Happens to a Broken Heart?   17
Chapter 2: Growing Up Toxic   25
Chapter 3: Living in Pain   35
Chapter 4: The Beatdown   50
Chapter 5: Death Has Come   61
Chapter 6: Dancing with the Devil   68
Chapter 7: Only the Beginning   79
Chapter 8: Oh, This House Is Not a Home   94
Chapter 9: God Always Has the Last Word   109
Chapter 10: When the Doctors Said No, God Said Yes   117
Chapter 11: A Jury Not of My Peers   127
Chapter 12: Homelessness Is in My Rearview Mirror   133
Chapter 13: My Life with Jah-Quar   139
Chapter 14: Farewell, My Star   148
Chapter 15: A New Direction   157
Chapter 16: Until We Meet Again   165
Chapter 17: What God Has for You Is for You   172
Chapter 18: And Then Came the Blues   180
Chapter 19: 9/11   183
Chapter 20: Premonitions   187
Chapter 21: The Good Cop   197
Chapter 22: This Ain't *New York Undercover*   205
Chapter 23: No Ordinary Love   218
Chapter 24: Movin' On Up   229
Chapter 25: Forty, Fabulous, Farrakhan   238
Chapter 26: On to the Next   251

Chapter 27: The Call   263
Chapter 28: Another New Beginning   267
Chapter 29: Loss After Losses   272
Chapter 30: The Road to Resolution   280
Chapter 31: The Details of the Detail   289
Chapter 32: Messages from the Messenger   297
Chapter 33: No More Blues   308
Chapter 34: The Power of Prayer and Forgiveness   316
Chapter 35: Thank You, Rats   325
Epilogue: When It's All Said and Done   335

Acknowledgments   341

PROLOGUE

Scream All You Want

I had an eerie feeling as soon as my taxi driver pulled up in front of the house. The steely sky was thick with snowflakes, and the thought of leaving the cab and walking to the door made me shiver. The whole drive over, a voice inside me had been saying, *Don't do it. Don't go in there, guuurrrl. You don't need anything from him.* But on that cold January morning in 1993, I had no choice but to ignore the warnings. I needed my ex-fiancé to give me back my belongings. They were all I had.

A few weeks earlier, I had told Larry that I was ending our relationship. Years of arguments and abuse had finally convinced me that my two daughters, my unborn son, and I were better off on our own. I was five months pregnant when I left the home we shared on Long Island and moved to a hotel nearby. Since then, I had been living in a small room with seven-year-old Morgan and two-year-old Melissa.

I spent that time wondering how my children and I would survive. I was grateful to have a friend who had given me some money so that I could stay in the hotel temporarily, but now those funds were running out, and I had no job, no other place to live, limited education, and no stable family to support me. But Larry and I had been talking on the phone every night, and he seemed to be starting to understand why I couldn't be with him any longer.

One night, I called him with the hope that he would let me drop by the house to pick up some clothes for myself and my daughters. He answered the phone on the first ring, and when I asked how he was doing, he told me he was worried sick about us.

Despite everything he had done to me, he sounded so pitiful that I almost felt sorry for him. But when he asked me to tell him where I was, I told him I couldn't. "All you ever do is beat me and rape me when I don't want to have sex with you, and I can't take it anymore," I said.

"I'm so sorry, Trina. If you come back, I promise I'll never do any of that again."

I didn't believe him. "You've been doing it for too many years for me to trust you," I said. "And now that I'm pregnant again, I don't want this baby to go through what the girls have seen. I need a better life for us."

"I just love you so much." He was sobbing now. "The thought of not being with you makes me crazy."

For more than an hour, we stayed on the phone. "Please come home," he kept saying. "Please." But the sound of his voice made me sick. Now that I had gone several weeks without seeing him, I knew I was strong enough to survive on my own, no matter how hard it might be.

We talked a few more times over the next several days, and Larry finally stopped begging me to come home. All he wanted now, he said, was to be part of our children's lives.

When I asked him again if I could stop by our house and pick up some clothes, he agreed, so I said I'd come over the next morning. After that, I told myself, I would cut our ties for good and begin to rebuild my life.

I woke up to snow blanketing the ground and more accumulating each hour. I was physically and mentally exhausted, yet I knew I couldn't postpone what I had to do. Morgan had stayed overnight with a neighbor who lived across the street from Larry; I was planning to pick her up after I saw him. I dressed Melissa and myself in our warmest winter clothes and called a taxi.

During the short ride to Larry's, the driver tried to make small talk, but all I could hear was the sound of my own heart pounding. Despite the peaceful tone of my recent conversations with Larry, our house was still soaked through with pain, violence. It beat to a constant soundtrack of insults, objects crashing to the floor, and children screaming. Larry had kept me isolated there, forbidding me to work or see any of my friends, abusing me relentlessly. That house had come to represent loneliness and sadness, rather than the happy home I had hoped it would be when we first moved there.

A month earlier, I'd had a violent dream that Larry tried to kill me and I survived. I'd had visions like this before, dreams and premonitions, starting when I was a little girl. I had dreamed that my grandmother would be a victim of the Bed-Stuy slasher in the 1980s, two days before he assaulted her in front of her apartment building. I also knew that the child I was currently carrying was going to be a boy, because I had a dream about a baby in all blue, floating in water.

I hadn't been able to forget my dream about Larry, and it came to me again as the taxi pulled up to our house on Gray Avenue. My breath fogging up the back window, my toddler sleeping against my side, I shuddered as I looked at the house. *Just go in, get your stuff, and get out*, I told myself. *Everything will be better after you do that.*

I took a deep breath, picked up Melissa and the empty bags I had brought to pack my things in, and carried them up the front steps. When I turned my house key in the door lock, nothing happened. I jiggled the handle, but the key still wouldn't work. Just as I realized that Larry must have changed the locks, the door opened from the inside and he appeared.

I got straight to the point: "Let me just put the baby down, and then I'll pack up my stuff."

He didn't respond, though as he stepped aside to let me enter, I noticed his eyes. His pupils were the size of quarters—he looked like a madman. Even then, I told myself that as long as I was courteous and quick, I was doing the right thing by being there—I just had to get it over with.

I dropped my bags in the living room and then carried Melissa into the room she and Morgan had shared. She was still asleep, so I laid her on the bed and slipped out the door. I went into the master bedroom across the hall and opened the armoire where I kept my clothes.

All the drawers were empty.

Oh no, I thought. *No, no, no. This isn't right.* My stomach churned, and my pulse began to race. I walked toward the adjacent living room to ask Larry where my clothes were. When I came around the corner, his service revolver was aimed right at my face.

"This is the day you gonna die, bitch," Larry said, and shot me in my stomach—*boom, boom, boom*, three times, with perfect precision, as if I were one of the targets at the shooting range he had to practice at for his job.

I fell onto the couch, clutching my middle, thinking of my unborn baby—the baby Larry and I had conceived together. I looked down and saw that my stomach had gone flat, like a balloon that had popped. I could smell gun smoke, but I didn't see any blood. I had never even seen anyone fire a gun before, let alone at me.

All I could think to say was, "I'm not even bleeding."

Larry just looked at me with eyes possessed. "Shut up, bitch."

I pushed myself up off the couch and ran into the bedroom, where the telephone was, to dial 911, only to discover that Larry had cut the wires. I rushed back into the living room and over to the windows, thinking I could jump out, but each one I tried was sealed; Larry had nailed them shut. I started to yell for help, but Larry just laughed at me.

"You can scream all you want," he said. "Nobody's going to hear you. No matter where you go in this house, you won't be able to get out."

I started to shake; I felt like I was having a nightmare, but it was the real-life manifestation of the dream I'd had about Larry a month earlier. He had sat in this house and locked it all down. Everything he had said to me on the phone had been part of a scheme to lure me here.

In my dream, I had survived. But now, as I contemplated his words—"This is the day you gonna die"—I thought, *He's absolutely right. No one is going to save me.*

Larry knew he had me trapped now, and he was just getting started. "You don't love me? You don't want to be with me? I gave you everything you wanted, and it still wasn't enough! You fucking bitch!"

As he pointed his gun at me again, I thought, *If he's going to kill me over this, I should at least pretend to be willing to reconcile.* So I pleaded with him: "I *will* be with you, Larry! I promise!"

The fourth bullet hit my arm and sent me collapsing onto the floor. I tried to get up, but he started kicking me—in my face, my back, over and over, yelling, "Bitch, I hate you! You will die!"

I started screaming back at him: "You motherfucker! You lied to me! You set me up! Why the fuck are you doing this? You know I'm pregnant!"

Larry didn't respond; he just stood still, watching me, as if he were thinking, *You're so stupid. Don't you get that your life is about to end?*

I remember thinking that Larry must be planning a murder-suicide: first, he would kill me; then he would kill my daughter Melissa; then he would kill himself. I hadn't heard a sound from the bedroom where I had left the baby, so I assumed she was still asleep, though I imagined Larry would go right in there and shoot her too after he finished me off. *At least Morgan will get to live because she's not in the house right now*, I reasoned.

"Who's going to take care of the kids when I'm gone?" I asked him.

"My mother," he said. "Then I'll take care of them when I get out of jail. I'm only going to get five to fifteen anyway."

Five to fifteen years for first-degree murder? I thought. But he wasn't in the mood to talk anymore. He put a fifth bullet in me, this time in my butt.

Blood was pouring from my wounds now, but I still had enough adrenaline to crawl. I dragged myself across the floor uselessly, begging Larry to spare my life and the life of our baby, but his only response was to fire at me again.

I couldn't move anymore after that. I lay on the living room floor, a floor I had walked across countless times without ever realizing it might be the last thing I'd ever see, and began to fade in and out of consciousness.

A friend of mine had once told me about a movie in which a man had been shot and had played dead to avoid actually being killed. Larry began brutally beating me with a wooden board, which he must have purchased in advance and planted in the living room. I didn't know if he was still holding his gun, because I was too woozy to look. As he struck me in the head, I had the brief thought that maybe if I pretended to be dead, he would stop hurting me. It wouldn't be hard to do—I was so exhausted and in so much pain that I barely felt alive. My whole body was on fire from the bullets, as if people were holding torches to my skin. As I contemplated the possibility, everything went black.

I found out later that Larry dragged my unconscious body into our bedroom and stripped off my clothes, then took me into the bathroom and put me in the bathtub. After attempting to dress my wounds with Band-Aids—as if a tiny piece of plastic could have done anything to help me, or to cover up the atrocities he had committed—he left me in there to die.

People who want to fatally shoot someone will do it quickly—one bullet, in the head. Larry didn't want that for me. He wanted me to die, but he wanted it to happen slowly. He wanted to torture me first. He wanted to make me suffer.

Yet things didn't work out the way he wanted them to, because I had an angel watching over me. Larry's cousin Sha almost never came over, but sometime after I lost consciousness, he showed up unexpectedly at the house. He and Larry had spoken on the phone the day before, and something about the way Larry was talking had put Sha on alert, so he came over to check on things. When Larry answered the door, the first thing he said to Sha was, "Yo, I did it—I killed Trina."

Sha rushed into the house then, found me in the bathroom, and took me to the hospital. I don't remember the car ride, but Sha told me later that I woke up and started pleading with him: "Just let me die. I'm tired. Nobody's ever going to help me." But he just kept saying, "No, I'm not going to let you die. I won't let that happen to you." If he hadn't been there that day, I wouldn't be here now.

Sha drove me thirty minutes to a hospital in Patchogue, Long Island. When we got there, he didn't take me inside. He was afraid to be seen with me; he didn't want to become a suspect in an attempted murder. So he left me outside the doors to the emergency room, where the hospital staff found me.

I later learned that Larry had shot me ten times. The police retrieved ten shell casings from the crime scene and found bullet holes in my abdomen, my arms, my butt, and even my vagina. The father of my daughter Melissa, and of the baby I was carrying, had wanted to make sure I would never give birth again.

AND THEN CAME THE BLUES

At death's door, as I lay on the ground outside the hospital, my soul begged God to take mercy on me. Because this was not the end of my story, and it was also not the beginning of it. No, my story started many years earlier, in a broken family that didn't know how to love.

CHAPTER 1

What Happens to a Broken Heart?

My maternal grandparents grew up in adjoining towns in North Carolina but didn't meet until they moved to New York. They were married in the late 1940s and had five children together between 1948 and 1954. In the beginning, they loved each other and their children, and my grandfather took care of all of them. He worked as a carpenter while my grandmother, whom I always called Mommy, stayed home.

Mommy was a beautiful woman—light brown skin, straight black hair, slim build, five feet four inches tall—and it was a beautiful life, until two of their sons, Edward Jr. and Ivory, died at eighteen months and one year old, back to back, of sudden infant death syndrome. Then, when Mommy was five months pregnant with her fifth child, my mother, my grandfather left her for a white woman and never spoke to her or their children again.

With very little education and no money to support herself and her children, Mommy was evicted from her apartment and had to move with all of her kids into her mother's one-bedroom apartment. We called my great-grandmother, whose name was

Mary, Big Mother. She was dark-skinned and glamorous, with long fingernails always painted bright red.

My grandfather's mother, Nana, only made the situation more difficult. She was biracial—light-skinned, with striking green eyes and curly, brownish hair—and while she would have said she identified as mulatto, she obviously favored her white side. She treated all of her light-skinned grandchildren and great-grandchildren better than she treated the darker-skinned ones. I was the one exception; I was darker-skinned too, but she treated me like part of the "good" team. I always thought that was odd.

Nana had four sons; my grandfather was the oldest. Three of them were married, all of them had children, and none of them took care of their families, except Uncle Cee, who at least provided financially for his kids. Still, no matter what, those boys were perfect in Nana's eyes. Uncle Anthony and Uncle P both lived with her, and even though Uncle Cee didn't, he was over at her house every day with his brothers, eating the meals she was constantly cooking. She played the role of both a mother and a wife to all of them. Between her blind devotion to her children and her racist tendencies, when my grandfather met Frances, Nana was one of their biggest cheerleaders, rather than telling him to stop messing around, go home to his loving wife, and help her raise their kids. When they got married, they moved to a brownstone only five blocks from where Mommy lived, so she had to see him with his new wife all the time. Worse, my grandfather and Frances ended up adopting a biracial son, Michael, and my grandfather doted on him in a way he never had with his biological children. Whenever my grandfather saw Mommy, he acted like he didn't even know her or their kids. I'll never understand how he lived with that on his conscience, turning his back so suddenly on the people who loved him most, or why he couldn't see that his actions had consequences that would taint our family for generations to come.

My grandma, aka Mommy.

Meanwhile, Mommy didn't have anyone to turn to. She couldn't ask her own family for financial help. Her father had died when she was young, her mother was a factory worker who didn't have much income, and she had no siblings. Eventually, she went to my uncle Joe—a notorious Bed-Stuy drug kingpin, a man she had known since her youth in North Carolina, and someone who was like a brother to her.

He said, "Listen, I'm going to plug you in with NB"—one of the most notorious dealers in America from 1972 until his arrest in 1977. Mommy didn't do any drugs herself, but it wasn't uncommon for women in her neighborhood to get involved in that line of work because they had no other options. My aunt Crystal did the same thing after her husband left her with five kids. Lacking any other option, Mommy started bagging heroin for NB.

Mommy was fortunate to get out of the drug game when I was two, shortly before NB's empire was taken down. Eventually, she went to college and became a librarian at the Central Library on Grand Army Plaza in Brooklyn, where she became a supervisor and stayed until 1998. It was a perfect career for her because she had always loved to read, and it gave her a stable income. Once in a while, when I was little, she would take me to work with her. I would write stories, make stick people and houses for them, and read books. My love of reading started in that building. And everyone there revered Mommy, so they were always friendly to me. At lunchtime, she would take me to Blimpie and buy me my favorite sandwich—turkey and cheese, with lettuce, tomatoes, onions, and mayo on both pieces of bread. She had enough income by then that we could afford to eat out once in a while and go clothes shopping at Alexander's on Saturdays. On those weekend days, we would finish off our excursion at Woolworth, where I always ordered the same thing: a cheeseburger, fries, and a vanilla milkshake.

Mommy's financial circumstances were also improved somewhat by the fact that she was still legally married to my grandfather, despite his claims to the contrary, and that meant she was eligible to collect Social Security from him after he died. Frances and my grandfather had had a secret wedding ceremony, but they couldn't actually be legally wed because he and Mommy were never divorced, so when Frances went to get the Social Security payments for herself, the office told her she couldn't because her marriage wasn't valid.

Mommy always sent me to the corner where Frances and Grandpa lived to pick up the checks for her. Frances never let me come inside the house. She wouldn't even open the door or speak to me; she would draw the curtain to see who was on her doorstep, then slip the check underneath.

One day, I had an idea. When I heard her on the other side of the door, I called out, "Can I use your bathroom?" I didn't actually need to; I just wanted to get inside and take a good look around.

"No," her muffled voice called back.

Fine, I thought. I kicked the front door, hard, and ran all the way to the corner of her block.

Mommy once told me she thought those Social Security checks were my grandfather's way of apologizing to her for leaving. Between that money and her income from the library, she managed to survive, but her broken heart never healed from my grandfather's betrayal. He was her love, her life, her husband, her kids' father.

Mommy would always tell me, "People can look right at you and never know the pain that you're going through. They see you dressed up, they might see you smiling and think you're fine, but they never realize how much sadness you have going on inside you." I didn't fully understand what that meant until I was grown. Sometimes people just can't find a way to reconcile their exterior and interior selves, and when they don't, it destroys them. That's what happened to Mommy.

In no emotional condition to care for her children, Mommy raised my mother, Niecy, in a home with no rules, structure, or supervision. Niecy never knew her father, but she and Mommy were inseparable. Even after my mother began running around the neighborhood and doing drugs at a young age while Mommy was off working for NB, she still spent time with Mommy every day. That bond was not strong enough to keep Niecy safe, however, or to make her trust her mother with her biggest secret until it was too late for Mommy to help her. At sixteen, Niecy found out that she was pregnant and didn't tell a single person.

My first time going to Niecy's house.

The only person in her life who noticed what was going on was my godsister, Wilma. She told me a story, much later in my life, about a field trip she and my mother went on with their eleventh-grade class at the end of the school year, to the Great Adventure amusement park. It was summertime, hot outside, but Niecy wore a full poncho the whole day. A friend of Wilma's pointed at Niecy and said, "You know your friend is pregnant, right?"

Wilma said Niecy got on all the rides that day. She took me on the roller coasters with her. She just wanted to be a regular teenager and have some fun, and someone had ripped that chance away from her before she was ready to let it go.

Niecy gave birth to me in October 1970, at Beth Israel Hospital in New York. I was only five pounds when I was born, because she had never received proper medical care and had taken cocaine and smoked weed throughout her pregnancy.

Those roller coaster rides were our first and last mother-daughter bonding experience. Niecy didn't want me from the start. In the middle of the night, my grandmother's phone rang; it was a nurse from the hospital, calling to say that her daughter had given birth and left without her baby. Nobody knew where Niecy had gone. Mommy hadn't even known she was pregnant.

Mommy could have chosen to surrender me to the state, but that wasn't the kind of person she was. She wasn't about to abandon her own blood, the way her husband had. So she called my uncle Anthony and told him what had happened, and that she needed him to drive her to the hospital.

It was pouring rain that night. Uncle Anthony picked up Mommy, then Aunt Crystal, and the three of them rushed to the hospital to get me. There was far less protocol and red tape back then, and when they arrived, Mommy was allowed to name me. She had no idea what to call me until Aunt Crystal said, "Just name her Katrina, after my daughter." Uncle Anthony picked my middle name, Chantel, and Cooke was Mommy's last name. The doctors gave her permission to take me home, where she began to raise me as her own.

Mommy's pain—caused by a man who didn't have the integrity or the courage to honor his promises to her—drove her to alcoholism and destroyed her life. She was a good person who got a bad deal. Had she not, the younger generations of our family might have turned out differently. Every choice we make has consequences, and if we make bad ones, those choices don't affect only us; they also affect our children, and our children's children.

Being raised in Mommy's brokenness was the beginning of my toxic legacy, the start of a curse that extended through multiple generations in my family.

AND THEN CAME THE BLUES

My grandmother was the beginning of the first toxic generation.
Niecy was the beginning of the second.
I was the beginning of the third.

CHAPTER 2

Growing Up Toxic

One of the earliest memories I have is of attending the Together We Stand day-care center on Lexington Avenue in Brooklyn. It was eleven long city blocks from the house where I lived with Mommy, and she and I walked there together every morning, even in rain, sleet, or snow. We would count off the blocks together—one, two, three, all the way up to eleven—and then she would drop me off and continue on to the Central Library.

I can imagine what Mommy and I looked like to observers on those excursions: a beautiful professional woman and her adorable five-year-old granddaughter, holding hands while they strolled together out of their big brownstone on MacDonough Street.

Our building was three stories of red brick with shiny black trim and a shiny black gate. The exterior looked grand, like the home of a large, happy family. Mommy never left that house without looking impeccable, and she kept me just as nicely turned out, in little Buster Brown shoes and pretty dresses from Alexander's. Mommy always kept up with fashion, as I still do today. The environment people grow up in always has an impact on who they become: the where, the how, and, most of all, the why.

Despite our polished appearance, the inside of our home was a mess in every way. Just as Mommy said, the way a person looks on the outside doesn't always reflect their interior, and it was the same with our house.

After Niecy gave birth to me and left me at the hospital, she came back to Mommy's to live, but only for two months. Shortly after that, when she was only seventeen, she met a thirty-four-year-old man named Leo at Uncle Joe's, where he spent a lot of time, gambling and doing drugs, and moved in with him.

Mommy, my aunt Lilly, and I lived on the third floor of our brownstone. Lilly was Mommy's sixth and youngest child, ten years younger than Niecy and only six years older than I was. She was the product of a one-night stand between Mommy and a man who was never around, and she didn't like me because she was jealous of all the attention Mommy gave me. After all, Mommy was her mother, not mine, and Lilly was still a little girl. She was never able to forgive me for dividing her mother's attentions, or for the fact that the two of them were never as close as Mommy and I were, and she picked on me day in and day out. It was all about survival in that house. On the rare occasion I tried to interact with her, she would just snap, "Get out of here with your fresh-ass self," or, "You act too grown."

The bottom two floors of our brownstone were occupied by Uncle Joe, Aunt Helen, and their seven children. The adults lived on the first floor and the children on the second. Upstairs, where Mommy and I lived, was much quieter and neater. Uncle Joe was a well-known drug dealer, gambler, and pimp, and he had parties in his apartment almost every night. I rarely went down there, but whenever I did, there would be a pile of cocaine on the table, weed on the counter, and liquor in the cabinets. My whole family loved Al Green, so his music would always be playing in the background. There were usually one or two hookers hanging around, smoking cigarettes, dropping off the money they owed Uncle Joe for pimping them out. I could tell they were streetwalkers by the way they dressed: high, high heels, fishnet stockings, red lipstick, and revealing clothing.

That apartment smelled like fish every Friday night, when Aunt Helen would fry up a bunch of fish sandwiches on Wonder Bread while the men played cards in the kitchen. She sold those sandwiches, along with homemade french fries and cole slaw, for two dollars to her friends and neighbors. She would start cooking at around five o'clock in the afternoon, and people would come over all night long to pick them up, along with the bootleg alcohol that Uncle Joe sold.

On Fridays, I liked going to my aunt Crystal's house instead, when she would fry up her own fish, as well as crab. Aunt Crystal picked me up from day care most days when Mommy was working, and then Mommy would sometimes come over for dinner. She and Aunt Crystal would always drink white-label whiskey when they were together. Watching them and seeing how much fun they were having made me want to have fun too.

I was five years old when I started drinking the whiskey they left around. While Aunt Crystal cooked, I would sneak sips of her drinks. They tasted nasty, but I didn't let that stop me—I wanted to be like her and Mommy. After taking a swig, I would pop one of Aunt Crystal's peppermints to cover the smell of alcohol on my breath. If anyone ever noticed what I was doing, they never said, and since I never got caught, I didn't stop.

Just as there were no rules in Niecy's childhood, none existed in mine either. Uncle Joe was the source of a lot of the chaos in our brownstone. He was a handsome man with beautiful clothes, an intoxicating personality, and plenty of money from his work. Every time I saw him, he gave me cash. He also got most of the children in our family into drugs. He was proud of it, claiming that if he didn't give them drugs himself, the kids would try them anyway, and whatever they found on the street would be more dangerous than anything he gave them. He would start them on weed when they were preteens. By the time they were teenagers, the weed would turn into coke, and eventually the coke would turn into crack.

Even Uncle Joe, who was a big cokehead himself, ended up becoming addicted to crack. Fortunately, I was still too young for him to target me, but that didn't mean I was safe.

Growing up in a house full of people with no rules can be dangerous. Bad things go unnoticed simply because no one is watching. I grew up extremely fast—too fast—with no rules, no support, and no guidance, surrounded by addicts and criminals, abandoned by my own mother, lacking any structure or self-esteem. Although I didn't realize it until I was older, that environment made me a prime target for predators.

I was six years old when one of Uncle Joe and Aunt Helen's daughters, my seventeen-year-old cousin, Cherry, came upstairs to Mommy's apartment from one of Uncle Joe's parties and told me to get undressed.

"I need to give you a bath," she said. I couldn't understand why, because I usually washed up by myself, yet I did as I was told.

When my bath was done, she didn't give me a towel; instead, she made me stand there naked while I air-dried. The whole time, she just looked at my body. Then she massaged me all over with lotion, before telling me to get dressed.

After that night, Cherry came to "take care of me" every chance she could, and began to take things further and further. She would order me to touch or suck her breasts. I still remember how nasty they tasted. Or she would lift up my dress—the same kind of pretty dress I wore when Mommy walked me to day care—and lay me down and lick me all over, including inside my vagina. She would suck my toes, flip me over, and kiss me in places her lips should never have been. Tears flooded my cheeks, but I was too afraid to cry out loud because anytime I tried to refuse her, she said she would beat me. I was also terrified because Cherry was Niecy's best friend, and in my child's mind, I reasoned that maybe if I did what Cherry said, Niecy would be nicer to me.

I now realize that Niecy would never have taken the time to care about what was going on upstairs. She and the rest of my family were so busy getting high and drunk—they had no idea what was going on right over their heads, and I was too young to fully grasp what was happening to me. I just knew that I hated Cherry for what she was doing. She sexually abused me for two years, until I was eight.

The house I grew up in, and where I was molested.

Sexual abuse is a vicious cycle. Hurtful and self-destructive behaviors are passed down from one generation to the next, and they often don't stop until someone makes them stop—

until someone says, "This ends here." I eventually found out that Cherry had also molested one of my male cousins, who later became a molester himself. I sometimes wonder who abused Cherry.

This treatment at such a young age set the tone for what was to come for me. It made me realize that no one was ever going to protect me. I wish I could have seen the warning signs back then, but I was only six. Not until many years later would I realize that we have to dig deep within ourselves to defend ourselves from harm.

Niecy was beautiful. She must have looked like her father, because she was much taller and darker-skinned than Mommy. She had a gap between her two front teeth and wore big glasses that added to her appeal. She was very thin and bowlegged, and she always dressed well, like everyone else in my family. She would wear a nice shirt and a plaid skirt with two-tone shoes, or fitted jeans and a blouse with a belt and matching shoes and pocketbook. She was a chain smoker; if she wasn't holding a cigarette, she had a joint in her hand. And she always had a big stack of sterling silver bracelets on her wrist.

Niecy had an unforgettable presence. When she walked into a room, everybody knew she was there. She looked sophisticated and poised, even at just twenty-one years old. She would sit quietly, with her legs crossed, exuding a sense of *Don't get too close to me*. She worked for the New York Police Department as an administrative aide at the 5th Precinct, and on the side she was a salesperson for Avon perfume. I can still smell the fragrance she wore: Avon's Candid. I always knew when Niecy was at Mommy's house; I would follow that scent and the sound of her jingling bracelets to a closed door, where she talked with Mommy or Cherry on the other side. Peeking through the crack like a spy, I would sit there for as long as I could, watching the woman who had given birth to me and who acted as if I didn't exist.

All I ever wanted was Niecy's love, but she never showed me a single moment of kindness. Whenever she had time to come by Mommy's, it was only to say hello to her and to hang out with Cherry. Wherever Niecy was, Cherry was never far away—the person I wanted most to be close to, and the woman whom I wanted to get as far away from as possible. The two of them were cokeheads, so they would always end up downstairs, getting high at Uncle Joe's.

I knew not to play with Niecy, though that didn't mean I didn't try to get her attention. I began to steal candy out of her purse, just so she would notice me. The first time I did it, she said, "You better not steal my candy again." Of course, I did it again. The second time, she said, "I'm telling you right now, if you steal my candy again, I'm going to kill you. Just like I brought you into this world, I will take you out of this world."

When I was still five, Niecy gave birth to another child—my younger sister, Macey. Niecy brought her over to Mommy's every time she visited, and it hurt me to my core that Macey was wanted and loved while I was invisible. *What is wrong with me?* I asked myself.

Then, in the early summer just before I turned six, Mommy had to be away overnight and asked Niecy to take care of me while she was gone. As much as I wanted to be around Niecy, she still felt like a stranger, and between her rejection and Cherry's abuse, I was developing a strong distrust of women other than Mommy. However, when Niecy came to Mommy's house to pick me up, I had no choice but to go with her back to the apartment she shared with Leo.

The first thing I noticed was how dark it was. There were virtually no lights on. And the whole place smelled like incense. She kept it burning all the time to cover up the smell from the cigarettes and joints she was always smoking. The apartment was immaculate, yet that didn't stop it from feeling gloomy.

Leo was sitting at the kitchen table when we arrived, smoking a cigarette in the dark. I could tell that although he looked good on the outside, he had a dark energy on the inside, just like Uncle Joe. Leo always had on a suit and a cap. His shoes were always shined. He always smelled good. A Camel cigarette always dangled from his lips. He was tall and thin, with a tiny waist. Everyone thought he was a pimp because of the way he dressed and acted, but he wasn't; prostitutes would pay him to protect them while they were out on the streets, because he was well respected and no one would mess with him. Leo and Niecy looked perfect together, but I'd overheard Mommy telling people on the phone how the two of them argued all the time, and how he was cheating on her and abusing her.

Leo put out his cigarette, stood up, and walked down the hallway to the back bedroom. A few minutes later, he called to Niecy to join him. She carried my baby sister with her to put her in her crib. After their door slammed shut, I heard Leo calling Niecy all kinds of names. Then he began beating her, dragging her all over the bedroom floor. Her screams and cries echoed throughout the apartment. I stood alone in the kitchen, shaking and trying to stay quiet. I didn't know where to go because I had never been to their apartment before. Everything I had heard Mommy talking about during her phone calls was playing out just down the hall from me.

When Leo had finished beating Niecy, he left without saying a word to me. Niecy eventually came out of the back room and cleaned herself up. She walked over to her record player, and I watched how gently she placed the huge needle on the Al Green album she selected. That was one lesson I learned from her: how to treat vinyl properly.

As "Love and Happiness" began to play, Niecy started to prepare dinner. All the while, she didn't say a single word to explain what had just happened. I had seen many of my relatives high and drunk, but I had never witnessed anyone in my family being beaten. I immediately hated Leo for hurting Niecy, and began to blame him for the fact that Niecy wasn't in my life. In my mind, he had to be the reason she never spoke to me. He had to be the reason she didn't care about me. He had to be the reason she never hugged me, kissed me, or showed me any love. *It's because of him*, I told myself, and that made me feel a tiny bit better.

Later that evening, Niecy called me to the dinner table and set out a plate of food for me. Despite the beating she'd just endured, she had prepared chicken, rice, and brussels sprouts.

"I don't eat brussels sprouts," I announced.

"Don't tell me what you don't eat. You will not leave this table until you finish them," she said, before leaving the kitchen to go smoke weed in her bedroom. When I was sure she was gone, I stashed some of the brussels sprouts under the table and the rest in my underwear. When she returned, the plate was clean and she excused me.

A little while later, Niecy told me to watch my sister while she went to the store. After she left, I flushed the brussels sprouts down the toilet. Then I went into Macey's room and took her out of her crib. I struggled to carry her back to the kitchen, where I turned on the oven, opened the door, and placed her inside.

I can still remember how she screamed when her stomach touched the hot oven rack, but I left her there anyway. I was trying to bake her.

When Niecy came back from the store and didn't see my sister in her crib, she asked me where the baby was. I pointed to the oven. I now thank God that she hadn't been gone very long.

"You put my baby in the oven?" she asked.

I remained silent as she rushed to the stove and took Macey out. Amazingly, she didn't hit me or even scream at me—she just sent me to bed.

When Leo came home a few hours later, I was still awake. He must have seen Macey's burns, because I heard him ask Niecy, "What the fuck happened to my daughter?"

"Oh," she replied, "she fell on the stove while I was warming up her milk. I had to hold her because she was crying."

Niecy had barely finished her sentence before I heard the sound of Leo's fist hitting her face. I pulled my covers over my head, shaking and crying, because I knew what had happened was my fault. I had hurt my sister only because I was resentful and angry about my family, not because I wanted to cause her or Niecy pain. Macey has burn marks on her stomach to this day because of what I did to her.

Leo beat Niecy for what seemed like hours. I eventually crawled out of bed and hid in the doorway, watching as he pummeled her to a bloody pulp. When he was finished, he slumped in the same kitchen chair he had been sitting in when Niecy and I first showed up, and lit a Camel cigarette.

Feeling my eyes on him from the doorway, Leo turned around and said I could never come to their house again. After that, I didn't return until years later.

CHAPTER 3

Living in Pain

By the time I was almost eight, the partying downstairs in our brownstone had gotten out of control, and so had Uncle Joe's gambling—so much so that he lost the whole building in a bet. He had been a poker player for years. People bet heavy on cards, and back then, if you didn't deliver on a bet you lost, you got killed.

Mommy must have been devastated to have to leave her home, but all she said to me about it was, "We've got to move. Uncle Joe lost the house. I knew all that gambling would catch up to his Black ass someday."

We moved in with Mommy's boyfriend, Mr. Mitch, a tall, dark-skinned, handsome sanitation worker, also originally from North Carolina. Mommy never told me about him until right before we went to stay with him. He never came by our brownstone. In fact, I don't know if they were even romantically involved until we were all living under the same roof. But I didn't mind; his brick building was right around the corner from ours, and his apartment was similar, except now I had my own bedroom and didn't have to share with Aunt Lilly anymore.

Mr. Mitch's landlords were a mother and daughter from Bermuda. The mother used to play Minister Louis Farrakhan on the radio every day, and I would sit on the stoop and listen. *One day*, I told myself, *I'm going to meet that man.*

For more than a year after we left our building, Mommy, Aunt Lilly, and I didn't have a place of our own. Mommy was on a waiting list to get into a nearby housing project, and in the meantime we continued to stay with Mr. Mitch.

Although much was uncertain during that period, some light did shine through. For my eighth birthday, Mommy let me have a party at my favorite restaurant, McDonald's. It was the only birthday party I had ever had; I kept begging her and begging her until she gave in. She told me I could invite ten friends, but I invited more—two people from my block, some of my cousins, a couple of Mommy's friends and their grandchildren. Even Niecy was there. She didn't interact much with me, but this McDonald's was one of the few where people could have parties inside the restaurant, and it was right in her neighborhood in Bushwick, so I realized she must have been the one to arrange the event. She brought Cherry with her, but at least by then I wasn't living in a house where she could get to me. I avoided speaking to her or even making eye contact.

I wore a pretty party dress and Mary Jane shoes, and all of my guests and I got burgers, fries, and cookies to eat. I lined up all those cookies in front of me and didn't want to share them with anyone because I loved them so much; I even stashed some in a party-favor bag so that I could take them home and eat them later that night. Because I was the birthday girl, I had my first Big Mac ever, and it tasted so good that from that day on, every time I went to McDonald's, I ordered a Big Mac. Ronald McDonald came and did balloon tricks for us. We all pointed at his big red shoes and laughed. And because I was a bad kid and had to test my limits, I punched him in the stomach, and my friends did too.

People brought me all kinds of gifts—mostly nice outfits,

because they knew I was into fashion. I remember starting to open some of them and Mommy saying, "Wait until you get home so you can try everything on."

I almost never got to feel like a regular kid, but for two whole hours I forgot about the fact that Cherry had molested me, that Mommy was a drunk, and that Niecy didn't love me. I wanted that day to last forever.

When I was nine years old and Macey was four, Mommy and Niecy decided to send the two of us to Leo's mother's house in Virginia for the summer. I hated the idea. Macey didn't feel like my sister because we didn't live together. I had never even met Grandma Gigi before. And I was going to a whole other state, the farthest I had ever been away from home and the longest I had ever been apart from Mommy. The only thing that excited me about the trip was that I got to travel on an airplane for the first time. I had a window seat and looked out at the clouds for the entire flight.

Macey and I arrived at the tiny, crowded brown house on a humid, ninety-degree afternoon. As soon as I met Grandma Gigi, I could tell she didn't have any plans to make the summer fun for us. She didn't welcome us warmly or seem to have considered that two little girls from New York would be bored out of their minds in a home full of people they didn't know, including Grandma Gigi's sixteen-year-old daughter Riley; and Grandma Gigi's three nieces and a nephew, whom she was raising.

Every day, we followed the same routine. We watched TV all day, and if we wanted to go outside, we had to sit on Grandma Gigi's stoop. The only time we ever went anywhere was to church on Fridays and Sundays. I had almost never been to church before, but now, Grandma Gigi made us pray every night before bed. On Sundays, we weren't allowed to wear pants, watch TV, or wash any clothes. Grandma Gigi treated Macey and me like her servants. She was obese and could hardly walk, and would bark out orders for us to get her soda or ice cream from the refrigerator.

I complained to Grandma Gigi, telling her I wanted to go home, but after a few days of listening to me whine, she decided I was being disrespectful. That finally got her up off the couch. She went outside, picked a switch from a tree, and beat every inch of my butt, shutting me up for the rest of the summer.

Grandma Gigi always seemed to have enough energy to snatch up Macey and me and beat us. One time when we were on our way to church, Macey wanted to sit next to the window in the car, but she forgot to lock the door, and as Grandma Gigi began driving, the door flew open and Macey fell out.

Grandma Gigi stopped the car, yanked Macey back inside by her arm, and locked the door without saying a word. She never even asked if Macey was all right. The whole time we were at church, she didn't utter a word about the incident, though as soon as we got home, she went outside and got herself another switch. She beat Macey for falling out of the car, and she beat me for letting Macey fall. I couldn't wait to go home. I would take the drinking and drugs and neglect going on there any day over Grandma Gigi's abuse.

Riley was just as mean as her mother. One day, Macey and I were sitting with her on the stoop when one of Riley's friends strolled by. When she asked if Macey and I were Riley's cousins, Riley replied, "No, the little one is my niece. She's my brother's daughter. The big one is her sister."

I couldn't understand what she meant. *Leo is my father too*, I thought. *Why didn't Aunt Riley say we were both his daughters?*

Later that evening, the question was still bothering me, so I asked Aunt Riley why she had told her friend that I wasn't her niece.

"Because you ain't," she snapped. "When my brother met your mama, you was already born."

I felt sick to my stomach, and I ran inside and cried. Leo had never shown me any affection, but neither had Niecy, so I just assumed that was how my parents were. No one had ever actually told me that Leo was my father, yet no one had said he wasn't, either, so I had always figured that because he was with Niecy, he was my daddy—a daddy who didn't care about me, but my daddy nonetheless.

My body was so numb from this revelation that the next time Grandma Gigi beat me with her switch, I didn't even feel it. In fact, I became so numb after that incident that I started acting out as much as I could, because it was the only way I could think of to feel alive.

As soon as I got back home to New York, I asked Mommy who my father was. She said she didn't know. "And even if I did," she added, shrugging, "it wouldn't matter because he wouldn't have done nothin' for you anyway."

I heard Mommy's words loud and clear, but I couldn't absorb them. My father had to be out there somewhere, and he couldn't be any worse than Niecy and Leo. After that, I wondered about every single man who came around my family, and I asked everyone—I mean *everyone*; I didn't care if it was the mailman—if they knew who my father was. But nobody could give me an answer, and after a while, Mommy got sick of hearing me ask about it.

"Listen, little girl," she finally said, "when I found out your mother was pregnant with you, I asked her who she got pregnant by, and she said to me she didn't want to talk about it, so I never asked her again."

I wasn't willing to give up. "So, your young daughter had a baby and you didn't even question her about it?"

"For what?" Mommy snapped. "Your father knows who you are, and he knows you're alive. If he cared about you, he would have come around!"

"Well, why didn't I just live with Niecy, then?"

Mommy could have made something up, but she must have thought it was best to be brutally honest with me. "Your mother didn't want you, Trina," she said. "That's why I took you."

"But why didn't she want me?" I asked.

Mommy just said, "You've got to ask her that. She left you in the hospital."

I started to have the same sick feeling I had experienced when I found out that Leo wasn't my father. I had not yet found God, but I had learned about prayer at Grandma Gigi's. She had told us that if we prayed for something, it would come to us. I knew that was true, because I had prayed to come home to Mommy's and it had worked. So now I began praying to God and asking him to bring my father to me, begging God to show me who he was. *Do I look like him? Talk like him? Walk like him? Does he like the same foods I like? What's his favorite color?*

The more questions I asked, the more I prayed, the more obsessed I became with my mission to find out more. Eventually, I became suspicious. If no one could answer my simple question, maybe my father was someone who shouldn't have been my father.

The only person I didn't ask was Niecy, because I was too afraid. Not only did she not want me or love me enough to tell me much of anything, I also feared she would tell me she didn't know either, and I didn't think I could handle that.

One afternoon in early 1980, Mommy came home from work waving a letter in the air before she'd even taken off her coat. "Child, we're moving into the projects!"

"Which projects?" I asked.

She said we would be living in the same place as Aunt Dorothy. Mr. Mitch was planning to keep his house but would be with us most of the time. We would have only two bedrooms, meaning I would have to share with Aunt Lilly, but it was going to be our first real home in more than a year.

On a sunny morning in March, Mr. Mitch packed up his car and transported everything we owned over to the Brevoort projects. Our new address was 340 Bainbridge Street, apartment 7D. The russet-colored brick building had seven floors with five apartments on each floor.

Our first night there, Mr. Mitch and Mommy slept in one bedroom and Aunt Lilly and I slept in the other. As we began to settle into our new space, I usually had the room to myself because Aunt Lilly was always out in the street. But just because we had a new home didn't mean it was a happy one. Soon after we moved to Brevoort, I began to notice that Mommy was drinking alcohol more frequently than she used to. She said that my grandfather was the one who had introduced her to it, and that she had been only an occasional social drinker with him. Within a few months, she was drinking every night and every weekend, so heavily that she blacked out sometimes. Monday through Thursday, she drank Night Train Express wine. Friday, Saturday, and Sunday, she drank white-label whiskey. Everybody in the neighborhood knew what she was up to—she never hid it—but even in a drunken stupor, she still smelled good and dressed well. And somehow, she never missed a day of work.

Mommy's routine was the same every day. She would wake up at five o'clock in the morning, turn on 1010 WINS, light a Kool cigarette, and brew Maxwell House coffee. After she poured her coffee, she bathed, then put on her face while wearing a special robe she had for just that purpose. She never wore a lot of makeup—all she needed was a little foundation and her signature red lipstick. She ironed her clothes every morning and always had a complete outfit—if she wore a skirt, it had a matching jacket to go along with it. Nothing about her appearance was ever out of place.

Every night when she came home from work, she would put on a little lounge gown, pour herself a drink, light up a fresh cigarette, and get dinner on the table. Mondays we had leftovers. Tuesdays through Fridays, she would cook. She liked to make fish on Fridays if we weren't going to my aunt Crystal's. We always had food no matter what, although when she cooked on the weekends, she would always burn it because she was too drunk.

When Mommy and her friends went out drinking, they frequented the Casablanca Lounge in our neighborhood, and they often took me along. Mommy would let me sit at the bar with her like I was a grown woman. She would order her drinks, and, as usual, whenever she got up, turned her back, or walked away, I helped myself to whatever was in her glass. Sometimes she would look at her cocktail and say, "Now, I *know* I didn't drink this that fast!" But I never let on that I was the one stealing drinks, and once she was intoxicated enough, she stopped noticing. Sometimes she managed to stumble home; other times she fell down on the way or just passed out right on the bar.

But any routines Mommy adhered to, good or bad, were just a facade covering up a crumbling soul. Her drinking began to affect her relationships, and that included her relationship with Mr. Mitch. Despite Mommy's claim that he would continue to spend much of his time with us even after we moved out of his apartment, we started to see less and less of him over our first few months at Brevoort. Then one morning, Mommy woke me up early and told me to get dressed because we were going to his house.

When Mommy rang the doorbell, her friend Ms. Brown answered the door. Mommy asked why she was there, and Ms. Brown didn't respond; she simply told Mommy that Mr. Mitch was upstairs in bed.

Mommy was not a confrontational woman. She was humble and soft-spoken. She didn't go after Ms. Brown that day; instead, when Mr. Mitch appeared on the top step, she asked him what was going on. He tried to make excuses, yet Mommy knew he was lying. She was a sweetheart, but she wasn't a fool.

I felt sorry for Mommy. Mr. Mitch was the second man to break her heart by leaving her for another woman.

When Mr. Mitch came to our apartment a few days later, Mommy wouldn't let him in. She talked to him briefly through the door, but that was the last time I ever saw or heard from him. After the grief my grandfather had caused her, Mommy had no tolerance for another betrayal.

We were still living at Brevoort when I started junior high at a Catholic school called New Bed-Stuy. Mommy sacrificed a lot for me to go there, but all my friends went to the local public junior high school, JHS 35, and talked about how much fun they were having.

I asked Mommy if I could go to public school too, and to my surprise she agreed. By then, alcohol was her top priority. She was drinking so much that whenever she sent me to the liquor store, the people working there knew exactly who I was. "Oh, that's Ms. Cooke's granddaughter," they'd say. "She wants a pint or half a pint." As long as I got those bottles for her, she let me do whatever I wanted.

As soon as I enrolled at JHS 35, I started getting into trouble. I didn't like studying, and my teachers didn't seem to care whether their students got an education, so that made it easy for me to cut class. Whenever I got the urge, I would just walk right out the door. I was in the principal's office almost every day for something stupid. I often picked fights with other kids; all anyone had to do was mean-mug me, and I'd be on them, punching and pulling hair. Eventually, I hit a teacher with a chair—ironically, for speaking rudely to the school principal, Ms. Williams, whom I actually liked—and Ms. Williams suspended me.

My school had called Mommy several times to tell her about my bad behavior, but she always said she wasn't willing to take time off work to visit the principal's office. This time, Ms. Williams announced that the only way I could return to school was if my mother—not Mommy, but my actual mother, Niecy—addressed the issue. That was something I definitely didn't want to happen, so, in a panic, I went to Julie, my next-door neighbor in my building, and asked her for help.

Julie was in her late twenties. She was beautiful and fashionable, and we always talked about clothes and her daughter's father, whom she was madly in love with, even though he was always cheating on her.

I felt comfortable enough with Julie to ask her to pretend to be my mother and meet with the principal. Our lie went over so smoothly that I didn't learn a thing from the punishment, and not long after that, I got suspended again, for having two fights in one day. This time, the school called my house and Mommy told Niecy what I had done. I knew I couldn't lie my way out of this one, because if Niecy went to my school, she would find out what I had asked Julie to do.

When we arrived at the school, Principal Williams realized immediately that Niecy and Julie were two different people and ratted me out.

"Who the fuck you have come up here pretending to be me?" Niecy said, and I had no choice but to tell her the truth. Niecy assured Principal Williams that she wouldn't have any more problems with me, then dragged me out of the office and straight back to the Brevoort projects. She hurried me up to Julie's apartment and banged on the door until Julie opened it.

"You stay the fuck away from Trina!" Niecy yelled. "If I find out you've been hanging out with her, I'll beat your ass!"

I remembered the time Niecy had threatened to kill me just for stealing her candy, so I knew she was serious. As much as I loved Julie, I steered clear of her after that—at least, until I found myself in a situation where only she could help me.

* * *

When I returned to school after my second suspension, I stopped getting in so many fights. I had learned my lesson. To distract myself, I started spending time with an older boy named Sam. He was eighteen, five foot eleven, and light skinned; he had nice clothes and a funny personality. I saw him almost every day on the way to school because he was always perched in front of Ms. Lucky's, the store where I bought candy right across the street from JHS 35.

One day, Sam asked me if he could walk me home from school. I was only thirteen, and I couldn't believe someone five years older was showing interest in me. For the next two weeks, he walked me home, telling me how pretty I was and how nicely I dressed, so the day he asked me to go to his house after school, I said yes.

When we arrived, he introduced me to his family, then took me to his room, where he had sneakers stacked to the ceiling and a closet full of clothes. When he took off his shoes, I tried to ignore how bad his feet smelled.

We watched TV for a while, and then Sam started kissing my neck. He whispered in my ear, "Take off your pants." I didn't want to, but I was afraid that if I didn't, he wouldn't like me anymore, so I did what he said.

Sam crawled on top of me right away. Rough and heavy, he forced himself into my vagina until I started bleeding. I hadn't even gotten my period yet, and for a moment I thought he had brought it on; I didn't realize he was just tearing me apart.

Once Sam was finished, he rolled over without saying a word. I put my clothes back on and lay next to him in silence while he fell asleep. *Is he ever going to talk to me again?* I wondered. *Or did he just want to have sex with me?* Maybe this was just normal behavior for teenagers after sex. How could I have known? My only experiences with intimacy so far had been nonconsensual.

At around three a.m., I got up and walked home by myself. Sam didn't offer to go with me, and I didn't ask him to.

The next day, I was too embarrassed to go to school and see him standing in front of the candy store, so I told Mommy my stomach hurt. I realized she didn't believe me because she knew I had come in late the night before, but she let me stay home anyway.

Eventually I had to go back to school, and there was Sam, standing right where he always was. I thought he might not speak to me, but he invited me again and again back to his house, where I continued to allow him to have sex with me. I always went home alone, and I always felt awful afterward, but in my mind, he was my first boyfriend and this was what I owed him.

What I didn't know was that my boyfriend had a girlfriend, a big girl named Cheeks who was a little older than Sam. He always said that she just had a crush on him, but one day when the three of us were together, she asked him why I hung around him so much.

"I don't know. I guess she just on my dick," he said, shrugging.

Not long after that, Cheeks approached me in front of Sam's house. "Hey, little bitch," she said, "get out of here! You always in my man's face!"

"Who you calling a bitch, you fat Black bitch?" I yelled.

Those words set everything off, and we started fighting. Even though she was bigger than I was, I was stronger, so Sam jumped in on her side. Of course that pissed me off even more.

After a couple minutes, Sam's brother broke up the fight. "Go home, Katrina!" he said.

"Yeah, take your ass home! Every time I see you, I'ma beat your ass!" Cheeks chimed in.

"Yeah? How you gonna do that when you couldn't even do it the first time?" I shouted back.

That was the end of my relationship with Sam. I would still

see him by the store—the only place he ever seemed to be—and he would try to get me to come to his house, but I wouldn't do that anymore. I didn't want to feel sad about him; I wanted to make him jealous. I started dating a seventeen-year-old named Tis. He had been trying to talk to me before I started messing with Sam, though I had always ignored him. Now, I started giving him some play. Before long, I was cutting school regularly so that we could go to my house and have sex while Mommy was at work. He lived with his mother and his siblings in a small one-bedroom apartment, so we could never do our business inside, yet we did hang out on his stoop a lot. He and his sister Star, who was six years older than he was, became my very close friends during that time. We would listen to Run-D.M.C. and sing along to the Stephanie Mills song "Sweet Sensation" on her boom box.

After I had been sleeping with Tis for about a month, I got my period for the first time. I was afraid to tell Mommy because she had never talked to me about menstruation or sex. She discovered that my cycle had started only when she saw blood in my underwear one day while doing laundry. She went and bought me pads, but she never mentioned it again, and neither did I.

A month or so later, in February 1985, I started throwing up and couldn't get out of bed. At first, I thought I had a stomach bug. I hadn't gotten my period recently either, but since it was still a new thing for me, I assumed that it had just gone away and would come back later.

For weeks, whenever I wasn't in school, I lay on the couch, nauseated and exhausted, with a bucket by my side in case I couldn't get to the toilet quickly enough to throw up. I sometimes saw Mommy looking at me out of the corner of her eye. Even in a drunken stupor, she must have seen the obvious signs, but she never said anything. On the rare occasion that anyone came to the house, I would go into my bedroom and close the door.

After about four months of being sick, I couldn't deny to myself that I was pregnant. That made me feel even sicker, but I didn't want to tell anyone. I was too ashamed and too confused and too young to know what to do. I was only fourteen years old. I was still playing with dolls. And I had grown up believing that I was worthless, that I would never amount to anything, that I destroyed people's lives.

Whenever Tis called, I refused to talk to him. When he dropped by the house, I told Mommy to lie and say I wasn't there. After a few months of that treatment, he gave up and stopped coming around.

As much as I didn't want to talk about it, I also knew I didn't want to keep the baby. I had to get advice from someone who wasn't part of my family. Eventually, I went over to Julie's apartment and confided in her that I was pregnant. Once again, she pretended to be someone else. She let me use her Medicaid card and took me to get an abortion, but when they asked for a picture ID, we left the clinic because we didn't look anything alike.

I didn't know what to do. I began deliberately falling down the steps in my building, hoping that I would have a miscarriage. I would start at the top of the stairs, lie on my belly, and go *bump, bump, bump*, all the way down. I did that over and over for a week, but it didn't work.

As my stomach continued to grow, I stopped going outside and spent every day on the couch. It was summertime by then, and I was thankful that I didn't have to go to school anymore.

Mommy had still not uttered a word to me about my condition, until one day when I was about seven months along. As I was walking to the bathroom, she glanced at me and said, "You pregnant."

I just looked at her and didn't say a word.

A few days later, Niecy came over to the house. "Your daughter is with child," Mommy told her.

"What are you talking about?" Niecy asked. She looked right at me, possibly for the first time ever.

"Look at her," Mommy said. "Isn't it obvious? You should know. You did the same thing when you were pregnant with her."

As much as I had always wanted Niecy to talk to me more, all I wanted now was for her not to speak. "Are you pregnant?" she asked.

"I think so," I mumbled, looking down at the floor.

As she leveled her gaze at me, I saw the previous generation of trauma forming storm clouds in her eyes. "I'm taking you to get an abortion tomorrow," she said, and stormed out of the apartment.

CHAPTER 4

The Beatdown

The next morning, Niecy showed up at Brevoort to take me to the doctor's office. The whole walk there, she cursed me out, calling me a stupid motherfucker and every other name she could think of. "Bitch, you getting an abortion, so don't even think you keeping this baby!" she yelled. "You're an embarrassment to this family."

"Oh yeah? *You* were an embarrassment to our family when you had me," I snapped back, my mind racing. *Are you serious right now?* I thought. *You've never even talked to me, and now, all of a sudden, you're screaming at me in the street?*

When we arrived at the doctor's office, the nurse made me pee in a cup and drew my blood. Niecy accompanied me into the examination room, where I put on a gown and waited for the doctor to come in. He performed a quick exam without saying much, then instructed me to get dressed and meet him in his office.

While I was putting my clothes back on, I avoided looking at my belly. I had been staying away from mirrors for months because I couldn't bear to see my reflection. Although I was carrying small, I knew that if I caught a glimpse of my new shape, it would make everything too real. I just kept thinking, *This can't be happening. This can't be happening.*

Once I was dressed and Niecy and I were seated before the doctor, he told us that I was twenty-seven weeks pregnant, due in about two months.

"But she's getting an abortion," Niecy said.

"I'm sorry," the doctor said, "but Katrina is too far along for that."

Niecy's eyes narrowed for a moment. Then she turned and hit me so hard, she knocked me right out of my chair.

The doctor remained in his seat and never said a word as he watched me fall to the floor. I curled into a ball as Niecy stood over my body and hissed, "You *will* give this baby up for adoption, so don't get attached."

All of the humiliation that I had already experienced that day still wasn't enough to satisfy Niecy. When we left the hospital, she took off her thick leather belt and began to beat me right on the sidewalk. People nearby gaped at us as she dragged me along, yelling, "This stupid bitch is only fourteen, and she's pregnant!" as if that would justify her actions. Everyone watching her must have thought she was crazy, yet that didn't mean anyone intervened to stop her from hitting me again and again.

Niecy was making such a scene that eventually a police car pulled up to the curb. As the officers rolled down their windows, I thought, *Finally, someone's going to help me.*

But then Niecy explained to them that I had gotten pregnant at only fourteen years old. She said, still brandishing her belt, "If you have a problem with what I'm doing, you can get out the car and get some too." Whether they were afraid of getting hurt or figured I deserved to have my butt whooped for being young and stupid, they simply drove off without saying another word.

Does anyone even care if I live or die? I wondered. *Even the police won't help me.* I couldn't have known then how many times in the future I would have the same thoughts.

When Niecy finally stopped beating me long enough to

catch her breath, she asked who had gotten me pregnant. I reluctantly revealed that Tis was the baby's father.

She said, "Tell me his address."

When we got to Tis's house, Niecy banged on the window until Tis's mother answered the door. Niecy pushed her way inside, yelling, "Do you know your son got my daughter pregnant and she's only fourteen? She can't get an abortion! She's putting the baby up for adoption!"

I anticipated a similarly dramatic reaction from Tis's mother, but she only shrugged. "Tis isn't home, but I'll tell him." Maybe she just thought, *Boys will be boys*. Maybe she had other problems on her mind. Whatever her reason, she seemed as unfazed by the news as Niecy was rattled.

"You do that," Niecy said. "You also tell him to stay the fuck away from my daughter, because he ruined her life. And fuck you too."

When we got back to Mommy's apartment, Niecy started beating me all over again. She was so enraged that she just couldn't stop. It was as if all those years she had given me the silent treatment came to a head on that one morning.

Mommy tried her best to calm Niecy down and protect me from her blows. When Niecy told her, "She's putting that baby up for adoption," Mommy looked right at me with sad eyes. It was the first sign of compassion I had seen from anyone in months.

"Is that what you want, Katrina?" Mommy asked.

"It don't matter what she wants!" Niecy yelled before I could answer. "I'm not taking care of no baby, and neither are you!"

Mommy didn't say anything to that. She knew better than anyone that when Niecy made up her mind about something, no one could get in her way.

That night, I cried myself to sleep. Niecy was right—I *was* stupid. I had gotten myself into this situation, and now I was trapped.

* * *

I felt like a prisoner in every way: in my own body; in Mommy's apartment; and among my family and friends. When I admitted to the Macmillan sisters who lived in the building across from us that I was pregnant, their mother told them they weren't allowed to hang with me anymore because I was "too damn fresh." For years after that, I couldn't shake her characterization of me. *Maybe I really am worthless,* I thought.

My friend Shanice was the only one who still called or visited. The fact that I was pregnant didn't seem to bother her nearly as much as it bothered me. My pregnancy felt eternal, especially because I wasn't doing any of the things other expectant mothers do to bond with their unborn children. Niecy's warning, *Don't get attached*, kept echoing in my head.

Although my isolation and shame kept me inside almost all the time, one day I had a craving for a pickle, so I headed to the neighborhood deli. I didn't realize until too late that it was Brevoort Day, where all the families in our housing project gathered to barbecue outside. Before I could hurry back upstairs, a girl named Sharon approached me and told me she was Tis's girlfriend.

"I just had a son by him, and you're fucking up my family by having this baby," she said.

"I don't know how I'm doing that," I responded. "I don't even want Tis."

"That's not what he said."

"I don't care what he said to you—I'm telling you, I don't want him. He calls every day, and I barely talk to him."

If Sharon had chosen to believe me, we could have resolved the issue right then, but she couldn't let it go. Instead, she told me that I had better stay away from Tis, or else I would have a real problem. That was all I needed to hear. Too many people had already kicked me around, and I wasn't going to let another threat slide. Instead, I decided to get Tis back. The next time he called, instead of dismissing him, I kept him on the line, acting sweet and working him over to ensure that his alleged girlfriend wouldn't have his attention much longer.

I was fourteen. I should have been playing with dolls, not boys. But, having spent my formative years being molested, beaten, and neglected, I had no idea how to love or respect myself. All I wanted was for someone to notice me, and I was willing to do anything to make that happen.

During the final weeks of my pregnancy, I became a popular topic of gossip around my neighborhood. On the rare occasion that I left Mommy's apartment, I heard people whispering and giggling about me when I walked by. And Niecy only became more embarrassed by me as my due date approached. But I didn't care much what Niecy thought, because she had never been a mother to me. If she had, I might not have gotten pregnant in the first place. She was the one who had given me up at birth. She was the one who had chosen not to have a relationship with me. She was the one who didn't love me. I was only a child. How could she blame me for my mistakes when she had abandoned me to raise myself?

One cool and sunny Friday afternoon in September, I was at Mommy's apartment alone while she was at work. I had been having lower abdominal pain off and on all day, and when Mommy came home from the library, I told her about it.

"You're in labor," she said immediately. "You're about to have the baby."

Mommy called a cab, and as she and I exited the building, I saw a group of people sitting on a nearby bench, watching me. A girl called out, "Good luck, Trina! I think it's a boy!"

I knew she wasn't being sincere; she had never been nice to me. *They just can't help taking one last low blow at me*, I thought, wincing as I got into the taxi.

When we entered the emergency room, Mommy told the nurse

I was in labor, and an attendant quickly brought me a wheelchair and took me to the delivery room. My contractions came rapidly, though my cervix wasn't dilating. The hospital staff decided to keep me there overnight so that they could monitor me.

By the next morning, I was officially in labor and the pain from my contractions was severe. I screamed and cried, yet no one seemed to care. One nurse told me to shut the hell up. "You weren't making that much noise when you was making that baby!" she said, scowling at me.

On Sunday evening, two days after I was admitted, Mommy left the hospital. She had stayed with me as long as she could, and she had to be at work early the next morning. I was alone in the delivery room late that night, fourteen years old, crying and doubled over in pain, with no family or friends to comfort me or hold my hand, when my daughter came into the world.

Morgan Cooke was born in September 1985. She was five pounds, two ounces, and nineteen inches long, and the minute I saw her, I knew I didn't want to let her go. All those months I had spent trying to feel detached from her dissolved in an instant. I could not believe my body had created such a beautiful living thing, and while I had no idea how I would take care of her, I just knew that I didn't want to leave her.

Every morning when I woke up, I went to the hospital nursery to peek through the window at my daughter. She was so quiet and tiny. I begged the nurses to let me hold her, but they forbade me because, unbeknownst to me, Niecy had already arranged for Morgan to be adopted straight from the hospital. I discovered that she had forged my signature on the papers.

I shouldn't have been surprised that Niecy had betrayed me or that she'd had no qualms about breaking the law, but as soon as I found out what she had done, I became determined to figure out how to stop the adoption from happening. I might not have been allowed to touch my baby yet, but there was no way I was letting some couple who hadn't even met her walk out of the hospital with her in their arms.

I thought about this for the entire week I was in the hospital. During that time, Mommy visited me every day, as did the Macmillan sisters, much to my surprise. Tis came to see me too. He must have made his usual daily call to check on me after Mommy got back to her apartment, and she must have told him that I had gone into labor.

The first time he saw Morgan through the nursery window, he came back to my room and told me she was too light-skinned to be his. "I don't think that baby's mine," he said, frowning. "I think that baby's Sam's."

"Get the fuck outta here," I snapped from my bed. "I haven't been with Sam. This baby is yours."

That must have shaken him out of his delusions, because then Tis told me he wanted us to be a family. "I miss you," he said. "I want us to be together."

"Well, this girl Sharon told me that y'all are together and that I best stay clear of her because she already has your baby."

"I'm not with her. I don't want her," Tis said.

"But what about your baby with her?"

"Oh, I'll take care of my son, but I don't want to be with her. I want to be with *you*. I want to raise our daughter together."

I shook my head. "That's not going to happen. Niecy already put Morgan up for adoption. I don't want to give her up, but there's nothing I can do about it."

Tis took my hand. "Well, even if we can't keep the baby, I still want to be with you."

I hadn't thought any further than wanting Tis to choose me over Sharon, but now, as he made his choice clear, I felt so vulnerable, so in need of comfort from somebody, I realized he was my best option.

I said, "Okay, then I guess we can be together once I get out of the hospital," and that settled it.

* * *

On the day I was supposed to go home and say goodbye to my daughter forever, I pleaded with the nurse on duty: "I know I'm not supposed to hold my baby, but can you please bring her to me? I promise I won't say anything."

The nurse was hesitant but eventually told me she would be back shortly. When she left my room, I called my aunt Lilly. To this day, I don't know why she was the person I chose to call. She and I had never been close, and by the time Morgan was born, Lilly was addicted to crack. But that day, she did something that would change my life and my daughter's life forever.

When she answered the phone, I started crying. "Aunt Lilly, I don't want to give my daughter up for adoption."

"Okay," she said, as if we had nothing more to discuss. "Then I'll come get you."

"Okay," I replied. I hung up the phone, wondering if Aunt Lilly would actually show up. *She better get here soon*, I thought.

When the nurse returned with Morgan, she placed her in my arms and then left my room again, closing the door behind her, to give us some time alone. I gazed at my daughter's beautiful face and her tiny closed eyes, stroked her soft, dimpled cheeks, and breathed in the sweet scent of her clean newborn skin. It didn't matter right then how young I was; as I kissed her all over, I understood the infinite bond between mothers and their children.

Shortly thereafter, Aunt Lilly appeared in my room. She was wearing a long, loose-fitting, Muslim-style black dress that I had never seen on her before. She looked like she was in disguise—and then I realized why.

"Mommy told me I could come get you," she said, holding out her arms. "Give me the baby and then get dressed."

I stood up and handed Morgan over to her. I don't know whether it was the crack, a sudden sense of family obligation, or something else that made Aunt Lilly feel invincible that day, but she lifted up her big dress, put my baby underneath it, and walked right out of my room to the nearest exit. I wasn't far behind her; the nurse who had given Morgan to me was off checking on another patient, so I hurried into my street clothes and ran out of the hospital without looking back.

I burst through the door of Mommy's apartment, ran into her bedroom, and found Morgan lying on the bed. I could not believe how easy it had been for Aunt Lilly to just walk out of the hospital with her.

Too easy, it turned out.

An hour later, someone started pounding on the door. I could hear Niecy screaming from the hallway: "You stole that baby from the hospital!"

The hospital staff must have called her and the police when they realized what we had done. Knowing full well what Niecy's wrath looked like when she unleashed it, Aunt Lilly and I refused to let her in. But shortly after that, the cops arrived and Aunt Lilly had no choice but to open the door. I cowered in my room as they stormed through the apartment like they were doing a drug raid. A three-hundred-pound, six-foot-four officer burst through my door and asked, "Did you take that baby out of the hospital when she was meant to be adopted?"

"But it's *my* baby!" I tried to explain.

"Tell me what happened," he said, standing over my bed.

"I had a baby, and my mother put her up for adoption. She signed my name on the papers without telling me."

Niecy came into my room then, holding a batch of papers, and started shoving them in the officer's face.

"Look at that handwriting," I told the officer. Niecy had unique handwriting that looked nothing like mine. "That's not my writing."

"Is it true that you signed those papers for your daughter, ma'am?" the officer asked.

"Yes," Niecy said. "But she's only fourteen years old. She can't take care of a baby. The people who want to adopt her are a married couple who can give her a good home."

The officer asked Niecy to step out of the room so he could speak to her privately. Miraculously, Mommy happened to come home early from work just then. When the officer explained to Mommy what was going on, she said she had told Aunt Lilly that it was okay to bring the baby home to her apartment. Mommy might not have intervened when I was pregnant and Niecy first announced that I would have to give up the baby, but I imagine she had been worrying privately about my well-being since then. It was the first time in a long while that I felt like someone actually cared about me.

Even when Niecy only got angrier, Mommy just shrugged. In the same nonchalant tone she had used when she had first told me I was pregnant and then that I was in labor, she said, "You didn't want Trina, and I had to raise her, so I'll just help her raise this baby too."

The cops didn't seem to know what to do with all of us, three generations of Cooke women—and now a fourth, counting Morgan—all fighting in a small apartment. They asked Niecy and Mommy to step out into the hallway with them while I waited inside.

I never found out what the cops said to Niecy and Mommy out in that hallway, but after what felt like an eternity, Niecy came back in, walked calmly into the bedroom where Morgan was still sleeping, picked up the baby as if she were her own child, and left. Niecy had never even met Morgan before then, had never visited me in the hospital, but she took one look at her and fell in love at first sight. Only a few hours earlier, she had been ready to give the baby to a couple of strangers; now, all the love she had been withholding from me for fourteen years poured out of her and right into her granddaughter. It was the second time that day that someone had disappeared with my daughter, and in that moment, not only did Niecy reopen the deep wound she had cut into me by neglecting me for my entire life, but she killed all the magic I had felt with Morgan in the hospital. Of all the things Niecy had taken from me, the bond I might have had with my daughter was the greatest loss.

A few months after Morgan was born, Niecy found out that she was pregnant and Morgan came back to Mommy's to live with us. But by that point, I had lost my ability to fully connect with my daughter.

I also gave up on the possibility of having a relationship with Tis. We tried to be a couple after I returned from the hospital, but two months later he started smoking crack and was hooked instantly. He was only eighteen. I wasn't willing to put myself or my daughter in jeopardy, so I broke up with him. He was so addicted by then that he didn't even care.

The following fall, I entered ninth grade. I tried my best to stay in school, yet now that the burden of motherhood was on my shoulders, it was a constant struggle. Mommy was still working full-time, and I didn't have any money to pay a babysitter, so that December I dropped out to help raise my daughter. I spent my days hanging out at Mommy's and with my friends, drinking and occasionally sniffing cocaine. I had no job, no income, and no purpose.

Before I quit school, my guidance counselor had suggested that I join an organization called Job Corps in upstate New York, where I would be able to get my GED and some job training. After about nine months at home, I decided to enroll in the program. On a certain level, I knew I needed to do something productive with my time, and I didn't want to give up on my education entirely. Even though Mommy was still drinking all the time, she promised to make sure Morgan was cared for while I was gone. I should have guessed that no one there would look after me.

CHAPTER 5

Death Has Come

I hated Job Corps. As much as I wanted to continue my education, the coursework was challenging, and I was distracted by thoughts of home. Then one of the teachers, an older white man with a bushy mustache, began sneaking into my room at night. He would show up with snacks for me whenever my roommate wasn't there, and then would try to kiss me. But my experience with Cherry had taught me to recognize the warning signs of sexual abuse, and now that I was ten years older, I wasn't going to allow myself to be a repeat victim. Every time the teacher appeared in my room and tried to climb onto me, I would say, "Get off me." Fortunately, my roommate had an uncanny knack for appearing just when things were about to get really bad.

Seven months in, I was so fed up with the whole situation that I called Niecy for the first time ever. I begged her to let me come home. "This place isn't for me," I told her.

"Listen," she hissed into the phone, "I can't deal with your shit right now. I have too much stuff going on here at my house."

When she hung up, I asked myself why I had even called her in the first place. She had never helped me with anything in my life, so why would she start now, especially when she was juggling so many challenges of her own: a new baby, my brother

Jack; a partner, Leo, who was still cheating on her and beating her up regularly; and a diagnosis that she hadn't shared with anyone yet?

I called Mommy, but she didn't answer. I realized that no one was going to help me get home, so I decided to leave on my own. I asked to be released, much to the dismay of the Job Corps staff, who received government funding for each child in their care, and they gave me a one-way Greyhound bus ticket from Oneonta to Port Authority in New York City.

When I got back to Brooklyn, I decided to move in with my friend Shanice. Her mother had left her alone in her apartment in Brevoort, right across from Mommy's, so she had plenty of room, and Aunt Lilly's crack addiction was so bad that I didn't want to sleep under the same roof with her. She was always stealing Mommy's money. Mommy even took to hiding cash in her vagina to prevent Aunt Lilly from getting it, but Aunt Lilly figured that out quickly and would just reach into Mommy's underwear and pull it out. Mommy was so drunk most of the time that she wasn't quick or strong enough to fight her off.

Mommy and Aunt Lilly weren't the only ones with substance-abuse issues. A few weeks after I moved in with Shanice, she reintroduced me to cocaine. I had dabbled with Tis and other friends shortly after Morgan's birth but had stopped doing coke before I left for Job Corps. Now that I was back, I did it every weekend. It made me feel free and fun and as if all my problems had disappeared, when in reality, I had nothing going for me. I didn't have money, and getting a job never really crossed my mind. I was just waiting to turn eighteen in two years so I could be eligible for welfare. In the meantime, I let each day slide into the next, watching TV and sleeping. Shanice's niece and nephews moved in with us for a short while, after her sister went to prison. Sometimes when Shanice was asleep, her nephew Robert and I would go into the bathroom and kiss. I liked him, but messing around with him was just something I did to pass the time. Mostly I hung out on the bench outside our building and chilled with guys who I knew would give me coke.

Despite my aimlessness, I made a habit of visiting Mommy and Morgan every day. Each time, I knew what I would find. Mommy would be drunk, Aunt Lilly would be scoring crack in the street, and Morgan, who was two by then, would be watching TV alone on the floor. I was always happy to see her, though I still couldn't recapture that bond I had felt with her in the hospital.

One day, I entered the apartment and walked in on the usual scene. I picked up Morgan from the floor, kissed her beautiful face, and asked if she had been a good girl.

"Yes, Mommy," she said, smiling at me.

I heard a sniffling noise, and looked over at Mommy. She was crying.

"What's wrong?" I asked.

"Your mom is real sick. She has breast cancer," Mommy said.

Cancer. The word sliced through me, yet at the same time, I wasn't entirely surprised, because six months earlier, I'd had a dream that showed me Niecy wouldn't be alive for much longer. I hadn't dwelled on it at the time, but now that I knew about her condition, I realized that my dream was actually one of my premonitions.

All I knew about cancer was that eventually you died from it. I thought about my sister and baby brother, Jack; their father, Leo, had become a crackhead by then. Who was going to take care of them if Niecy died?

Mommy told me Niecy was in St. John's Hospital, so the next day I decided to go see her. When I walked into the room, a nurse was administering her medications. I approached her bed cautiously and asked, "How are you feeling?"

She spoke softly as she explained to me that she didn't know how long she had to live.

"When did you find this out?" I asked.

"When I was pregnant with your brother," she said.

She told me that her doctor had suggested she have an abortion so that she could begin treatment right away, but she had wanted to have the baby, so she had refused. Now, the cancer had spread to her lungs and other parts of her body.

As I listened to Niecy explain her condition, I felt my entire head grow hot. I was losing my opportunity to have a relationship with her. I didn't want her to see me cry, but I needed a hug. I needed someone to tell me everything was going to be okay. I was too young to become a motherless child. But all I said when I left the hospital was "I'll see you later."

After the visit, I broke down. Niecy was Niecy, but she was also my mother. And I had so many questions for her: who my father was, why she never wanted me, and why she had taken my daughter from me in the first days of her life. Most of all, I wanted to know what had happened to *her* to make her treat me so badly. Asking these questions didn't seem right while she was on her deathbed, but not asking meant I would never gain any of the closure I wanted so desperately. Niecy had never really been mine, but I had had hope. Now, her illness was robbing me of that too.

I visited Niecy in the hospital every day. Even as the cancer was destroying her body, she was still able to muster up enough energy to be nasty to me. It seemed second nature to her—her comfort zone—and I just sat back and took it because I wanted to spend as much time as I could with her.

The last time I visited Niecy, she gave me two dollars and asked me to go to the store and buy her some chocolate donuts and a Welch's grape soda. When I got back, she rolled her eyes at the donuts and frowned.

"Damn, you so stupid," she snapped. "You can't even get donuts right."

Even though all of her physical strength was gone, she might as well have punched me in the stomach. I had never been able to make her happy, and I wasn't going to magically start now.

Hanging my head and avoiding eye contact with her, I placed the donuts on the dresser, told her I would let her rest, and left. That was the last time I saw her alive.

On February 22, 1988, I woke up and got dressed. I was planning to finally go search for a job, but when I looked outside and saw that it was cold and dreary, I decided to save it for another day. I left Shanice's and headed over to Mommy's place instead. When I got there, she told me Niecy had passed away at nine o'clock that morning.

I was seventeen years old, with a two-and-a-half-year-old daughter, no mother, no father, an alcoholic grandmother, and a crackhead for an aunt. And even though Niecy had never acted like a mother to me, just knowing that she existed had kept me going. Now that she was gone, I felt empty.

Mommy numbed her grief that day by hitting the bottle hard, and by ten thirty a.m., she was already sloppy drunk. People called and stopped by to offer their condolences, but no one could make me feel any better. For an entire week, all I did was cry and fixate on the questions that I had never asked Niecy.

On the day of Niecy's funeral, I was the last one to enter the funeral parlor. I almost didn't approach her casket because the sight of her would confirm that she really wasn't coming back. When I finally decided to peek at her, she didn't look anything like the beautiful, tall, well-dressed woman she had been when she was alive. She was a skeleton—only fifty-six pounds, half what she had weighed when she was alive—and she was wearing a wedding dress. At one time, Niecy and Leo had planned to get married, but, not surprisingly, they had never made it down the aisle. When your main priority is getting high, exchanging vows is not important. But since Niecy had gone so far as to buy herself a wedding dress, Mommy decided to bury her in it.

The service was flooded with people. Although Niecy had not had many friends, Mommy was beloved by everyone in the neighborhood, and all of them, as well as my grandfather's brothers and other relatives, turned out to support her. Some of my friends from the projects came too. Ironically, Leo, the one person everyone expected to show up, was absent. I kept turning around in the church, expecting him to walk in, though he never did, and I wouldn't find out why until many years later.

During the reading of the eulogy, I could hardly focus. I felt like Niecy had gotten off easy because she had never had to answer any of my questions or be accountable for her cruel behavior toward me. All of the conflicting emotions I'd had toward Niecy for the past seventeen years came to a head in that church, and I started crying so hard that my aunt Millie and my godmother had to take me out into the hallway to console me. When they said they thought it was best that I didn't attend the burial, I agreed and went home instead. But afterward I felt robbed. They should have let me sit with my grief, rather than trying to squelch it. They should have allowed me the opportunity to see Niecy's casket lowered into the ground, even if I was hysterical at her graveside.

After the burial, when everyone came to Mommy's house for the repast, countless people approached me, saying, "Don't worry—we've got your back," and telling me to call them if I needed anything. But I knew they were just saying what people say at funerals. I knew that when the ceremony ended and the real, deep grief settled in, I wouldn't be able to count on them.

When everyone finally left, I leaned my head on Mommy's shoulder and she squeezed me tightly.

"This is the third child I've buried," she said, wiping her eyes. "That's a pain you never want to feel. I just pray I don't lose any more."

"Well, with the way Aunt Lilly is going with that crack, you may bury a fourth one soon. I hope she gets off that stuff," I said, shaking my head.

"Me too," Mommy said. Then she let out a little chuckle. "Plus, I'm tired of her stealing everything that isn't nailed down."

After Niecy died, Leo kept Jack, and Aunt Dorothy took in Macey. But, like so many other people I knew at the time, Leo had let his crack addiction take over his life. One day about two months after the funeral, he stopped by Mommy's with Jack. "I'm going to the store," he said, and hurried off.

He never returned. We later found out that after Niecy died, Leo took up a collection on the block where they lived and used that money to get out of town, leaving his children behind.

Mommy couldn't support yet another child, so Aunt Dorothy agreed to let Jack live with her and Macey. She lived in Brevoort as well, in a nearby building, and I was able to see my siblings frequently, until Aunt Dorothy moved to Florida with them two years later. By then, I was trapped in a relationship that would almost kill me.

CHAPTER 6

Dancing with the Devil

I couldn't shake the feeling that something was missing. Now that my premonition about her had come to pass, I was carrying the weight of the dead around with me. I kept thinking about how I would never have a relationship with my mother and how my daughter was going to grow up without a grandmother.

A year after Niecy passed away, I moved back in with Mommy, Aunt Lilly, and Morgan. Shanice's mother had been in an accident and wanted to move back into the apartment Shanice and I were sharing, so I had to leave.

Mommy was still drinking as heavily as ever, but she was also taking care of my daughter. Every day, she dropped off Morgan at day care on her way to work, just as she had done with me when I was a child, and picked her up on her way home. She never complained or asked me to help, even when I was living with them again. I did basic tasks for Morgan, such as bathing her and putting her to bed from time to time, but I never made an effort to take her on excursions or play with her the way I should have, because I was still unable to summon any kind of authentic love connection with her. Niecy had taken that from me before she died.

Although I was grateful to Mommy for letting me come

back, that also meant I had to contend with Aunt Lilly again. Her crack addiction had gotten so out of hand that I had to sleep with the few valuables I owned: a pair of door-knocker earrings and a cable chain, as well as some gold bracelets and earrings that I had bought for Morgan. Lilly also had a new baby who we all believed our neighbor's husband had fathered. However, he could have been anyone's—Lilly was out on the street all the time. Fathers—no matter who they were—just didn't matter much in our world.

Aunt Lilly had also started dating a fellow crackhead named Stevie. I tried to avoid them as much as possible, but one day when I was in my bedroom, Stevie stuck his head in the door and said, "Hey, Trina, I got somebody for you."

I looked him up and down and responded, "You ain't got nobody for me." I assumed anyone he knew would be a crackhead too.

"For real, I do," he said. "He's my cousin. He's a corrections officer."

"Then what's he doing hanging out with you?" I asked. *He's a CO*, I thought. *That must be a cool job.* I didn't know many people who worked besides Mommy. Also, the Social Security checks I had been collecting since Niecy's death had run out, and I had almost no money. *Maybe this guy will buy me something nice*, I thought.

The following weekend, Stevie knocked on the door and said his cousin, Larry, was downstairs in his car. I didn't want everyone on the block knowing my business, so I told Stevie to have him come up. Then I ran to the window to see what Larry looked like.

He had a nice car, a gray Mitsubishi Galant with tinted windows, but my first thought when I spotted him was, *That's one ugly mutha*. When he came upstairs, I noticed his poor posture and his uneven complexion, though it was mostly just a feeling I got: *This man is not sexy. He has no swagger.*

When he asked me what I was getting into that night, I said, "Nothing much."

"Then let's go get something to eat from McDonald's."

Despite my utter lack of interest in him, I was just sitting around Mommy's apartment, so I decided I might as well go. I was moving aimlessly through life by this point, without purpose or direction, and I figured a man with a car and a job was better than nothing. What I didn't realize then was that someone who has no purpose is more vulnerable to getting involved with toxic and sometimes even dangerous people.

It was my first time ever riding in a car that wasn't a cab. Larry drove slowly through the streets with the stereo pumping so that everyone would take notice. The music was too loud for us to have a conversation, so I just took in the view.

After we got our food, Larry asked if he could see me again soon. I didn't have anything else to do, so I agreed and gave him my phone number.

The next weekend, Larry came over and invited me to go to Atlantic City. I told him that I didn't have any money for gambling, but he said he had me covered, and the allure of the money and of leaving Mommy's apartment for a day trip to New Jersey was all I needed to say yes. However, I insisted that Shanice come along with us.

"That's cool," he said. "Then I'll bring Stevie."

The four of us got in Larry's car and headed down to Atlantic City, while the thought *I'm finally out of the projects* ran through my mind like a news ticker. Larry kept his service revolver and his CO badge on display next to him for the whole ride, and turned the stereo volume all the way up again. He lowered it only long enough to ask me, "How fast do you think this car can go?" as he stomped on the accelerator. I smiled at him, egging him on, as the speedometer hit 120 miles per hour. Larry didn't have to worry about being pulled over by the police; his badge ensured that no traffic violation he committed would stick. I would see him talk his way out of much worse offenses in the years to come.

When we arrived at Harrah's Casino, Larry handed me a hundred-dollar bill. No one had ever given me that kind of money—money that I could just have fun with, rather than having to use for necessities. Although it was nearly weightless, I felt the bill's presence with every step I took. While Stevie attempted to flirt with Shanice over by the bar, I played blackjack. Larry stayed close to me the whole time, giving me advice, and helped me win five hundred dollars. He wasn't gambling himself, but he knew cards. Every time I glanced at him, he was staring at me, looking thirsty. I still wasn't attracted to him, but I thought I might be able to tolerate him if he kept treating me nicely and helped me get out of Brevoort.

From that day on, Larry was at Mommy's house every day when he wasn't working, even though he had his own apartment in his parents' house in Bed-Stuy. He seemed to have decided, without asking, that we were going to be a couple. Although he was beginning to look after Morgan and me financially and even gave Mommy money from time to time (after she quipped, "He looks like he done moved in; he needs to be paying me over here"), he never asked me anything about what I wanted out of life or from our relationship. All he ever talked about was his job. He bragged about how he physically and verbally abused the inmates at work, as if it was a game. I didn't realize back then that everything he did—from giving me money to showing off his car to keeping his gun and badge on display to boasting about hurting people—was meant as a display of power. And all that posturing was actually just an attempt to hide the truth: that he had no self-esteem.

Despite Larry's insecurity, I was in survival mode. I was living with a grandmother who was a drunk and an aunt who was a crackhead and starting to have children. I couldn't talk myself into being physically attracted to Larry, but I needed him to get me out of there. The first time we had sex, I had to get drunk and snort cocaine beforehand in order to tolerate even the five minutes it lasted, and after he finished, he rolled over and went straight to sleep while I lay awake, hoping all of my sexual encounters with him would be as quick as this one.

Two months later, in June, my period didn't start on time. My cycle had always been regular; the only time I had ever missed a month was when I was pregnant with Morgan. Then I started having morning sickness, and within a few weeks I could no longer deny the truth.

Please, not again, I thought. But this time, I was determined to approach the situation differently. I knew so much more than I had during my first pregnancy, four years earlier. With Morgan, I had sabotaged my chances of terminating the pregnancy by remaining in denial. This time, I knew right away what was happening, and I also knew that I had to make a plan.

I was on Mommy's health insurance, so I told her right away that I was pregnant again. She was about to go to work, making her coffee.

She turned away from the coffeemaker and looked me up and down, shaking her head, before she said, "I can't take care of another child. Take my insurance card out of my purse and go to the doctor. Get a referral for an abortion."

I nodded and did as she asked. This time, we would be a team.

When Larry came over to Mommy's that night after work, I took him into my bedroom to tell him about my plans. I knew he would agree to the abortion, because neither of us had ever discussed having children together—or much else. *This will be a quick conversation, and then I can move on with my life, hopefully without him*, I told myself.

But when I explained to him that I had been sick because I was pregnant, he beamed. I had never seen him smile so genuinely before.

Why does he look so happy about this? I wondered. "Anyway, I'm going to make an appointment to have an abortion," I continued.

"No, you're not," Larry said.

"Yes, I am. I don't want any more children." I was only eighteen, and one child was more than enough for me, especially given that I wasn't even a devoted mother to Morgan. I also didn't really like Larry and didn't want to have a baby with him.

But Larry told me that he wanted a family so badly that he was not willing to consider any alternatives. He immediately started trying to convince me to change my mind, promising me that he would take care of me, Morgan, and the new baby.

I said, "Why would you want that? We don't even really know each other. We don't ever have a real conversation."

The logic was plain to me, but his blinders were on. "Well," he said, "I need you and I love you."

"You *love* me already?" *Who does he think he is? I'm from the street. We don't say things like that.*

No matter how many promises Larry made, it didn't change the fact that this decision about my body and my future was not his to make. And why should I have believed anything he said about supporting me? I had never known the father of anybody's baby, including my own, to be involved in parenting.

"You know what?" I eventually said, swatting the air with my hand. "I'm tired of talking about this. Get the fuck out of here."

The instant the words were out of my mouth, Larry slapped my face so hard that I flew backward and flipped over my bed. When I could see straight again, I sprang to my feet and yelled, "Man, you crazy!" I ran right at him and started hitting him. We broke almost every fragile object in that room while we brawled.

Mommy came in after a few minutes, yelling, "What's going on in here?" The same man who had just told me moments earlier that he wanted me to have his baby was pummeling me like I was one of his inmates. He might have killed me and his unborn child with his bare hands had Mommy not jumped on his back and started punching him.

Larry finally stopped and bent over, hands on his knees, trying to catch his breath. "I'm sorry, Ms. Cooke," he said, panting, "but she's pregnant with my baby and she wants to have an abortion."

"Well, beating her isn't going to make her change her mind!" Mommy shouted.

Larry straightened up, shook his head at both of us, and stormed out of Mommy's apartment. After he slammed the door behind him, I stared into the empty space where he had stood. I knew he was violent at work, but Larry had never shown any aggression toward me. Everything would be different from now on.

Mommy sat on my bed and patted the mattress next to her. When I took a seat, she suggested that I rethink my decision about the abortion. "I believe Larry will be a good father, and it will get you out of these projects," she said.

Clasping my arms around my midsection, I began to cry. "Mommy, how can you say that after what he just did to me? He's crazy! And I don't want any more children right now. I don't even have a job!"

"But if you're with Larry, you won't need a job. He loves you. Can't you see that?"

"But I don't love him. I barely even like him."

She studied me for a moment, then shrugged. "Okay, if that's how you feel." Then she stood up and left my bedroom.

Sitting there alone, I thought about what she had said. In the moment, all I could focus on was how twisted her thinking seemed. She had just seen her granddaughter being savagely beaten and was telling me I would have a better life with him?

It didn't make any sense. I now realize that she was projecting her own feelings onto me, comparing Larry's unforgivable behavior with her own experiences with heartless men. *It's not that bad. At least you have a man who loves you,* she must have been thinking. *You can have everything if you say yes to him.* And it wasn't her fault—Mommy just didn't know any better. She had limited resources and limited energy, her man had left her, and she was drunk and broken. Any hope she had once had for a good life had dissolved. And even though Larry was revealing himself to be a bad man, he was someone who could do what neither Mommy nor I could do for me: get me out of Brevoort and launch me into a future with more opportunities.

Despite Mommy's words, I had not changed my mind. The next morning, I made an appointment with the doctor to get a referral for the abortion. Larry called all day, begging me to have the baby, but my mind was made up.

I didn't tell Larry when my appointment was, though as I sat in the waiting room at the doctor's office, I looked up just in time to see him striding in. His fists were clenched at his sides, and I could see the whites of his eyes.

How did he find me?

"Why are *you* here?" I asked.

Without saying a word, Larry grabbed me by my hair and dragged me out the door. I screamed for help, but not one person tried to stop him. *What is it about the people in these places?* I wondered. Were the other patients in the waiting room afraid to step in because they feared Larry would hurt them too, or did the sight of a battered young woman simply not affect people anymore?

Larry pulled me outside and shoved me into his car. I was so weak from morning sickness that I didn't have the strength to fight back. I felt like I might faint as I landed in the passenger seat.

While Larry drove through the streets of Brooklyn, neither of us said a word. I had no idea where he was taking me, and I didn't have the energy to ask. When he parked in front of Mommy's building, I thought maybe he had come to his senses, so I tried again to reason with him.

"Why do you want to have a baby with someone who doesn't want to have a baby with you?" I asked. "I don't even like you like that."

"Yeah? Well, after you have the baby, you'll change your mind."

"I am not having this baby, you asshole!" I yelled.

Larry followed me into Mommy's apartment. All I wanted was to get into bed and close my eyes. *I'm done with this pregnancy, and I'm done with him*, I thought. I glared at him and said, "I don't want to be with you anymore."

After he left, I lay down and tried to breathe deeply and relax my body, but my mind was still racing. I decided to make another doctor's appointment for later that week, when I knew Larry would be at work. I received my new referral three days later and scheduled my abortion. *After I get rid of this baby*, I told myself, *I never want to see Larry again*.

The morning of my abortion appointment, I heard Larry banging on the door of Mommy's apartment and yelling at me to let him in. I didn't want him to disturb the neighbors, so I cracked open the door. He pushed his way inside and started hitting me again. I wondered if he realized how little sense he was making. What if he hurt the baby he said he wanted so much?

He finally stopped beating me but refused to explain how he'd found out I was going to the clinic that morning. To this day, I still don't know. Either he'd had a hunch that I was trying to deceive him, or I was living with a spy who was feeding him information, most likely Aunt Lilly. I knew she would have accepted money from him to buy crack in exchange for anything she could tell him about my whereabouts.

Larry paced around the apartment, yelling about how I was having his baby whether I wanted to or not and rifling through drawers and cabinets. I didn't know what he was looking for until he went into my bedroom and found my doctor's referral on my dresser. Before I could grab it, he ripped it up and threw the little pieces of paper in my face. As they fluttered onto the floor around me, he hurried out the front door.

From my seventh-floor bedroom window, I watched him exit Mommy's building. As he walked to his car, I screamed at him out the window, calling him every name I could think of. Once he drove out of sight, I sat down on my bed and began crying uncontrollably. I felt like a prisoner. I was broke. I already had one child. I had tried everything I could think of to get out of this pregnancy. I had tried to reason with Larry. I had tried to go to the doctor. I had tried to talk to Mommy. Yet no one would let me make this choice for myself.

The next day, I decided that since I couldn't beat Larry physically, I should try to appeal to him emotionally. I called him and asked him to come over so we could talk.

When he arrived at Mommy's, I half expected him to hurt me again. It doesn't take long for behaviors that felt shocking just days earlier to start seeming normal. But his hands remained loose at his sides, and his face was soft as he spoke quietly to me, begging me to abandon my plans. "I promise you won't ever have to work if you just have this baby. Please, Trina," he said.

I can't fight him anymore, I thought, looking at his sad eyes. Without my doctor's referral, I would have to pay for an abortion myself, and I couldn't afford that. And I didn't want to be a single mother of two. If I was going to have another child, I wanted a more traditional path.

"Look," I began, "if you want this baby, you're going to have to promise me some things."

"Whatever you want, I will do," Larry said.

I paced the floor and took a deep breath while I formulated what I would say next. Because I hadn't even entertained the notion of having another child until a few minutes earlier, I hadn't thought through what my demands should be. But I sensed that I should aim high, since Larry seemed so amenable at that moment. If he was going to be my ticket out of the projects, I wanted to go all the way.

After a few more minutes, I stopped pacing and looked right at him, counting out my list on my fingers. "The first thing I want is a ring. I want to be married. I also want a house and a car, and I don't want to ever have to work. I also don't want any more children. That's it."

In the ensuing silence, my heart was pounding so hard that I was sure Larry could hear it. After what felt like an eternity, he smiled at me and said, "No problem."

Years later, I would wonder what would have happened if he hadn't uttered those two words, which set us on a three-year collision course that culminated in his shooting me. But in the moment, all I could think was *Well, that settles it. Family of four, here we go.*

CHAPTER 7

Only the Beginning

Over the next few months, Larry gave me everything I had asked for. He began the process of having a house built for us on Long Island, he bought me a car and taught me how to drive, and he bought everything our baby might need, including a five-hundred-dollar Aprica stroller. Since he was trying his hardest to please me, I promised myself that I would try to like him in return. But the first six months of my pregnancy were extremely difficult. I experienced morning sickness, emotional distress, and physical turmoil. Fortunately, my third trimester was much easier on me, and I finally felt well enough to get excited about having another child. I promised myself that I would be a different kind of mother than I was to Morgan. I read books and sang to the baby as my February 28 due date grew closer.

On Christmas morning 1989, I entered Mommy's living room to admire her decorations and the beautiful tree. We always put our tree up the day after Thanksgiving—a tradition I continue to this day. I inhaled the delectable aromas wafting in from the kitchen. Christmas was Mommy's favorite holiday, as well as mine. It was the one time of year when I felt genuinely happy. Despite Mommy's drinking, Aunt Lilly's drug addiction, and the stress we were all under, the atmosphere was always festive. Mommy played her favorite holiday songs day and night: Nat King Cole's "The Christmas Song," Otis Redding's "Merry Christmas Baby," and the Temptations' "Silent Night." She also always prepared a soul-food feast: Cornish hens with stuffing made from scratch, collard greens, macaroni and cheese, and sweet potatoes with marshmallows. She baked beautiful cakes too, and I was always waiting right there to lick the bowl.

I smiled to myself as I took in the moment, then startled a little when Larry approached me and gave me a kiss on my cheek. Ever since he had started getting his way in our relationship, we had been getting along much better. Then he got down on one knee and pulled a small, square velvet box from his pocket. He opened it slowly, revealing a sparkling diamond ring, and asked, "Will you marry me?"

My legs felt shaky. I thought, *No*.

I said yes.

Mommy came into the living room right away and beamed at me. "Are you happy now?" she asked, taking my hand to look at my ring.

"Yes," I said, all the while thinking, *No*. I had nothing to show for myself besides a shiny new car and the house that we were building. Yes, I had told Larry I wanted those things, but I still didn't have a clue about who I was or what I wanted to do with my life. And now I was about to be responsible for not just one but two more lives.

Glancing down at my diamond, I forced a smile for everyone. But I didn't have any time to process my new reality, because as soon as that ring was on my finger, Larry had another surprise for me. He told me that he would be moving Morgan and me out of Mommy's house the next day and into his parents' basement in Bed-Stuy until the construction on our new house was finished.

I tried to tell him that Morgan should stay with Mommy when we moved out, but Larry insisted that she come with us.

He had been sweet to her ever since he first met her, and I knew he wanted to be a father figure to her as much as he would be to our new baby. "Morgan is part of our family, Trina," he said. "Mommy doesn't need to be responsible for her anymore. You'll both have everything you need to be comfortable." Since he was about to be my husband—and since I knew now what he was capable of when I resisted his wishes—I agreed. At the time, he was forcing my hand in motherhood, but it turned out to be one of the few lasting gifts he gave me.

Moving into Larry's parents' basement was not one of those gifts. His mother couldn't stand me and had no problem showing it. Larry was one of four children and her favorite—and she made no secret about that. She thought I wasn't good enough for him. Most of the time, she didn't speak to me, even when she passed right by me inside the house. I frequently overheard her badmouthing me to her friends on the phone. I used to sit on the stairs leading down to the basement and eavesdrop as she said things like, "Oh, Larry's girl is living here right now, but we don't get along." She would call me a whore, claim I was with Larry only for his money, and say she wished he would get back together with his ex-girlfriend. She also suspected that Larry was not even the father of our baby, even though I hadn't been with anyone else, so she never expressed any excitement about the upcoming birth of a new grandchild.

Between Larry's abuse and his mother's verbal insults, living in that house was making me even sicker than my pregnancy. When I eventually mentioned his mother's behavior to Larry, he said, "My mother doesn't like you because she thinks you just want to use me."

Well, she's got a point, I thought. I was using him to get out of the projects and had given him a list of demands before we got engaged, yet I had never once expressed an interest in living under the same roof as his parents—that was all Larry.

"*Use* you?" I let out a strangled laugh. "You need to tell her that this is what *you* wanted. Don't make it seem like I wanted this."

Larry glared at me, and I knew I was in for another severe beating if I pressed the issue.

The only saving grace of our time at Larry's parents' house was that we had our own living room, bedroom, and bathroom, and needed their space only when I had to cook. Larry's mother worked the late shift at the post office every evening, except Sundays and Mondays, from five p.m. to one a.m. She would go upstairs and start getting ready for work around three, so I would use the kitchen after that. On Sunday and Monday mornings, I would get up early, before Larry's mother woke up, to cook for Larry and Morgan and me, so that I could be back in the basement before she came downstairs. Larry's stepfather was a sanitation worker whose shifts were from six a.m. until two p.m. He never mistreated me, though he was often under the influence of alcohol, and he would retreat upstairs to his bedroom after the six thirty news.

Those days and nights stretched on and on, and all the while, my body continued to expand as my baby grew. The walls felt as tight as my clothes, but I told myself everything would be fine once we were settled in our new home on Long Island.

In late January 1990, Larry and I got into a terrible argument. It started because I told him that I was planning to put our new baby on welfare. I was already receiving welfare for both Morgan and me, but I hadn't mentioned that to Larry. On this night, I told him that if both of our kids were benefiting, I could make a small financial contribution to our household through that subsidy. I planned to deceive the welfare system by claiming that Larry and I did not live together; that way, because his name would be on the baby's birth certificate as the father, the office would go after him for child support and I could collect that money.

Ever since I had agreed to keep Larry's baby, he had continued to degrade me verbally whenever I said anything that rubbed him the wrong way, but he had stopped being physically abusive. During this discussion, however, things escalated quickly. I should have known that Larry would never agree to my suggestion. He had to control every aspect of our relationship. He wanted to seem indispensable; he wanted to be able to say, "I bought Trina a house. I bought her a car. I give her everything," so that everyone, especially he, would believe I couldn't live without him.

When I brought up the welfare idea, we were on the main level of his parents' house. I was walking toward the stairs leading down to our basement apartment while we talked, and he kicked me hard in my back. I tumbled down every step and landed at the bottom of the staircase with a loud smack.

"You piece of shit!" I screamed at him, my body aching, tears streaming down my face. His mother must have heard all the noise I made as I fell, because her face materialized right next to Larry's in the stairwell above me. Rather than coming down to help me or even asking if I was hurt, she just glared down at me, as if I deserved to be right where I was.

I could feel bruises forming all over my body as I lay there, but I was used to that. What concerned me more was that a few hours after we went to bed, I began to have sharp pains in my abdomen and became convinced that my tumble down the stairs had killed my baby. The baby had always been an active kicker, and now it had stopped moving entirely. Eventually, unable to go back to sleep, I got out of bed and called an ambulance.

Once I hung up, I shook Larry awake and said, "I need to go to the hospital. My stomach is killing me. I think something's wrong with the baby. It's not kicking. An ambulance is on its way."

Larry sat straight up in bed. "No," he snapped. "I'll take you."

I knew what he was thinking—he didn't want anyone knowing why I was in so much pain in the first place—but I had already made the call. Back then, if someone ordered an ambulance, police were also dispatched to the pickup location. I had never asked anyone to intervene on my behalf the previous times Larry had beaten me, but this time was different, because another life was involved—a victim even more innocent than I was. So, when the ambulance arrived at Larry's parents' house, along with two white male police officers, I thought, *This is my chance to share my story and finally get some help.*

However, I was too naive to realize the clout that a law enforcement position can wield. One of the officers got into the ambulance with me, and the other one started talking to Larry. I told the officer who was with me exactly what Larry had done to me. He and his partner had thought they were simply responding to a routine medical emergency, not a domestic-violence incident, but once I explained that Larry had pushed me down the stairs, the officer who was with me left the ambulance to consult with the other officer. Larry immediately flashed his CO badge and told the officers a different version of the story. I never heard what he said to them, but the next thing I knew, they were telling me to get out of the ambulance because Larry was going to take me to the hospital after all. They got back in their squad car and, without one more look at me, drove away.

I was in so much pain that I could hardly walk, though I managed to get into Larry's car. Nearly the whole way to the hospital, we were both silent. Larry was speeding through stoplights, trying to act like a superhero, but all I could think about was how readily the police had disregarded me, and about how Larry must have twisted the story to his advantage. I promised myself then, *I'm done. I'm going to leave this guy. I'm getting out as soon as I possibly can.*

The only thing Larry said to me as we neared the hospital was, "You better not tell anyone in there what happened tonight."

I'm not scared of you, I thought. The police might not have protected me when they came to our house, but surely someone in the maternity ward would show me some compassion.

When we were admitted to the hospital, I told the first nurse who examined me that Larry had kicked me down a flight of stairs.

"My God, that's horrible," she said. "I'll tell the doctor."

After she left the room, I thought surely I had set in motion a chain of events that would hold Larry accountable for endangering my life and the life of our baby, but I was wrong again. When the doctor came in, he said nothing about Larry's abuse; instead, he simply performed a routine cervical exam and said, "You're in labor."

My due date was still a month away. *I'm not ready for this*, I thought. The baby needed more time to grow—if it had even survived my fall down the stairs. But my contractions were becoming more intense, and I was admitted to the delivery room. When Larry joined me, he never asked me how I was feeling or whether he could do anything for me, but he couldn't sit still. He paced around the room, smiling and rubbing his hands together. *Do you even remember what you just did to me a few hours ago?* I thought, glaring at him from my bed. While he carried on as if he hadn't just nearly killed me and our child, all I could think about was how much of a fraud he was.

As I lay there, I wondered if every argument Larry and I had was going to end up with him physically assaulting me. No one had ever taught me that when a man puts his hands on a woman, she should leave him immediately and never look back. While I knew it didn't feel right, I also thought it was just something men did to women.

For twenty-three hours straight, I labored, my rage and pain my constant companions. When I was fully dilated, the doctor barked at me repeatedly: "Push, Katrina! Push one more time!"

I groaned and sweated and focused all my energy on getting the baby out, and finally I succeeded.

"Is it a boy?" I whispered, as the doctor completed his work.

"No, it's a girl," the nurse replied.

I sighed. "I don't want another girl! I wanted a boy!"

Everyone in the delivery room started laughing, but I was serious. I had been hoping for a son this time, so much so that I didn't even have any female names or clothing picked out. But when the nurse handed me the baby and I saw how healthy she looked, how beautiful she was, I no longer cared.

I held my daughter tightly and kissed her on the head. No one was going to take this baby away from me, the way the hospital and Niecy had done with Morgan. "I love you, *I love you*," I whispered into her tiny ear.

Larry stayed at the hospital until I was recovering comfortably in my room. Then he went home to bring me the bag I'd never had a chance to pack. When he came back, he had a bunch of cigars with him and handed them out to anybody who would take one. His exuberance about the baby was so pronounced—manic, really—that as I watched him bouncing around the room, I couldn't help but think, *Things are going to change for us; he's going to clean up his act now*.

When it was time for us to decide what to name the baby, I let Larry choose her first name, since she was his first child and he had wanted her so badly. He named her Melissa, and her middle name after my mother.

The day after Melissa was born, so many people came to visit that I barely got any rest. Larry's mother was one of the first to arrive. I felt my whole body stiffen when she appeared at my bedside. *What is she even doing here?* I wondered. Then I remembered her suspicion that I had gotten pregnant by someone else and realized she must have come to see if the baby looked at all like Larry.

Sure enough, she never asked me how I was doing; all she said was, "Where's the baby?"

I sat up slowly, grimacing as my sore muscles protested, and shuffled down to the nursery with her to introduce her to her granddaughter.

"Hmm, she's very light-skinned," Larry's mother said, peering through the glass. "And she don't look nothing like Larry or you. I guess she must look like someone in your family," she continued, raising her eyebrows at me.

I rolled my eyes and said nothing. But if she could have read my mind, she would have known that I was glad the baby didn't look like her or her son.

The rest of the week that I was in the hospital was much more pleasant. Mommy came to meet her great-granddaughter, and other people visited. I spent as much time as I could just holding Melissa and making promises to myself about the kind of mother I wanted to be this time. I had a second chance to right the wrongs I had committed because of how young I was when I'd had Morgan, and how disconnected from her I'd become when Niecy took her away. Now that I was a little older and had decided that I wanted this baby, I was determined to be present for Melissa and to shower her with affection. I never wanted her to doubt for a second how much I loved her.

Over the first two months after Larry and I returned to his parents' house with Melissa, we settled into the usual routine of caring for a newborn. Larry was attentive to both Melissa and Morgan, reading them bedtime stories and running out to buy Pampers and formula whenever we ran low. We never wanted for anything. Our new house was not done yet, but his parents were preparing to move out of state, and they would allow us to remain in their house until we were ready to relocate.

In March, two months after Melissa was born, Larry came home from work one night and was agitated about something.

His mother was upstairs in her kitchen with her best friend, Amy. When Larry entered our apartment, I was lying down and Melissa was sleeping in her bassinet next to our bed, but he didn't want to go to sleep; he wanted to fight. He started arguing with me about something trivial, then grabbed me by the neck, cutting off my breathing. I was too weak from lack of oxygen to fight back as he began punching me in my face, screaming, "You're not going to be able to see when I'm done with you!" He hit my right eye again and again, until I couldn't open it anymore, and then he said to me, "Now I'm going to shut the other one too." He repeated the process until both of my eyes were swollen shut.

Melissa woke up in the middle of the commotion and started screaming because she was hungry. Larry finally stopped hitting me and sat down on the bed, panting. Although my head was throbbing, I had to go up to the kitchen to prepare Melissa's formula. I knew how my face would look to Larry's mother and her friend, but even more painful was when I realized the two of them had heard our entire fight and had done nothing to stop it.

When I got upstairs, Larry's mother was in the kitchen and Amy was in the living room, two rooms away. Amy took one look at me, glanced around to make sure that Larry's mother couldn't hear us, and whispered, "You've got to get away from that man. He's going to kill you."

I didn't say anything at first, because I didn't believe that Larry was capable of killing me. I knew he was likely to hurt me over and over, but it was just becoming normal for me to live like this. Besides, where else was I going to go?

Amy was staring at my battered face. "I want you to call me tomorrow," she said. "Can you do that?"

I nodded and walked into the kitchen, where I quickly got Melissa's formula ready, then went back downstairs.

I did as Amy had asked. The next day, when Larry was at

work, I called her. She reiterated what she had said to me in the kitchen the night before: "You've got to get away from Larry."

"But where would I go?" I asked. I knew I couldn't go back to Mommy's; she was still an alcoholic, Aunt Lilly was still on crack. Nothing had changed in their world.

Amy couldn't answer that question. "Just leave," she said. But she didn't offer for me to come stay with her or give me any other suggestions.

"Larry's mother let him do this to me," I told Amy.

"She don't know any different," she responded. "She thinks you need to help your own self."

The next month, just as my black eyes were finally healing, Larry started in on me again. He came home one night wanting to have sex, and I told him I was too tired because I had been home all day with Morgan and Melissa. Rather than accepting my no, Larry pushed me onto our bed, secured my arms behind my back with his work handcuffs, punched me again and again in my right eye, and then penetrated me as I lay there, limp and bloody.

This time, I called 911 to send the cops to the house because my fiancé was beating me. While I waited for them to arrive, I told myself, *No more. When Larry goes to sleep, I'm taking these kids and going to Mommy's.*

When the police arrived, they knocked on the door and I hurried upstairs to let them in. Larry followed me and stood right behind me in the doorway. I pointed at my black eye and said to the police, "Look what he did to me. This man is a corrections officer." I thought that if I could highlight what a hypocrite Larry was—a law enforcement officer who couldn't keep his rage or his hands in check—they would be more inclined to take me seriously. But, of course, my plan backfired.

"Let me talk to you for a minute," Larry said to the cops, nudging me aside. He always kept his badge inside a black chain wallet that he kept clipped to his left pants pocket, even when we were alone at home. Now, as he walked past me and gestured to the officers to follow him down the pathway that led to our front gate, I saw him flash his badge and I just shook my head.

"I'm leaving," I called out to him. "I'm leaving you because you keep beating me up."

One of the officers looked from Larry to me and, raising both his hands and backing up slightly, said, "You two have to work this out on your own."

Work it out? I thought. There was no reasoning with a man who was that sadistic. So, at three a.m., when I was sure Larry was asleep, I packed a small bag and walked two miles with both of my daughters.

When I got to Mommy's apartment, I banged hard on the door. Aunt Lilly answered; she was probably up smoking crack. Without a word, she let me in, then headed back to her room and shut the door. Mommy was asleep, so I peeked into her bedroom and told her I would explain in the morning why I was there. Then I lay on the couch with Morgan and Melissa, holding them tightly.

When Mommy woke up at five a.m. to go to work, she immediately noticed my battered face.

"Oh, I see why you're here," she said.

"I can't take it anymore. Larry is beating me all the time, and things are only getting worse."

I thought Mommy might tell me I had to go back to him, but she just nodded and said, "You can stay here as long as you want, Trina."

Of course, it wasn't long before Larry came banging on Mommy's door to get me.

"My kids are not staying here!" he screamed from the hallway.

"Get out of here!" I yelled back, my heart pounding. "We're not coming home!" I felt safe enough because project doors are virtually impenetrable, but I wanted him to stop making so much noise. Eventually I heard his footsteps retreating, and when I heard the elevator door close, I knew he was gone. I also knew he wasn't going to let me stay with Mommy indefinitely. He would keep coming back if I didn't return to him first.

Later that week, I asked my homegirl Tasher if she would go with me to Larry's house so I could get some clothes for myself and the girls. When we arrived, I knocked on the door, with Melissa strapped to my chest in a harness, and Larry's stepfather answered it.

"How can I help you?" he asked, looking me up and down as if he had never seen me before.

"I came to get the rest of my clothes," I told him.

He scowled at me. "You don't have no clothes here!" he said, then slammed the door in my face.

Tasher and I trudged back to Mommy's house. Larry called later that night and said, "If you want your clothes, you better come back home right away."

I clenched the phone as my breathing grew ragged. *How will I ever be free of this man?* I didn't have enough money to buy much for myself or my daughters, and no one else I knew had any to spare. Larry knew his income was my only livelihood and that I would have no choice but to make my way back to him.

After I returned, Larry began raping me habitually. Every few nights, he would force me to have sex with him, aggressively holding me down even when I told him I didn't want to. It was as if he couldn't even hear my voice. The fact that I was living with him and had a child with him didn't mean he ever had a right to have intercourse with me without my consent.

To escape my dismal reality, I started getting high on cocaine again. I had stopped when I found out I was pregnant with Melissa, but now I needed something to help me cope. I never did it when my daughters were awake, and I never copped the coke myself; I would go over to my friend Shanice's, give her money, and ask her to buy me some when she was out getting her crack.

I also began quietly developing an exit strategy: I would accumulate as much money as I could so that I could leave Larry for good. The biweekly two-hundred-dollar welfare checks I was receiving just weren't sufficient, so I got on food stamps. That got me an additional two hundred and fifty dollars per month. I would set aside twenty to buy a bag of coke and would cash in the rest. And Shanice always knew somebody who would trade me money for food stamps.

One day while I was visiting Mommy, I ran into a crackhead I knew named Lorie. I told her that if she could cop a bag of coke for me, I would buy her a ten-dollar bag of crack, and she agreed.

I thought Lorie might just vanish with my twenty, but she reappeared shortly and handed the bag to me right outside Mommy's building. I immediately went upstairs and snorted a little of it. Then I picked up Melissa. Not five minutes later, I began sweating and shaking so hard that I almost dropped her.

Mommy was standing right there. "What the hell is wrong with you?" she asked, furrowing her eyebrows and grabbing the baby from me.

"I don't know," I said. "I need to sit down."

Mommy got me some water, but I was trembling so badly that I couldn't even hold the glass. When I finally took a sip, I vomited right on the floor, then had to run to the toilet as my body began spasming with diarrhea. *I can't believe I'm going to die right here in this bathroom*, I thought.

I stayed in there, taking deep breaths and holding my body tightly. As soon as I stopped shaking so violently, I reached into my pocket, pulled out the bag containing the remaining cocaine, and flushed it down the toilet.

When I finally exited the bathroom, I lay down on the couch

and prayed. "If I get through this, I will never touch this stuff again!" I said out loud. I barely even knew what praying was or who God was back then, but I had to reach out to *someone* for help. And God must have heard me, because I didn't die that night.

I always wondered what was in that coke Lorie gave me, or if it was even coke at all. When I talked to my friends about it later, they told me it was probably just a bad batch, cut with something toxic. I didn't care—I was done. That was more than thirty years ago, and I kept my promise to never use cocaine again. It was just that simple for me. I realized if I didn't stop, it would kill me.

CHAPTER 8

Oh, This House Is Not a Home

In late July 1991, after almost two years of living with Larry's parents, Larry and I moved into our new home in Suffolk County, Long Island. I was finally getting out of the hood and into the suburbs. No one looking at that house, including me, could ever have imagined how this new world would change my life forever.

The morning of the closing, we arrived at ten o'clock. Larry didn't explain much to me about what closing on a house consisted of, but he did do a lot of yelling and fighting with me on our way there. I thought it would be a happy moment for him, but he was in one of his characteristic bad moods that day and everything was irritating him: I took too long getting dressed; the music in the car was too loud; the traffic was going to make us late. I tried to be cheerful and make the atmosphere positive because he was upholding his end of our arrangement—he had said he was going to get us a house, and now he had—but he just woke up angry.

A woman who worked for the mortgage company was there for the transaction. When she asked whose name the house was going to be in, I just looked at Larry. I didn't have any money to put toward the house, so it made sense when he informed her that only his name would be on the deed. A few minutes into the closing, however, the woman asked me to step outside so she could speak to me.

She took me a few steps down the hallway and around the corner, then stopped. "Listen," she said, keeping her voice low, "I don't know what your situation is with your husband, but your name should at least go on the deed. It will protect you if he tries to throw you out or sell the house. But don't get on the mortgage, because then you'll be partly financially responsible for it."

She must know that Larry has been abusing me—but how? I wondered. Then I quickly realized it must have been because I was wearing sunglasses inside the office. I wouldn't take them off because I didn't want her to see that I was battered, yet people can always tell. Without her trying to protect me, I would never have known what my options were. God sends angels into our lives in all forms. We just have to be smart enough to recognize them.

When we went back into the office, I deliberately didn't make eye contact with Larry because I knew he would want to find out what the woman had said to me. When she informed him that my name would go on the deed alongside his, I could feel him glaring at me.

"But not the mortgage," he said. That was Larry's narcissism talking; even though keeping me off the mortgage reduced my financial liability, the sense of power he derived from doing so outweighed the practicality of asking me to contribute.

The closing took about two hours, and when it was all over, the woman handed us the keys to our new home. *Please let this be a new start for all four of us,* I said to myself.

We drove straight to the house. While we were in the car, Larry asked me, "What did that lady say to you?"

I thought quickly and said, "She just told me, 'You should get on the deed. If something ever happened to Larry, that will make sure that your kids are still all right.'"

Larry said, "Oh, that does make sense," and I exhaled the breath I had been holding. After that, his mood improved and he started telling me about all the things he wanted to do with the house. He also told me he wanted to get a dog—a rottweiler. I said I wasn't comfortable with that idea. When I was a little girl, Uncle Joe had a Doberman pinscher named Lady. He loved her as much as he loved his own kids, until she attacked his baby girl, Danielle. Without a moment's hesitation, Uncle Joe pulled out his gun and shot Lady right in his kitchen while I watched. It was the first time I had ever smelled gun smoke. Uncle Joe dragged Lady's corpse outside, dug a hole in his backyard, and buried her there. I had never been able to erase that memory from my mind, and I had been scared of dogs ever since.

When I explained all this to Larry, he just shrugged and kept his eyes on the road. "That was then; this is now," he said. "We're getting a dog."

When I asked "Who's going to walk it?" Larry said, "You. You don't got nothing to do with your life all day. That's the least you can do to contribute."

We suspended our conversation as we parked on Gray Avenue. Our house was a ranch-style building on a full acre of neatly manicured, bright green grass. We walked to our front door, and when Larry pushed it open, a distinct "new" aroma filled my nostrils. We walked around, inspecting every nook and cranny. The walls were all painted white, and each room had beige wall-to-wall carpeting. We had three bedrooms, and the master had an en suite bathroom. We also had a full basement that Larry wanted to transform into a movie theater and game room—presumably to entertain the friends he didn't have.

"Do you like it?" he asked. The whole time he had been overseeing the construction, I had never even been to the house.

I smiled. "Yes, it's beautiful. It's just so far from the city."

"So what?" He shrugged. "There's no reason for you to go back to the city."

"But my grandmother and all my friends are there," I explained.

"Whatever."

Fuck you, I said to myself. *You will never keep me away from Mommy.*

That weekend, we moved our belongings from Larry's parents' place into the new house. For the next few months, we spent the majority of our time shopping for things we needed to fill the rooms. We also got the rottweiler Larry wanted—a female puppy whom I named Duchess. I registered Morgan at the local public school and began acclimating to my new world.

Larry was working double shifts most days. I had Melissa on a strict schedule: I would wake her up for breakfast and her milk and turn on one of her favorite TV shows. I always put her down for a two-hour nap at noon, and during that time I would clean the house and figure out what to cook for dinner. Morgan got home from school at four o'clock; by then, I would be preparing dinner. I would leave out extra food for Larry to eat when he finished work, along with leftovers for lunch the next day. By living in this routine each day, I created the illusion of a peaceful environment for myself and my daughters—as long as Larry wasn't there.

Living out on Long Island meant that I was an hour and a half away from all of my friends and relatives, and I couldn't ignore my isolation. To kill time and loneliness, I began driving to the city twice a month to pick up the welfare check that Larry didn't know I was getting. I would just tell him that I was visiting Mommy. He never wanted me to go, though he knew I'd be willing to take a beatdown if it meant I could see her.

I invited Mommy many times to visit us on Long Island some weekend. Not only did I miss her, I wanted to get her away from Aunt Lilly, who was still physically abusing her and stealing her money. But Mommy always had an excuse for why she couldn't come. She never said it, but I always assumed it was because visiting me would take her away from her liquor. Whenever I went to see her on a weekend, she was just as drunk as I remembered, and she was starting to look more physically depleted. Her apartment had fallen into disrepair; the same furniture that had been there since 1979, when we moved into Brevoort, was still there in the '90s, and she wasn't keeping the place clean like she once had. We never talked about my relationship with Larry; I know Mommy saw my black eyes, yet she didn't bring up the beatings, so I didn't either. That was just the way we always were—we loved each other very much, but we rarely talked about anything important.

A year passed in that house that didn't feel like a home. The walls and carpets may have been light-colored, but darkness and sorrow lurked in every corner. I needed to get out, so one day while Morgan was at school, I decided to drive with Melissa to a restaurant at the end of my block. As I entered, I heard Bob Marley's music playing and smelled jerk seasoning.

A young man came up to me right away, smiling, and said in a strong West Indian accent, "Darling, may I help you?"

"No," I replied, "I was just stopping by to see what kind of restaurant this is."

I was explaining that I lived up the block, when a voice on my right, with the same West Indian accent, said, "Make the beautiful young lady something to eat."

I turned to look at the man who had just spoken. He was tall, slim, and dark-skinned, and appeared to be in his late twenties. Then I glanced around the restaurant for whomever he was addressing. I knew he hadn't called me beautiful; Larry only ever said I was stupid, dumb, or ugly.

"I'm talking to *you*," the man continued, sensing my confusion. "Don't you know you're beautiful, my love?" He gave me the warmest smile I had seen in a long time.

I smiled back and peered down at the floor.

"Look at the menu and order whatever you want—on me," he said.

"Are you sure?" I asked.

"Yes, baby love."

I asked for jerk chicken, rice and peas, and salad, which the man readily paid for. As Melissa and I exited the restaurant, the man followed me. I noticed that he walked with a slight limp.

"My name is Divine. I'm from Jamaica. What's your name?" he asked.

"Katrina."

"Nice to meet you, Miss Katrina. You are very beautiful." He winked, and I felt my face flush. He walked me to my car and opened the door for me. *Is this guy for real?* I wondered.

"Here's my phone number. Let's keep in touch. You look like you could use a friend," he said as I got into my car. I didn't respond.

At that moment, almost anyone with a kind word could have made me feel good. Now that we were isolated from everyone, Larry's beatings were becoming more frequent and more severe. If I didn't have a black eye, I had a busted lip or a fractured bone. He sometimes kicked me so hard that he broke my ribs. Other times, he pushed me down and kicked me in my face, before saying, "You're a piece of shit," and walking away.

After these episodes, I often had to stay in bed the entire next day because I was so sore. While I lay there, I analyzed my options obsessively, but I could not see a way out; I just kept thinking, *My life is over*. I didn't have anywhere to go. I didn't have enough money to support myself and my daughters. I had no education. One day, I decided, *I'm going to buy some poison, cook it into my food, and kill myself*. Then I thought, *No, fuck that. I'm not going to leave my daughters alone in the world without a mother. I'll poison Larry instead*. But then, I knew, I would end up in jail and would never see my children. They were the only thing that kept me going—that is, until Divine came along.

I waited for a week to pass before I contacted him. From that first call, I held on to every sweet thing he said to me, repeating it to myself in the late hours of the night, until I started to think that maybe I really was beautiful after all.

Before long, Divine and I were talking on the phone for hours every day. His soft, heavily accented voice lulled me nearly into a trance as he told me about the struggles he'd had in Jamaica, growing up in an impoverished family, and how his dream as a little boy had been to come to America. Now that he was in New York, he was working at the restaurant and also selling marijuana to customers around Long Island, so he had lots of cash.

I eventually told Divine everything about myself, including the fact that I was engaged and had two daughters. I also revealed to him how miserable I was with Larry and told him about the physical and emotional abuse I had been enduring. When he said to me, "You can't live like this. I want to turn your misery into happiness," I thought, *This man is going to save me*.

We quickly developed what felt like a true friendship. Divine was living with a cousin, even though he didn't want to, and was in the United States illegally. I was in an abusive relationship and trying to raise two children. We leaned on each other and found comfort in one another, and no matter what I told Divine, he never judged me.

We talked on the phone whenever Larry was gone, and even when Larry was at home, I made up excuses to get out of the house to see Divine. I became better at deception than I ever could have imagined. I would meet Divine at his cousin's house, only a few blocks away from mine, or at the restaurant at the end of the block. Sometimes we just got in the car and drove around. While Melissa slept in the backseat, Divine and I would pick up wherever our last conversation had left off.

Knowing that I had almost no income of my own, Divine started giving me money from time to time. "Go shopping," he'd say, showing me his beautiful smile. I used some of it to buy clothes for myself and my daughters. I wore the clothes from him only when I was with him, never with Larry, and the rest of the time I hid everything in the girls' room and hoped Larry would never find any of it. And I saved some of the cash to prepare for my escape.

The first time Divine and I made love was shortly before Thanksgiving. We were at his cousin's house one afternoon, and it just felt like a natural extension of the closeness we had been building. As we lay in bed in his dark room, I had my back to Divine. I happened to look over at the dresser, and I saw a prosthetic leg propped up against it, like a piece that had fallen off a mannequin. I wanted to sneak a glance at Divine's legs, but they were under the covers. I knew that he walked with a limp, and he had told me that he had gotten shot in Jamaica, yet he had never mentioned that it had cost him his leg. He must have finally gotten comfortable enough with me to take off the prosthesis, and I didn't want to compromise his trust or, worse, say something that would embarrass him or cause him to break up with me, when we had a good thing going, so I didn't say a word. I just shook my head the slightest bit, wondering, *How did he get that thing off so fast?*

Divine's leg didn't stop me from wanting to be with him, though. On the contrary, our sexual relationship was compassionate and tender, so different than the violent rape I had been experiencing at home, which only solidified my desire to leave Larry. I was finally with someone who was appreciating my body, not hurting it. The more time I spent with Divine, the more I wanted to be a better person, for myself and my children, and the more I despised Larry because I was finally starting to believe that I deserved more than he could ever give me.

As time went on, Divine and I talked about spending our

lives together. Since I knew he didn't have a green card, I wasn't sure if he truly loved me or if he was simply looking for his official ticket to America, but it didn't matter. As long as he could take me out of my current situation, I was all in. He told me that if I ever decided to break up with Larry, he would support me financially. I couldn't move in with him because he was living with his cousin, but he assured me that he would give me enough money to get my own place.

Meanwhile, my life with Larry was getting progressively worse. One night after he split my lip open for refusing to have sex with him, I called the cops again. This was the third time I had done so, but we were in a different jurisdiction now: Suffolk County. Maybe here, things would be different. When the officers showed up, Larry did exactly what he had done the last time: he asked to speak to them outside, he told them he was a CO, and they never even came back into the house to talk to me. *Damn*, I thought as I watched them drive off, *they even respect the badge here on Long Island.*

That night, I decided I was going to leave him for good. In the morning, while Larry was at work, I packed a few bags of clothes for the girls and me and drove us back to Bed-Stuy.

Less than twenty-four hours later, Larry was banging on Mommy's door, demanding that I come outside with Morgan and Melissa. Aunt Lilly, crackhead that she was, opened the door for him, and Larry burst into my room and dragged me out of the apartment as my children and Mommy watched. When Mommy tried to intervene, he pulled out his service revolver and held it against her head. "I will blow her fucking brains out if you and the girls don't come with me right now!"

He's gone and lost his damn mind, I thought, trembling. Larry had beaten me and raped me, but he had never threatened me with his weapon. And I had certainly never thought he would threaten Mommy. I had to protect her. I had to go with him.

On the ride back to Long Island, I was silent. I kept my

whole body turned away from Larry while I stared out the window. Morgan and Melissa had fallen asleep in the backseat, but I was wide awake. *I've got to kill this dude. I've got to get away from him.* I spent the drive envisioning different scenarios in which I murdered him and got away with it. I pictured shooting him in the head with his gun when he was asleep, or wrapping our telephone cord around his neck and strangling him. *If I don't kill him,* I told myself, *he's going to kill me first.*

As weeks passed, I fixated on these thoughts. Inside my head, he was already dead and gone; in reality, as weeks went by, nothing changed. Larry still wanted nothing more than to own me and control me. I woke up every day and asked myself why I was still living in a house with a man I despised. Every time he got on top of me, I felt so nauseated that I had to take Pepto Bismol. But I knew the answer to my question: it was because I had nothing and no one and was broken.

We tend to take certain support systems and relationships for granted because we don't recognize the true value of people who bless us with a sympathetic ear, good advice, and positive energy. Today, I know that these gifts are essential elements of a good life. Back then, I didn't have a single person I could count on until I met Divine.

When Larry and I had been going through the process of building our house, we had met a Latino couple named Jake and Jen. Our homes were both located in the same new development, and they had closed on theirs the same day we closed on ours. They had also relocated from Brooklyn and had young children of their own. Jake worked for Emergency Medical Services in the city, and Jen was a stay-at-home mom like I was. I never went to her house because Larry forbade it, but periodically she and I organized playdates at my house for all the kids. They would come by when Larry was off work, and we would all watch TV together.

Despite my proximity to Jen, I never disclosed any of the details about my relationship with Larry to her. She and Jake seemed blissfully in love, so I didn't think she would be able to relate to my situation.

One evening, Jen and Jake stopped by without their children. They hung out for a few minutes, and as soon as they left, Larry demanded that we go into our room to have sex. I was tired and just wanted to go to bed, but when I told him that, he smacked me upside my head and dragged me off our couch.

This time, I started to fight back. The fact that Divine had told me I had his full support if I decided to leave Larry gave me the fuel I needed to defend myself. *Fuck it*, I thought. *I'm going all out tonight.* I kicked Larry again and again, aiming my foot right at his testicles, screaming as loudly as I could.

As our furniture began to break and household items crashed to the floor, Morgan and Melissa came out of their room, screaming and crying. Enraged that I had the audacity to defend myself, Larry was punching me like he was fighting a man in the street. After some time, he moved from our living room into our kitchen. One of our kitchen chairs had a loose leg; he ripped that piece off, exposing the nail that had attached it to the seat, and surged toward me, hitting me in the head with it. The nail cut me deeply on my forehead; as blood spurted from the wound, I lay on the kitchen floor and soon felt too weak to move.

After a while, I got up and tried to get the telephone to call an ambulance, but Larry was right there. "You're not calling anyone!" he yelled, snatching the receiver away from me. He sent the girls to bed and called Jake. Within moments, Jake and Jen came back over. When Jen saw my head, she covered her mouth with her hand and started screaming, "Oh my God, oh my God!"

Jake kneeled down next to me and did his best to clean the wound and close it with bandages, but after he had done all he could, he told Larry, "I think she needs stitches."

"Well, she's not going to the hospital, because they'll call the cops," Larry said.

Jake tried to convince Larry that I needed additional medical attention, but when Larry wouldn't consent, Jake bandaged me up as Jen looked on with tears in her eyes. Jake advised me not to go to sleep for a while and promised he would check on me the next day. "Thank you," I whispered as they left. I wanted to add, *Take me with you.*

No sooner had they pulled out of the driveway than Larry forced me to have sex with him. It didn't matter that he had just busted my head wide open; he would rather have endangered my life than fail to satisfy his animalistic urges. As he pounded away inside me for the longest five minutes of my life, I distracted myself by thinking about how I could get out of our relationship. I thought back to Larry's mother's friend Amy's prediction that he was eventually going to kill me, and this time I knew she was right. I also knew that he would kill Mommy if she tried to protect me, so going back to her house wasn't an option. I decided I would ask Divine for help.

Shortly after that night, I discovered that I was four months pregnant. I had noticed that I had missed my period for a few months, but I had chalked it up to stress. Because I was so far along when I found out, I knew right away that it was Larry's baby, as it had been conceived before I had even met Divine. I shouldn't have been surprised, given how often Larry was raping me, yet I kept thinking about the kind of environment I would be bringing another child into. I decided to keep the baby, but I didn't mention my pregnancy to Larry. I promised myself that as soon as I had enough money saved, he was never going to see me or the kids again. I didn't mention my pregnancy to him, and I prayed for a boy. During my pregnancies with my daughters, I had always experienced crippling morning sickness, but this time I felt fine. That convinced me that I was finally having a son.

I knew I would eventually have to tell Divine that I was pregnant, but I wasn't ready, because I still needed his support. *What man would be crazy enough to be there for me while I'm having another guy's baby?*

One day while we were on one of our drives, I blurted out the news, then stared straight ahead at the road, my heart pounding.

Divine turned to me in the car and took my hand. "Well, you don't have to tell anybody that," he said.

"But I'm already four months along," I said.

"So what? Once you leave Larry, everyone will just think it's my baby."

I gaped at him as he calmly steered the car. *This man is actually going to take responsibility for a baby that's not even his?* I had hardly ever known any fathers who showed up for their own kids, let alone another man's child. "Are you serious?" I asked.

"You know I am," Divine said, smiling at me.

That was the moment I knew I could safely hatch an exit plan.

Between the cash Divine had given me and the welfare checks I was still collecting, I had managed to squirrel away five hundred dollars, which was the most money I had ever saved at one time. It was the holiday season, and I told myself that after the new year, I would start a new life.

In mid-December, Larry's sister Karen came to visit. Larry behaved himself in front of her, but when I had a moment alone with her, I told her everything he had been doing. Unfortunately, she wasn't surprised. I also confided in her that I had met a man who was much nicer to me than Larry was. "I really want to be with him," I said. "But even if that doesn't happen, I'm still leaving your brother. I can't take it anymore."

When Karen didn't jump to defend Larry, I was so desperate for an ally that I decided I could trust her. I even went so far as to take her to a party Divine was having. We were there all night, and as we were leaving, Karen turned to me and said, "I like Divine. You should be with him. He'll make you happy." At the time, I had no idea she was setting me up.

When it was time for Karen to leave, Larry drove her to the airport. While he was gone, I packed up everything I could and checked into a nearby motel with Morgan and Melissa. I didn't want to venture too far because I wanted to be able to see Divine. He came by every day, and I would sit in the car with him right outside our room and talk to him, trying to formulate my next steps. But I kept getting stuck about what to do, because the only place I could think to go was Brooklyn, and I knew living there wouldn't be safe for us either.

After a few days, I called Mommy because I knew Larry would have gone over there to look for me. He had, of course, but this time he hadn't pulled a gun on her. Mommy said I should have told her where I was going, and I told her that I didn't want to put her in danger; Larry could have forced her to reveal my whereabouts. I assured her that I was okay and told her that no matter what, I wasn't returning to Larry. "If he comes back to Brevoort, don't answer the door. Also, don't bother calling the cops, because they'll be useless," I said, and hung up.

We stayed in that motel for two weeks, but my money was dwindling and my children needed more clothes. I called Mommy again, and she told me that Larry had stopped coming by to look for me. We both thought maybe he had finally given up.

Christmas passed, and on January 2, 1993, I decided to call Larry. He still didn't know about my pregnancy, and I didn't feel right keeping it from him anymore. To my surprise, he didn't verbally abuse me. Instead, he sounded upbeat and glad to hear from me, and when I told him I was pregnant and that I thought we were having a boy, I could hear him smiling through the phone.

He said, "Trina, I know we haven't been getting along and that you haven't been happy. I want you to be happy. And I want to be in our son's life. Everything is going to be different now. I'm going to change." He said everything I had been wanting to hear, though he never asked me to come home or to get back together with him. I had suspected that he was cheating on me with a fellow corrections officer whom he used to carpool with, and when he didn't put any pressure on me during our phone call, I thought, *He must be with her now*. I was actually happy for him—and for myself.

We even talked about what we should name our baby. "How about Larry?" Larry said.

"No." I had let Larry name Melissa, and I knew what I wanted my son to be called. "His name will be Justice."

I thought surely Larry would fight me on this, but he simply said, "Justice? Okay," and that settled it.

Larry made me promise to call him every day after that, just to tell him how the girls and I were doing, and I did what he asked. Each time we spoke over the next week, he was a person I actually enjoyed talking to. *Where was this man the whole time I was living with him?* I thought. We were even able to laugh together when I joked, "You bought Melissa an Aprica stroller; you know you're going to have to buy this new baby the same one, right?"

Larry just chuckled and said, "Oh, my son is going to have *everything*."

Our conversations were so easy and fluid that when I called Larry the following Friday, January 8, and asked if I could come over to pick up some clothes for myself and the girls, he agreed immediately. "Come over around eleven tomorrow morning," he said. "I'll be home then."

And that was how I found myself back on Gray Avenue, shot ten times, and left for dead.

CHAPTER 9

God Always Has the Last Word

I floated into consciousness on a sea of fluffy white clouds. I saw bright lights hovering over my head and heard the muffled echo of voices. "God, You can do it! God, You are a healer!"

My eyelids were so heavy that I could hardly open them, yet through my blurred vision, I made out a small group of women standing around me, wearing long skirts and holding Bibles. "God, You can do it!" the women chanted. "We trust You!"

Who are these people? I wondered. *And where am I?* I scanned my memory for the last thing I could recall, and I conjured an image of myself lying on the floor of my living room on Long Island, shot by my fiancé. *Am I dead? Am I in heaven? Or is this hell?*

I forced my vision to focus, but even that small effort was exhausting. Still, the women must have noticed it, because they screamed out, "Oh my God! Thank You, Jesus!" They laid their hands upon me and began to pray even more intently.

I still did not have a relationship with God, but when those women put all their energy into saving my life, I felt ever so slightly lifted up. It was one of the first hints of the magnitude of my faith journey.

***

A few days later, I was still weak and groggy, but I was in stable enough condition to be removed from my deathbed, transferred out of the intensive care unit, and placed in a regular hospital room. There, I began to slowly piece together what had happened to me since Larry had shot me. I learned that I had fallen unconscious after the fifth bullet entered my body on January 9 and had been in a coma ever since. Now it was January 18. I had a lot of catching up to do.

"Girl, you are a miracle!" one of my nurses raved when I asked her who had sent all the flowers and balloons crowding my hospital room. "People from all over have been delivering gifts to you. Your story was all over the news. Your fiancé tried to kill you."

I knew that much, but this conversation with the nurse revealed the extent to which Larry had premeditated my murder. I learned from her that in addition to shooting me five more times and beating me even after I lost consciousness, Larry had also put our dog, Duchess, in the basement ahead of time on the day I agreed to come over to collect my belongings, because he knew she would have tried to protect me if she had seen him hurting me. Only because Larry's cousin Sha happened to show up at the house that afternoon had I not bled out in my own bathroom.

"Do you know where my kids are?" I asked the nurse.

"Let me get Dr. Jude," she said. "He can tell you more."

She left, and a few minutes later, a tall, handsome white man with glasses entered my room. "Good morning, Katrina. How do you feel?" he asked.

"I don't know," I said. "I'm trying to find out where my children are."

Dr. Jude's face was inscrutable, his voice flat, as he reeled off one piece of bad news after another: "I'm sorry to say that your baby boy didn't survive. You will never be able to have more children. You will also never be able to walk again. You will never have a normal life. But you are alive."

"But why?"

"Because you were shot ten times. You still have six bullets in your left side. I didn't want to take a chance removing them; it could have been fatal."

What? What? Why am I still alive right now? My fiancé shot me and left me for dead. He killed our son. I'm paralyzed from the waist down. If I'm never going to walk again, I have no purpose. I can't take care of my daughters or myself. I don't even know where my kids are right now. I'm never going to have a normal life. Just one of those pieces of information would have been nearly impossible to process, but all at once? I thought I had already experienced the lowest points of my life. And now Larry had won. I probably would have tried to kill myself if I didn't have two daughters; they were the only reason I could think of to go on living.

"A social worker will be here soon to speak to you about your children," Dr. Jude continued, "and we will arrange for you to do rehab from your home."

I could barely hear him. His voice was fading in and out like it was in a vacuum, *wah-wah-wah-wah*. I leaned back against my pillow and closed my eyes as tears leaked out. *Home? I don't even have a home.* "How long will I have to stay here in the hospital?" I finally managed to ask.

"That depends on how your body heals," he said.

He gave my chart a final look and then turned to exit, but before he crossed the threshold of my room, he turned around and looked at me with a slight smile. "I honestly never thought I would be here talking to you," he said.

When the social worker came in, she told me that my daughters had been sent to live with Larry's mother in the South. The day I was shot, the police had contacted her and she came up to New York to get the girls and take them back down to her house. My only consolation was that although Larry's mother had been hostile to me, she had always been kind to Morgan and Melissa, so, I reasoned, at least they were with a relative they knew, someone who would treat them well, rather than in the foster care system and at risk of being abused. And because I was in no physical condition to care for them, I did not have a leg to stand on, literally or figuratively. But I also promised myself that I would not lose my daughters for good, no matter what I had to do to get them back.

The final piece of the puzzle of the day Larry shot me did not fall into place until years later, when his cousin Sha finally told me his account of what had happened. Evidently, Sha had called Larry a few hours before I arrived with Melissa. He said Larry sounded manic on the phone, speaking too quickly to make any sense, so Sha decided to go check on him. When he got to the house, he encountered a scene right out of a horror movie.

"I did it," Larry said when he answered the door.

"Did what?" Sha asked.

"I killed Trina."

"You *what*?"

"I killed Trina," Larry repeated. "She deserved it."

When Larry let Sha inside the house, he found me unconscious. "There was blood everywhere. You were naked and soaked in it," he told me.

When Sha realized that I was still alive, he dragged my body out to my car—which had been parked alongside the house ever since I moved out to the motel—and rushed toward Brookhaven Memorial Hospital. Although I remembered nothing of the drive, Sha told me I kept saying, "Just let me die." But Sha told me, "I'm not letting that happen."

When we got close to the hospital, Sha knew he would be considered an accessory to murder if he escorted me inside. So, as much as it was not in his nature, he left my unconscious body on the street outside the building and fled. He sped back to Gray Avenue to drop off my car and was there when the police arrived to arrest Larry.

Helicopters hovered over the house to prevent Larry's potential escape, though he didn't even try to run. When the police knocked on his door, he was watching TV and drinking a Pepsi. He opened the door calmly and, with a sinister grin on his face, asked, "What took you so long?"

It turned out that after the hospital staff found me outside the emergency room and shortly before I slipped into a coma, I had given them two key pieces of information. I have a vague memory of doctors and nurses crowding around me, saying, "She's pregnant!" over and over and asking me, "Who did this to you?"

"My fiancé," I managed to say.

"And where does he live?" they asked.

I answered just before I lost consciousness again.

That was all the police needed to arrest Larry. They also took Sha in for questioning, and he shared more details about the day that clearly identified Larry as my attempted murderer.

Mommy learned what had happened to me from the six o'clock news. Shortly thereafter, the hospital called to let her know I wouldn't live through the night. Just as she had for three of her five children, she began to make arrangements for my funeral. But when she arrived at the hospital the next day to identify my body, she learned that I was still alive, albeit in a vegetative state. The staff told her what they eventually told me: that even if I survived, I would never walk again, have more children, or be able to live a normal life.

Once I was awake, Mommy and I talked on the phone every day. Long Island was too far from Brevoort for her to visit me in person, but hearing her voice and knowing she had not had to bear the burden of losing yet another child brought me some comfort.

Many other people came to see me and show their support. The woman who had been leading the prayer group at my bedside when I emerged from my coma turned out to be a cousin of Larry's named Lena. Although I had never met her before, she and her powerful faith community had prayed me back into consciousness and visited me numerous times, tirelessly continuing their attempts to heal me. Jake and Jen, the neighbors on Long Island who had helped me after Larry punctured my head with the kitchen chair leg, also visited.

My most frequent visitor of all was Divine. He came every day while I was in the coma, and continued to after I woke up. The first time he saw me conscious, he wept. "I'm so sorry this happened to you. I can't believe he did this to you. You don't deserve this. How can I make it better?"

It was the first time I had ever seen a grown man cry, and I cried right along with him, but I was still too weak and confused from my coma to have an in-depth conversation with him.

Then one day, a short, slim white woman entered my room. "Hi," she said, "I'm Keri." When I replied, "Nice to meet you," she said, "Actually, we've already met. We spoke right after your emergency surgery. I took a dying declaration from you before you fell into a coma. I'm happy to see you alive now."

"What's a dying declaration?" I asked. "I don't remember that at all."

"It's a statement someone makes when they believe they're about to die and are therefore unable to testify in court," Keri explained. "The statement speaks to the circumstances surrounding the cause of their impending death."

She must have been here when I named Larry as my attempted murderer and stated my address, I thought. "Why are you here now?" I asked her.

"I'm the district attorney assigned to your case, and I want to make sure your former fiancé spends the rest of his life in prison for what he did to you. A man who can gun down the mother of his children and kill his unborn child doesn't deserve to walk the streets ever again."

It was another first: the first time I had found someone who seemed willing to advocate for me, because law enforcement certainly was not.

I learned later that while I was incapacitated, a detective had shown up at the hospital. Although I do not remember his visit, he submitted a handwritten statement, dated January 24 and signed with my name, detailing the events of January 9. That day, I was not even physically able to write anything—I was paralyzed and newly awakened from a coma. What I eventually discovered was the police had taken a version of Larry's statement and falsified it to make it appear like it was my statement instead. Imagine my surprise when I discovered that a document I had never written, signed, or even laid eyes on later became part of the evidence in Larry's trial.

It was just the police's latest attempt to protect one of their own. I learned that when they arrived at Larry's house to take him to the station, they let him sit down while they read him his rights and arrested him. He had just shot someone ten times, yet they were concerned enough for his physical well-being to ensure that he was comfortable. Meanwhile, every time I had called them after one of Larry's brutal beatings, they saw me with black eyes, open wounds, and bruises all over my body, but they'd never once had the decency to allow me to share my story. For each time the police dehumanized me by turning their backs on me, they humanized Larry. And they were doing it again now, by aiding and abetting an attempted murderer.

Larry's mother was equally determined to protect her beloved son in the wake of his arrest. I thought surely, after he had shot me ten times in cold blood, after she had taken my children to live with her, she would have come to the hospital to express her condolences in person, to finally show a bit of humanity toward me. I wanted to see her walk through my door so that I could ask her, "What excuse do you have for your son's behavior now?" But she would not give me the satisfaction. She wanted me gone as much as Larry did. And many days I thought the two of them were right—that I would have been better off dead than trapped in a prison of my own body and mind.

CHAPTER 10

When the Doctors Said No, God Said Yes

On February 1, 1993, twenty-three days after being admitted to the hospital, I was released. At Lena's request, Larry's mother reluctantly agreed to let me move into her house in Brooklyn, on one condition: that I wouldn't press charges against her son for what he had done to me.

Larry was already being held in a Suffolk County jail and would stay there because he had no option for bail, but even if he had been free, I knew I couldn't agree to his mother's terms. However, I said yes for the time being because I had no other place to go. The great irony of Larry's attempt to murder me was that it was his family, not mine, who came to take me out of the hospital.

When Lena and her husband, Harry, arrived at the hospital on my discharge date, I was in a wheelchair. They got me settled in the backseat of their car, and I sat silently for most of the ride. But then I looked down at my atrophied legs and began to bawl. You never know how valuable your limbs are until you're no longer able to use them. Now I was more fragile than I had ever been.

We had to stop at Gray Avenue before we could continue

on to Larry's mother's house in Bed-Stuy. I had still not had a chance to retrieve my clothes. When Lena and Harry wheeled me inside, all I saw was blood—covering the white walls, the beige carpeting, the furniture. I remembered the first time I had seen the inside of the house and how pristine it was.

The one possession of mine that remained in the house was a pair of red Reeboks. Larry's mother had come while I was in the hospital and removed everything else that belonged to my daughters and me. She had taken the girls' clothes down South with her and had thrown away everything of mine, assuming that I would soon be dead and would have no use for it.

When I entered Larry's mother's house in Brooklyn, heaviness engulfed my whole body. *How can I be back here?* I thought. *Nothing about this feels right. I shouldn't even be alive.* Lena squeezed my shoulder and told me that praying to God would allow me to have a full recovery, yet I didn't believe her.

Social services assigned me a nurse, a twenty-four-hour home attendant, and a physical therapist. For the first month after I was discharged from the hospital, I spent my time sitting in front of the television in my wheelchair. I saw no point in trying to do anything else. My stomach was torn apart; my whole lower body was numb. The home attendant would sponge-bathe me, and the nurse would empty my colostomy bag, change my bandages, and administer my pain medication. There was nothing more to my life than that—no agency, no physical strength, and seemingly no hope.

But my physical therapist, Lee, changed everything. He was young—I was his first-ever client—and he was not about to let me sit around feeling sorry for myself. He came over three days a week at eleven a.m., just as my favorite game show, *The Price Is Right*, was starting. At first, I made Lee sit and watch it with me while I refused to let him help me. But eventually he got frustrated.

"I come here every other day, and you never want to do therapy," he said. "At least let me try this." He lifted one of my legs slightly and moved it around to stimulate the muscles.

When I felt nothing, I said, "See? It's not working. The doctor says I'm never going to walk again. What's the point of doing therapy?"

But Lee must have felt something deep in my leg—some tiny reflex that I couldn't detect—because he said, "If you give me a chance, you will walk again." I still didn't believe him, but the conviction in his voice made me trust him just a little bit more than I trusted everyone else who had tried to give me hope.

I began to pay attention to what Lee asked me to do, and somehow he transferred his will to me. By the time Lena took me to see an orthopedist named Dr. Watson one month later for a follow-up appointment, I was still in my wheelchair, but I was able to rise up out of it and stand before him for a few moments.

He flew backward in his chair when he saw how much progress I had already made. "You are one lucky girl!" he said, his eyes bulging.

"It's not luck," Lena told him. "It's God."

I now know firsthand that God has a way of bringing people into our lives who can turn our most challenging situations around. It is our job to listen, be open, and let God have His way. During my rehabilitation, I started going to the Beulah Church of God on Marcy Avenue in Brooklyn. At the first service I went to, all I did was cry. I just kept thinking, *All for some freakin' clothes.* I couldn't yet see that if I had not gone to Gray Avenue on January 9, Larry would have just found another way to try to kill me.

Every time I returned to church, my faith strengthened, and soon I decided to get baptized. I still could not walk on my own, so the deacons carried me to the baptism pool. That same day, I felt a tingling sensation in my feet and my legs for the first time since I had been paralyzed.

God had proven Himself to me, and I vowed that I would not give up on Him.

By the end of April 1993, I was walking with a walker. By the beginning of that summer, I was walking with a cane. By the end of the summer, I was walking on my own.

Then one day, Larry called me from jail. To be forced to hear his voice again after what he had done to me felt like a cruel joke.

"Trina, I need your help to get me out of jail," he said.

"How am I supposed to get you out of there?" I asked.

"When the courts ask who shot you, just say you shot yourself," he instructed. "My mother will write a letter with all the details; all you need to do is sign it. Then I'll get released and we can be together."

"That's not going to happen," I said.

"Why not?"

"Are you serious? Why do you think? You shot me ten times and killed my baby!"

Ignoring this, Larry tried to charm me: "You won't do it? But I'm just trying to help you. If you help me come home, I'll take care of you." The more I resisted, the more desperate he sounded. "I can't be here. I can't do this. Don't do this to me, Trina."

Fortunately, before he could say anything else, our time was up and the call ended.

That same night, Lena rang and told me she had spoken with Larry's mother, who had said that if I wasn't willing to cooperate with Larry's request to write a letter for him, I was no longer welcome to live at her house, effective immediately. Lena said that I could stay with her and Harry in their apartment in Mount Vernon, New York. They came to pick me up the next day.

I spoke to Larry one more time after his mother kicked me

out. It was a few months later; I was at Lena's one day when he called her. He began by telling her I'd been cheating on him, as justification for what he had done to me. When he found out that I was staying with her, he asked to speak to me directly, and once more attempted to soothe and charm me.

"Trina," he began, "I love you and miss you. Once I get released, I want us to be together again. I promise to take care of you from now on. And I will never hit you again."

Hit me? I thought. *How about* shoot *me?* In the past, I would have cursed him out. But now I was a Christian. I just passed the phone back to Lena.

Larry's mother still had custody of Morgan and Melissa. I had had no contact with either of my daughters; she had not allowed it. And although I had made great progress with my mobility, I was still in no position—physically or financially—to take care of two children. I didn't know when or if I would ever see them again.

But then, two months after she'd kicked me out of her house, Larry's mother returned my children to me. She had been trying to legally adopt them but had changed her mind. I believe she relinquished them to me because she wanted to destroy me. She knew I had no way to provide for them, and she enjoyed seeing me broken and destitute. But I was not about to give her that satisfaction.

The first time I saw my daughters again, I held them in my arms and wept. I thanked God for the mercy that my face had healed from Larry's final beating and that I was able to walk on my own, sparing them the sight of their mother as a disfigured and paralyzed woman. They were still so young—only three and seven—that they seemed unfazed by our separation. All they asked me was, "Where have you been?"

I left Lena's and moved into a transitional family shelter in the Bronx so I could get on the list for a Section 8 apartment.

My girls and I needed to start over, and we could only do that in a place that was truly ours. I told myself again and again, *As soon as I find us an apartment, I can figure out my life.* Each day, I would use the subway tokens the shelter gave me to take the train to Mommy's at Brevoort. I rarely entered the apartment because it had fallen into such disrepair. Instead, I would spend the day sitting on a bench outside her building while my daughters played nearby, or I would visit my friend Shanice. Once in a while, during those long July and August days, I could trick myself into thinking I wasn't homeless.

The minute we returned to the shelter, though, I was reminded of my grim reality. Sometimes the girls and I had to bathe in a McDonald's bathroom because people were defecating in the showers at the shelter. My welfare benefits gave me only two hundred dollars to live on every two weeks, and when that money ran out, our only food options were cheese sandwiches or peanut butter and jelly on stale bread from the shelter. Sometimes we had nothing to eat at all, or I would forgo food so that I could feed the girls. Even though I had found God, I was still broken.

I began to blame myself for what had happened to us. Maybe I should not have gotten involved with Divine, who had virtually disappeared after visiting me every day in the hospital. Maybe I should have stayed with Larry. At least my girls and I would have had a home and food. I was the reason my daughters were suffering. Many times each day, I asked myself if it would have been better for everyone if Larry had killed me. I felt as if Satan was testing me by taking away everything I had—my home, my health, my children. I wanted to have Job's resolve not to curse God for my circumstances, but I had to work hard to find that forgiveness within me.

In the midst of my despair, I was assigned a social worker, Vanessa, to help me transition out of the shelter. She was so kind to me; she said, "If you have already applied for Section 8,

I can help you get a voucher for an apartment." Yet even then, the process of finding a new place to live was not as easy as I thought it would be; as I came to learn, many landlords were not willing to honor Section 8 vouchers. I just wanted some stability for my daughters. They had been through enough already.

I was hoping to stay in Bed-Stuy, but that didn't seem likely, so one day I looked at a place in Brownsville. I had never considered living there because it was one of the worst parts of Brooklyn at the time—drug infested, with low-ranked schools and many residents living below the poverty threshold. But anything was better than living in a shelter.

The apartment was on Strauss Street, in a nice, clean building owned by a Jamaican man named Tom. He and his wife, Sharon, were in their late forties and had two teenage kids. It was a two-family house and my apartment was on the second floor. The two bedrooms weren't big, though the living room was a nice size.

I walked through the apartment room by room, claiming it. After inspecting the entire space, I told Tom that I wanted it.

"It's yours," he said, and walked out without so much as a goodbye.

Once he was gone, I started jumping up and down and thanking God. Tom probably didn't think much of the place, but to me it was everything.

I moved in on November 1, 1993. Once I received the keys and was officially unpacked, I exhaled deeply. Leaning against the kitchen sink, I began to cry. All I could do was thank God for leading me out of so much darkness.

The welfare office gave me a thousand dollars to purchase everything we would need to furnish our new home. After the furniture was delivered and set up, I went to get the girls, who despite my reservations had been staying at Mommy's, and took them back to the apartment.

"This is our new house," I told them, beaming as I showed

them around. They walked through the space in awe; it had been months since I had last seen such hope and joy in their eyes.

"Does that mean we don't have to sleep at the charity place anymore?" Morgan asked, practically vibrating with excitement. When I assured her that we were never going back to the shelter, they both hugged me tightly.

With my baby cousin: out of the shelter and into our new apartment.

That first night, I tucked the girls into their beds, and then slept soundly in my own room for the first time in what felt like an eternity. I smiled to myself in the darkness as I drifted off. Larry was in jail, so I didn't have to worry about him coming after us. My body was healing in a way that no one had ever expected. And I had been saved. I had learned that God, my Lord and savior, brings good energy and heals all pain. He also teaches us to forgive and to love. He teaches strength and faithfulness. He heals the sick. He does whatever we need Him to do.

The holidays that year were full of magic for us. For Thanksgiving, I used my food stamps to buy as many groceries as I could, and I cooked and cooked. The girls and I had been starving for so long, I wanted us to have more food than we could even eat. I made macaroni and cheese, candied yams, collard greens, turkey, chicken, and so much more—all the same holiday dishes that Mommy used to make. And when Christmastime came, I took a taxi with Melissa to Belmont Avenue one day when Morgan was at school, and we picked out a tiny tree. We took it back home with us in another cab and decorated it. We had everything we needed. We had a home, we were together, and we were safe—at least for the moment.

Not long after we moved in, Tom started coming upstairs a lot, asking to inspect my apartment for no real reason. One day out of the blue, he came too close to me. Stroking my arm, he said, "You're so sweet and nice. I want to take you out. You should let me come stay with you up here sometimes."

I took several steps back and put my hands out to stop him from coming any closer. He was a married man with a wife and children living right below me. I lied to him and told him that I had a man and wasn't interested in spending time with him.

Although Tom backed off and never propositioned me again, he launched a series of microaggressions against me. Sometimes I would come home to find him standing in the hallway outside my front door, and he'd just look me up and down. He started playing petty games with me, like not sending heat to my unit or withholding hot water. Then one day he entered my apartment with his master key, without asking my permission. I had just gotten out of the shower, and when I asked him, "What do you think you're doing?" he said, "This is my house. I can do what I want in here." That was the moment when I realized, *I need to get out of here, or this man is going to rape me someday. And it's not like the cops will help me if I call them.*

Tom could have his house, I decided. I called the same realtor I had used before and asked him if he could find me a new place because my landlord was giving me a hard time and my lease was about to expire. The realtor showed me a couple of new apartments, and I chose one in East Flatbush, on Rockaway Parkway. The four-unit building was not particularly well maintained, but it was better than having a stalker for a landlord. My unit quickly passed the Section 8 inspection, and my daughters and I moved in right away.

CHAPTER 11

A Jury Not of My Peers

In February 1994, a few months after my daughters and I moved into our apartment on Strauss Street, Larry's case was scheduled to go to trial. Keri had remained in contact with me ever since I had been discharged from the hospital. She had been urging me to testify in court because she knew that without my firsthand account of the shooting, we didn't have a case. But I kept refusing. "They're never going to lock Larry up. Cops always get off easy," I told her. I just wanted to move on with my life and avoid further trauma. In the 1990s, police officers were simply not going to prison for their crimes the way civilians were. Even now, in the 2020s, it happens in only the most publicized cases.

But Keri simply said, "No, no—there's far too much evidence against Larry for that to happen." No matter how many times I protested, she kept insisting. She finally grew so frustrated with me that she screamed at me one day, "I will hunt you down like a dog and drag you onto the witness stand myself if I have to!"

Ironically, that was the moment when I decided to do as she asked. I realized that anyone who was willing to tolerate as much as Keri had tolerated from me must believe in me more than I believed in myself. She told me she was confident that justice would favor us. "So when you walk into that courtroom, make sure you hold your head up," she said.

Larry had been charged with attempted murder in the first degree, and as much as I trusted Keri, I knew that his mother had hired a high-profile attorney to defend him. Keri warned me that Larry's lawyer would make me out to be some sort of gold digger from the projects who had used Larry as a means to escape poverty. And while I could admit to myself that that may have been my original plan, no one deserved to be physically and emotionally abused—let alone shot ten times—for it.

On the day of the hearing, Lena and Harry drove me to the courthouse in Suffolk County. Lena prayed during the entire drive, but I could not bring myself to participate and remained quiet. I was imagining myself coming face-to-face with Larry in the courtroom. I was remembering how he had told me while he was shooting me that even if he went to prison, he would get only five to fifteen years because of his job. *What if he's released from jail?* I thought. *What am I going to do if he comes after me again?*

My stomach churning, I got out of the car, smoothed out my white shirt and black skirt, and tried to keep my expression neutral as I entered the courthouse. Inside the courtroom, I saw Keri and a few other people, but Larry and his mother were not present, nor was the judge or a jury. Larry was in a holding pen outside the room and would be brought in shortly.

I had heard that the judge was newly appointed but already had a reputation for handing down lenient sentences to law enforcement officers. *This is never going to work*, I thought. Just as I had so many other times, I felt the odds stacking against me as the judge entered the courtroom. Everyone rose as he approached his bench. Next, a bailiff brought out Larry in handcuffs. I gaped when I saw him. He looked twenty years older than he had the last time I had seen him. His skin was dry and sallow, his shoulders were slumped, and he shuffled along as if all the stress he was under would not permit him to walk any faster. I wondered if his appearance was genuine or just a ploy to get sympathy from the judge.

I wanted Larry to look at me. I wanted him to see me as I sent him this silent message: *You tried to kill me, but look, I'm alive. You paralyzed me, but look, I'm walking. Everything that you tried to do to me wasn't done in the end.*

He eventually glanced in my direction, and while he would not make eye contact with me, I could see the fear on his face. He and his mother must have thought they could manipulate me, through their scare tactics and blackmail attempts, into avoiding the hearing, but there I was, a ghost before him, reminding him of what he had tried and failed to do.

I saw him lean over and whisper something into his attorney's ear, and then the attorney asked the judge permission for him and Keri to approach the bench. The two lawyers spoke quietly to the judge for a few minutes, and then Keri came to me and said, "Let's go outside for a minute."

"What's going on?" I asked, my heart rate accelerating.

"Just come with me."

I followed her into the hallway, and she said, "Larry has changed his mind. He's going to cop a plea."

"So he's not even going to go in front of a jury?" I asked. "I thought I was supposed to testify."

"Look, you know I want what's best for you, Katrina, and that means keeping Larry in prison. I'm still going to ask the judge for a sentence of twenty-five years to life, but just know that the judge is going to take into consideration that Larry has never been in trouble before, that he's a law enforcement officer, and that his lawyer is deeming this a crime of passion."

I was starting to feel like I couldn't breathe. How could someone grant any allowances to a man who had gunned down the mother of his own children? I kept fighting to live, yet people all around me, society itself, seemed to believe my life was worthless. I could only pray that Keri's words illuminated the truth.

When we reentered the courtroom, Keri spoke on my behalf, explaining to the judge that Larry had shot me ten times—once in the arm, once in the buttocks, three times in the stomach, once in the hip, and four times in the vagina—and that I still had six bullets in my body. She told him that Larry had known that I was five months pregnant at the time of his crime and that he had no remorse for what he had done to me. She also mentioned that I had no family support and had been homeless until recently. All of these factors, she claimed, justified her request for the maximum sentence of twenty-five years to life.

Larry's lawyer countered that I was an uneducated gold digger from the projects and that I was such an awful person that my own family didn't want anything to do with me. He said Larry had shot me out of passion because I had used him, so he was asking the court for five to fifteen years because—just as Keri had predicted he would say—his client was a hardworking corrections officer and a responsible homeowner who had never had any trouble with the law.

After less than one minute of deliberation, the judge looked right at Larry's attorney and said, "Your request will be granted." The sound of the gavel echoed throughout the courtroom, a door slamming on my future happiness.

I rushed out of the courtroom and doubled over in the hallway, trying not to scream. *I knew this would happen*, I thought. *I knew I would never win.* I tried to imagine if the situation were reversed; if I had been the one to shoot Larry. I didn't have a criminal record either, but I also wasn't a CO. I knew the court would not have shown me any mercy.

When Keri came out to find me, she was even angrier than I was. I didn't want to say, "I told you so," but when she kept apologizing for disappointing me, I had to remind her that I had known this would happen. The government was designed to protect law enforcement, and the system had failed me again and again—from cops choosing to ignore the sight of Niecy brutally beating me in public, to Larry flashing his badge to avoid punishment for abusing me, to today, when the judge had granted an attempted murderer the lightest punishment possible. Keri might have believed that my case was so cut and dried that the maximum sentence was the only possible outcome, but to me, my loss was inevitable. I felt like I had been left for dead all over again.

Twenty-eight years later, in February 2022, a *48 Hours* episode called "The Good Cop" aired. Along with millions of other viewers in the United States, I watched the televised version of my story unfold. All that time since Larry's hearing, I had been under the illusion that I knew the complete version of events, yet the program revealed otherwise. I learned that Larry had allegedly told the judge that he still loved me and that he was nothing without me, but also that he had no regrets and would have killed himself if he had the courage to do so. I also discovered that after I refused to perjure myself and write the letter Larry's mother asked me to write, claiming that I had shot myself and that I did not want to press charges against her son, she wrote it herself, signed it with my name, and gave it to the defense attorney, who passed it along to the judge. This was the third time someone had forged my signature on a legal document; first, Niecy signed the papers authorizing Morgan's adoption; next, the detective who came to the hospital wrote and signed a false statement on my behalf about Larry's crime; and now this.

I was still in touch with Keri, and I called her after I watched the episode. "Keri," I said, "where did that letter come from?"

"What do you mean?" she asked. "I thought *you* wrote it."

"I didn't write it. Larry's mother did. I didn't even know about it until just now, when I watched the show."

Keri was silent for a few minutes. Then she said, "I can't believe I didn't ask you about this back then. I just assumed it was your own writing. I thought you didn't want to testify because of what that letter said. I'm so sorry."

Keri didn't know that the letter was fraudulent, but Larry must have sensed that as soon as he saw me in the courtroom the day of his hearing. Realizing that I did in fact want him to be prosecuted and convicted to the fullest extent of the law, he would have understood that he was better off making a plea deal right then than running the risk of letting a full trial play out. And he got what he wanted: he shot me with his own service weapon and was given a sentence akin to what a burglar or the perpetrator of a computer crime would receive. That wasn't justice—that was a crime in itself.

The day Larry was sentenced, Keri promised me that she would go to every one of his parole hearings to make sure he served the full fifteen years. She kept her promise, but even after everything he had done to me, he was released after only twelve.

CHAPTER 12

Homelessness Is in My Rearview Mirror

After my daughters and I moved into our new apartment in East Flatbush, I attempted to establish a routine for their sake. I took Morgan to school every day and kept Melissa home with me. I continued going to church. I also saw Divine one more time. He picked me up, gave me some money for groceries, and took me to the supermarket. While I was happy to see him, we didn't discuss anything substantial—not our relationship, and not what had happened to me. We just picked up right where we had left off, making small talk. I realized that Divine had been only an escape from Larry and that I had mistaken need and desperation for love. I assumed he had realized the same, because he didn't try to contact me again.

None of my daily activities filled my free time or brought me joy. I mostly slept or watched TV, barely engaging with Melissa while she played in the apartment. Although I was physically more stable than I had been a year earlier, I had spent so long without any purpose that I didn't even consider getting a job. I just kept collecting my checks and waiting for something to change.

Then one day my homegirl Shanice called me and told me that her nephew Robert had asked for my phone number.

"I thought he was in jail," I said.

"He is," Shanice responded, "but he says he wants to ask you a question."

Back in the day, when I was a teenager staying with Shanice, Robert was the boy I used to make out with in her bathroom, but I was twenty-four now and hadn't seen him in years. He had gone to prison for alleged murder at eighteen. When Shanice said he had something to ask me, I assumed he wanted to talk about me getting shot, and since we had a little bit of a history, I told her I wouldn't mind speaking to him.

About five minutes after I hung up with Shanice, I received a collect call from Rikers Island. I accepted the charges, and Robert launched right in.

"What's going on, Ms. Cooke?" he said. That kicked off a conversation that lasted for hours. We reminisced about how we had liked each other when we were young and how we used to kiss in the bathroom at Shanice's house. Robert also reminded me about how he had always said he wanted to marry me.

"And I'm a grown man now," he added, "which means we can make it happen."

I laughed off his comment, but when he asked me to visit him so we could see each other in person, I said yes. The very next day, I left my daughters at Mommy's house and took two trains and a bus to Rikers Island. If I could warn that girl now about what she was getting herself into, I would tell her, "Get yourself and your kids into trauma therapy. Go find God. Go get healed. Stop focusing on finding a man." But back then, I wouldn't have been able to hear any of it. I didn't even consider the fact that I was going to see a man who was incarcerated at the same facility where the man who had shot me had worked. I just thought it was a nice distraction and a reason to get out of the house for a day.

When I arrived at Rikers, I spent two hours in a holding area while other visitors were admitted. My turn finally came, and I sat alone on the visiting floor for another eternity while I waited for Robert to come out. All of a sudden, I felt arms encircle me from behind. I turned around and found myself face-to-face with a light-skinned, curly haired man with muscular arms. He was so beautifully put together that I felt dizzy when he smiled at me. The dingy prison walls fell away, and it was just the two of us.

We sat down and talked for an hour straight. Robert told me that he was appealing his twenty-year sentence and that he was likely to win and come home soon. When the guard said our time was up, I blurted out, "I'll come back and see you the next time you can have visitors." And that was all it took for me to think I had found my forever man.

Robert was a thug, and I needed protection. I told myself, *When Larry is released, Robert will be my muscle*. And that was as well as I thought I could do. What other man would want me? My scars were permanent. Larry had told me many times that I didn't have the first idea about how to have a healthy relationship, and I believed him. Dating a man in prison felt like the right fit for my worth.

From then on, Robert and I spoke on the phone four or five times each day and I visited him every week. After I used my food stamps and my welfare check to buy groceries and other necessities, I always made sure I had enough money left to go to Rikers. I also kept up with the details of his appeal, and anytime he had to go to court, I was right there alongside his lawyer.

As Robert and I officially became a couple, I also grew close to his mother, Jamie, who had just come home from doing her own ten-year bid for robbery. She was a former heroin addict who had turned her life around and gotten sober, and she was always willing to take care of my daughters when I needed her to. Robert had a daughter too, a three-year-old named Megan whose mother, Missy, had gotten pregnant shortly before he went to prison. Sometimes when I went to visit Robert, Jamie would watch all three girls; other times, Robert would ask me to bring Megan with me to see him. She was too young to understand that Robert was her father, but she became attached to me and my girls, and while Missy and I were cordial to each other, she was too busy having other babies to have much time for Megan, so the girl eventually started living with us. Jamie came over every day to babysit. It was just easier that way. Much as I was still struggling financially, I couldn't help but think that if not for what Larry had done, I would be a mother of three by now anyway. Megan helped to fill the void that my unborn son had left in me when Larry killed him.

Three months after Robert and I had first reconnected, we were in the visitation room at Rikers one February day when he took my hands in his from across the table and said, "Trina, I love you and I want you to be my wife."

Warmth enveloped my whole body. I started to smile and couldn't stop. I remembered when Larry had proposed to me that Christmas several years before. He might have had a ring, but I had never liked him. *This must be what it feels like to be in love*, I thought. So of course I said yes.

Robert told me to go to the Queens courthouse and get a marriage license. He said that his mother would pay for it. All I could think about was the fact that I was finally going to be somebody's wife. That was a promise I had never thought anyone would ever make to me. And because both Robert and his attorney seemed convinced that he would be released on appeal sometime soon, I believed I would finally have the white-picket-fence future I dreamed of. Robert was loving and attentive every time we spoke. He showed no signs of being abusive. He was a soft-spoken, calm, humble man who rarely even used profanity. To this day, I believe he did not want to be out in the street; both of his parents were dope addicts, and when his mother went to prison, he had to live alone with his siblings and was forced to sell drugs to have enough money to eat. And now that my future mother-in-law had gotten clean, she was a good woman, much more loving to me than Niecy had ever been. But most of all, there was no one in my life who had the sense to tell me I was making a big mistake.

Robert asked his sister, Kayla, whom I had known since childhood but never gotten along with, to take me to pick out our wedding rings. She told me she could only spend two hundred dollars for both rings. When the bands I liked best came out to $220, she grumbled but eventually consented. I knew she was doing it for her brother, not for me, though I was still grateful.

Jamie gave me money to buy a dress. I didn't feel right wearing all white, since I wasn't a virgin, and Robert had said, "Will you wear something short? Even though we can't consummate this marriage, I can at least cop a feel." So I bought a white shirt and a black patent leather miniskirt, along with opaque white tights and black patent leather Mary Jane shoes. I didn't really care what I wore. I was just happy to be somebody's wife.

On March 31, 1995, I got up early. Jamie had stayed over at my apartment the night before so she could take my daughters to school, and I had asked my sister, Macey, to go with me to Rikers and be a witness at my wedding.

As we made the trek to the island, I barely spoke to Macey. I was too caught up in thinking about the fact that by the time I took the bus home later, I would be Mrs. Brownlee. I had been visiting the prison constantly, but now it would forever be the place where I got married.

We arrived just before nine o'clock. The ceremony was scheduled to begin at ten, and Macey and I needed to get all of the usual clearances. The guards searched us and placed us in the main waiting area, and eventually a minister and a corrections officer escorted us to the chapel building. We walked down an endlessly long, musty corridor and ended up in a poorly lit room adjacent to the chapel. I sat there with Macey, rubbing my palms together, trying not to sweat or cry.

When the guards brought Robert in, he was wearing a crisp gray jumpsuit and had a fresh haircut. As soon as I saw him, I thought, *There's my husband.*

The minister entered the room and instructed us to join hands. We exchanged the traditional vows, slid our rings onto each other's fingers, and shared a brief kiss. The entire ceremony lasted all of three minutes. But I was married, someone wanted me, and that was all I cared about.

Afterward, Macey went home and I returned to the jail building to visit with Robert. We were hugging and kissing and holding hands, and one of the COs kept having to come over and say, "Break it up." Every time he stopped us from touching, we laughed. Robert told me again and again that he loved me, and he promised that as soon as he was released from Rikers, we would be together forever.

CHAPTER 13

My Life with Jah-Quar

Not long after my daughters and I moved into our apartment in East Flatbush, I had a dream that the man who owned the bodega on the corner was sitting outside his building with three other men. As I walked by, he smirked at me and said, "You will be mine one day." I just laughed and rolled my eyes.

I knew the man in the dream was the local bodega owner because I had seen him working in the store. He was a nice-looking, medium-height Rastafarian with brown skin. My dream was telling me that this man and I would get together, but that I would be sad for most of our relationship. Yet instead of avoiding him, I found myself wanting to know more about him.

The very next day, as I walked to the end of my block, my heart began to pound. The bodega owner was sitting outside his store; he was wearing the exact jeans and shirt he had had on in my dream, and he was with the very same three men. I tried to hurry past him, as if to avoid the inevitable, but when he called out to me and said, "You will be mine one day," I froze.

In a heavy Jamaican accent, he said, "You know, I been watching you long time now. Who you live up the block with?"

"My three daughters," I said, because Megan was still living with me at the time.

He told me he liked me, but I knew he had a wife because I had seen her working in the store too. When I mentioned her, he smiled and said, "I'm not married. She's my girlfriend, but if you would be my woman, she wouldn't be my girlfriend anymore."

I couldn't suppress my urge to laugh, no matter how many women he had probably said the same thing to. Besides, it was nice to get some positive attention from a man who wasn't incarcerated. Although I had faithfully kept up my visits to Robert at Rikers, and although he kept assuring me that he would win his appeal any day, the long trips were starting to get tedious. I couldn't even do something as basic as walk down the street with my husband, let alone share a home or children with him.

After that encounter, the bodega owner started popping into my thoughts. I began coming up with reasons to go to his store. Sometimes I was in there twice a day. If the man's girlfriend, Jodie, was working, I wouldn't say anything and neither would he. But I would check her out on the sly. She was pretty—light-skinned, with brown eyes and long black hair. She was also Jamaican, though she had a British accent. If she was in the store alone, I would engage in small talk with her, and she was always friendly. Under other circumstances, we might have been friends.

But then I found out from some neighbors that Jodie was married to someone else, a blind man. Their apartment was right across the street from the bodega; they lived on the fourth floor and had a son together. Every day before she left for work, she would sit her husband in a chair facing the window overlooking the street. That way, she could see him from the store throughout her shift. But in the meantime, she was having a full-fledged affair with her boss.

As soon as I discovered this, I decided the Rasta was up for grabs. So one day when I went to the bodega and found him working alone, I asked his name.

"Jah-Quar," he said.

"How do you spell that?" I inquired, looking him up and down.

"J-a-h Q-u-a-r," he said, smiling.

"Is that the name your mother gave you?"

"That's the name Jah Rastafari gave me."

Jah-Quar asked me when I was going to let him stop by my house, to which I replied, "Never. I'm a married woman."

"You married? Then why I never see your husband?"

"Because he's in jail on Rikers," I replied. I told him that Robert was serving a twenty-year sentence and that even though he was supposed to be released early, it hadn't happened yet.

None of this seemed to faze Quar one bit. He was from the street too. As we spoke, he told me he had noticed that I never wore pants and said he liked women who dressed like I did, in long skirts and dresses.

"Then why does your woman wear tight jeans all the time?" I asked.

"That's why she's just a girlfriend," he said.

Over the next few weeks, I started asking around about Quar. Everyone in the neighborhood seemed to know something about him. I found out that he had slept with many of the women in our community. He especially liked young girls because he could control them. He was wealthy; he owned four buildings and three stores, which included the bodega, a gift shop, and a juice bar. I also discovered that he was one of the biggest weed and cocaine dealers in Flatbush. He had so much money that he could spend thousands of dollars every week without any impact on his bottom line. He knew that I needed money and that he could manipulate me that way. But I didn't realize that then. All I knew was that I was a lonely young woman with no job, a husband who might never come home, and three little girls, and Quar felt like a breath of fresh air. I had used Larry to get me out of the projects. I had used Divine to hatch a plan to escape from Larry. I had used Robert to protect me from future threats from Larry. And now I was looking at Quar to save me from my current isolation. Lacking any substantial goals, feelings of self-worth, or interest in working, I convinced myself that a well-to-do, forty-five-year-old man wanting me to be his woman finally gave me some value.

It was only about two months before our relationship became physical. The first time we made love, I lay in bed afterward, thinking, *You just decided to be the perfect wife a few months ago. Look at you now, cheater*. But before long, Quar and I were spending every night together. At first, I let him come over to my apartment only once my daughters were asleep. They were five and nine by then, and they knew I was married. Regardless, I was soon taking both of them over to his house, three doors down from mine, to sleep there most nights.

I began to make excuses to Robert about why I couldn't visit. I would tell him on the phone that I didn't have any money that week. Ironically, Quar would never leave my apartment without putting a hundred-dollar bill on my dresser, so I actually had more cash than usual, though I rarely spent it on trips to Rikers.

Everybody from the block quickly realized that Quar and I were involved, because we did nothing to hide it. Some people even encouraged me to be with him, despite the fact that I was married. Aunt Lilly's kids' father, Jah Mike, told me, "Oh, he's a rich man. He'll take care of you and your kids. You can finally have a better life if you stay with him." Meanwhile, Quar was becoming more and more critical of my marriage to Robert, asking me why I would waste my time visiting someone with a life sentence. I would never respond, because deep down I knew he was right. Being married to Robert was the equivalent of being alone, and I didn't want to be alone. I wasn't in love with my husband, I was in love only with the *idea* of having a husband—and Robert could never be a husband to me as long as he was living in a cell.

By the end of 1995, even though I was still married, I wanted to make things official with Quar. But in order to do that, I had to steal him from Jodie, who was still his girlfriend. The next time I saw her working at the bodega, I didn't say a word to her. I just jumped on her and started punching her in the face. Quar stood right there and watched the entire thing; when Jodie threw a bottle of soda at me, I ducked, and it hit Quar in the head.

Jodie had shown me nothing but kindness, yet I believed I had to fight for Quar to prove that I was serious about him. Because he was showing me a taste of the lifestyle I had always dreamed of, I wanted to hang on to him for as long as I could, and I wanted him all to myself.

After that, Jodie never came around again. Brawling just wasn't in her nature. I became Quar's official girlfriend, and she and her husband soon moved away. Not until much later did I realize that you should never steal someone's man because karma will always come back around to administer justice. I had no idea that my next challenge was imminent.

The next time Robert's appeal came up for review, the judge offered him a plea deal of five to fifteen years. He had already been in prison for four years, and the most he would have to do was seven more. But he was so confident that he would be released that he wanted to take a chance.

I went to the court every day of the week-long trial. On the final day of deliberation, I had to leave to pick up the girls from school, and when I got home, Robert's brother called to tell me that Robert had been found guilty of murder once again and would be transferred to a prison in upstate New York. My hand shook so badly that I dropped the phone, and when I hung up, I sat down on the floor and sobbed. *How could I have been so stupid?* I asked myself. *How did I get myself into this mess?* Robert and I didn't even really know each other. We had never even been physically intimate. And despite my dalliance with Quar, I was still lonely. In fact, the only one winning in this situation was Robert. I was giving him my time, sending him packages of money and other items he asked for, and had taken care of his daughter. I was beginning to resent him.

But he was my husband and he had always treated me well—and in my mind, having a man was better than having no man—so I decided not to confess to him that I was leading a double life. *Now that I have money,* I told myself, *I'm just going to make sure that Robert always has enough food and other necessities in prison, and then if things don't work out with Quar, I'll still have a husband.*

When Robert called me the night after his trial ended, he acted as if nothing had happened. I asked him how he was feeling, and he said, "It is what it is—nothing I can't handle." But then he added, "So wassup? You gonna leave me now?"

When I assured him that I wouldn't do that, he promised that as soon as he got upstate he would put in for trailer visits—weekend visits for married inmates and their families. The family stays inside the trailer with the inmate, and the visitors are permitted to bring food, water, and whatever else they think the inmate might need. It was just one more hollow attempt at giving our marriage a semblance of normalcy.

Once he was sent upstate after his sentencing, I signed up to be the coordinator of the prison bus, so I was able to travel to see him for free. I returned to my former schedule of visiting him every week, and he was able to secure our first trailer visit very quickly. When I finally had the chance to make love with my husband for the first time, I forgot all about Quar for two days. Even though I had been having sex with someone else every chance I got, the idea of doing it with the man I was legally married to felt pure and right—and, of course, Robert was all mine, unlike Quar. Robert was also selling dope in prison and sending money home, so between him and the weekly five-hundred-dollar allowance Quar had begun to give me, cash was flowing my way.

Robert and I were granted trailer visits every month, though it wasn't long before my weekly trips upstate started to wear me down. I couldn't imagine keeping them up for another sixteen years or more. But I did keep up with those trailer visits. Whenever I went for one, I told Quar I was staying at Mommy's house for the weekend, and he never questioned me.

Quar might not have suspected what I was doing, but it was inevitable that Robert would find out I was being unfaithful to him. A man from my neighborhood who bought weed from Quar told Robert that I was messing around with him. When Robert confronted me, I pretended not to know what he was talking about, but I also saw his suspicion as an opening. I started giving him more attitude when we talked. If he asked me to visit him upstate, I wouldn't tell him I couldn't afford it anymore; instead, I would say, "Nah, I don't feel like coming this week." After all, what could he do to me? He was inside, and I was a free woman—or at least acting like one. If I behaved badly enough with Robert, I reasoned, he would eventually ask me for a divorce. Only a few months into our marriage, that was what I wanted.

The day I arrived upstate with a hickey on my neck was the tipping point. It was a hot day in the early fall, and I was wearing a turtleneck to conceal it, but Robert spotted it right away.

"You got a hickey on your neck?" he asked, grabbing my arm and pulling me closer to him.

"That's not a hickey," I said, reaching up and swatting at it as if I could brush it off.

Robert, who had always been so gentle with me, hauled off and smacked me in the face, right in front of the prison guards. I went back to Quar's house and acted as if nothing had happened.

I wasn't the only one who was pretending. The more material possessions Quar gave me—including a green Nissan Sentra so that I wouldn't have to take public transportation with my daughters anymore—the more women he seemed to pick up on the side. He wasn't very slick about it, and I would always catch him.

One day, a young woman came into Quar's bodega when I was working there. She looked me up and down and said, "You know I'm fucking Quar, right?"

That was my first experience with karma. By letting me know that she was messing with my man and that she wanted him all to herself, this girl was simply repeating a pattern I had started with Jodie. But Jodie had backed down, and I wasn't about to.

"Yo, I'm not leaving him or whatever you think is going on," I said.

We started arguing loudly, and somebody overheard us and went to find Quar. When he came into the store, he waved his hand at the girl and said, "Get out of here. I ain't messing with you. I don't want you." Then he turned to me and repeated, "I ain't messing with her."

That was all the invitation I needed to come out from behind the cash register and jump the girl. Quar helped me beat on her, two on one. *When Larry gets out of prison*, I kept telling myself, *I'll be safe because I'm with a gangster now—not Robert, who's in prison himself, but Quar, who has his freedom. I have money, I have clothes, and most of all, I have protection.*

I had always been taught that women have to make compromises for a man; Quar was committed to being a womanizer far more than he was committed to me, and he had no intention of changing. As his infidelity grew, so did my allowance. Eventually, he was giving me five thousand dollars every week.

Each time I caught Quar cheating and he apologized, I would say, "Okay, you better not do it again." And then, of course, he would just do it again anyway. He also began to abuse me verbally. "You got shot up," he'd say. "Nobody else wants you. You're nothing." He told me that I was ugly, that the scars on my stomach from the shooting would turn off any other man. He said, "You got too many kids," even though I had only two. And he always concluded his tirades with "So you might as well stay with me."

Despite his gaslighting, I told myself it was a step in the right direction because at least he wasn't physically abusing me. I told myself I had God's support because I was faithfully going to church every Sunday and Tuesday. But really, I was just riding the dime with a man who was never going to care about anyone besides himself.

CHAPTER 14

Farewell, My Star

I woke up on Saturday morning, July 1, 1997, to the sound of the doorbell ringing nonstop. Quar got out of bed and went to the peephole to see who was there. He came back into the bedroom and told me it was Shanice.

"What's she doing here? Something bad must have happened," I said.

I went to the door and opened it. With tears in her eyes, Shanice said, "She's gone."

Jamie, Robert's mother, had died early that morning. She had moved to Atlanta a few months earlier, after finding out that she had full-blown AIDS. She figured that she had contracted the virus from using dirty needles years prior, when she was a heroin addict, and left New York because she hadn't wanted people she knew to see her looking sick.

I brushed my teeth and quickly got dressed while Shanice waited outside on the steps, and then drove with her over to Robert's grandmother's house. On the way, I realized that it was Jamie's fortieth birthday. She had died on the same day she was born, bringing her life full circle.

I started thinking about my own mother and how similar Niecy was to Jamie. Both were dark skinned. Both were slim. Both were quiet and poised. Both had been teenage mothers.

And they had both passed away far too young. I used to look at Jamie and think about how she and Niecy would have been the same age if Niecy had lived. Because of the rejection I had experienced, I was too afraid to label my relationship with Jamie as a mother-daughter one, so instead, I thought of her as an older sister. She may not have been formally educated, but she offered me all the wisdom she had, and stayed by my side in a way that few people ever had. Even though I was married to her son, she had never judged me for starting a relationship with Quar. She told me, "You're still a young girl with a lot of life ahead of you. You need to take care of yourself. My son isn't going to be around. He can't do anything for you. Quar has money. He can take care of you."

The next day, I drove five hours to the Auburn Correctional Facility. I hadn't been to visit Robert in a while, but calling the jail to tell him that his mother had passed felt wrong. I invited his cousin Jay to go with me. We were quiet during the drive. I rolled down the windows to take in the fresh summer air, and I thought about how I was going to tell Robert that his beloved mother had passed.

As I parked at the facility, I turned to Jay and asked, "Are you ready?"

He shrugged. "Not really."

I took a deep breath, and we got out of the car.

Robert entered the visiting area looking as handsome and youthful as ever. When he approached, I stood up, as I always did, to greet him with a hug and a kiss. Jay hugged him too, but Robert stepped back and squinted at us. Since we had never been to the prison together, he knew this wasn't a routine visit.

I took a deep breath and said, "I have something to tell you."

When I shared the news, Robert got very quiet and looked me in my eyes as a single tear slid slowly down his face. I pulled him toward me and held him tightly to try to absorb some of his pain. Since he was locked up, he wouldn't have much involvement with the funeral arrangements, though he did ask me to call the prison and let them know of Jamie's passing so that he could at least attend her funeral. I promised him I would.

Jay and I stayed with Robert for hours, and right before our time was up, Jay left so that Robert and I could have our final moments alone. We didn't say much, but right before I left, I told him that I loved him and that I would be back to see him soon. "I'll never leave your side," I said, even though it was a lie. I was too broken, and too far gone with Quar, to be a good wife to Robert, yet I felt a moral obligation to support him through the loss of his mother, despite what was going on in my personal life and despite the fact that I knew our days as a couple were nearing an end.

On the drive back to Brooklyn, visual snapshots from my visit with Robert and memories of Jamie preoccupied me. They might have been flawed people in some ways, and Robert and I might not have been meant to stay married, but they had given me all the love they had. My stomach churned at the thought of losing both of them. My mother-in-law, my friend, my daughters' caregiver, and my confidant was gone. She had left not one void but many, because she had played so many different roles in my life. She must have known that she was going to die soon, because when she had confided in me that she was infected with AIDS, she'd also said she had mailed me a letter. "Don't open it until after my funeral," she had instructed.

The night of Jamie's service, I went home and soaked in my bathtub after putting my daughters to bed. Then I opened her letter. It was long and instantly brought tears to my eyes, and while much of it will remain private for the rest of my life, the crux of it was this:

Dear Mrs. Brownlee,
    This is your beautiful mother-in-law. Mrs. Brownlee,

you know I loved you and your girls and I ask of you to please take care of my son and grandbabies. Stay beautiful and know that I love you.

Jamie's death reverberated throughout our Brooklyn community. Even Quar, who had known her for only a couple of years, was genuinely sad to hear that she had passed away. The fact that she was his girlfriend's husband's mother seemed not to taint his opinion of her one bit. If anything, I believe he was relieved that I was preoccupied with her death for a couple of weeks, because my grief took my attention off his cheating ways.

One night a few weeks after Jamie died, I woke up at two thirty a.m. to find that Quar wasn't in our bed. I left the apartment and walked to the corner to see if he was at the store. When I didn't find him there, I sat on the front steps of his building for the next several hours, watching and waiting.

At six thirty a.m., I saw Quar slipping out of the apartment of a woman who lived next door. My adrenaline surged. Before he could even register the sight of me, I ran down the steps and jumped on his back, screaming and hitting him and calling him every insulting name I could think of: community cock; fake Rastafarian; no-good, lying-ass nigga. For once, he didn't even try to lie to me about what he'd been doing. But his silence didn't feel like retribution. All I could think about was the dream I had had right before I met him, which had warned me that he would bring me great sadness, and the bad karma I had brought upon myself by stealing him from his girlfriend.

But I wasn't finished. I went to Quar's gift shop. He loved plants and birds and sold numerous varieties of each. I scooped up as many of his plants as I could and lined them up in the middle of the street. Hell hath no fury, indeed.

As soon as Quar realized what I was doing, he ran out into

the middle of the street to try to collect as many of the plants as he could before they were run over. I stood there, stone-faced, while he cursed me out, thinking, *You hurt me, I hurt you. Your plants are getting killed, just like you killed my heart.* Some of Quar's friends and employees had gathered out on the sidewalk to see what all the commotion was about, and they couldn't help but laugh at the spectacle.

"The next time you mess around on me, I'm going after your birds," I called to Quar. "I'm gonna wheel your birdcages right into the middle of this street."

"I'm going to kill you if you kill my birds!" he yelled, still trying to salvage his damaged plants.

"Well, then you'd better leave those other women alone," I responded.

I continued to watch him until it was time to get my daughters ready for school. Once I dropped off the girls, I went on a shopping spree with my daily allowance. When I returned, Quar was sweeping the sidewalk outside his store. He straightened up, holding his broom, and said quietly, "I need to go to Chinatown. And I need you to come."

"Why would I go anywhere with your cheating ass?" I countered. I tried to brush past him, but he held up a hand. "Please," he said. "This is important."

What's going on in Chinatown? I wondered. *We never go there.* In fact, I hardly ever left Rockaway Parkway unless it was to go shopping. I was intrigued enough to let my curiosity get the better of me, so I finally said, "Fine, I'll go."

Quar and I jumped into his old van and headed to Chinatown. While he drove, he turned on an oldies station on the radio and began to sing to me, which he did frequently. He had an excellent voice and had wanted to be a professional singer when he first came to the United States. As the Temptations' "My Girl" played, Quar crooned the lyrics and we both began swaying and snapping softly to the music in a twisted little duet. My whole body softened, and I found myself thinking, *I am his girl. I always will be.*

When we got to Chinatown, Quar double-parked in front of a jewelry store on Canal Street. "Come on. Get out," he said.

"You can't park here," I told him. "I'll just sit in the van and wait for you."

"Don't worry about it. We'll only be here for a few minutes."

"You still haven't told me why we're here."

Quar didn't answer; he just got out of the van, so I followed him. Once we were inside the store, he said, "Pick a ring. We're getting married."

My whole body grew hot, and I put my hand on my thundering heart. "Are you serious?"

"Of course I'm serious," he said.

I had to clamp my palm over my mouth to hide the fact that I was beaming. Even if Quar had finally decided to commit, I didn't want to give him the satisfaction of seeing how happy he was making me.

A saleswoman came over to introduce herself. When she asked, "How can I help you?" I said, "I guess I'm here to get an engagement ring."

I tried on a number of rings until I found the one I liked best: a princess-cut diamond on a gold band. It was too big for my finger, so the saleswoman said she would size it for me.

After she finished, Quar and I were on our way. Back in the van, he smiled at me and said, "I have something else for you."

"What is it?"

"When we get home, I want you to book flights to Florida for us."

Quar's family lived in Florida. His mother had recently been killed in a car accident, but his father and siblings were still there, so I assumed he wanted to go visit them. As soon as I got home, I called a travel agent and bought two tickets.

A few days later, we were in Kissimmee, where Quar purchased a beautiful four-bedroom house for us. He told me he wanted us to move into it once we were married.

"But what about your business? What about your stores and your houses?" I asked.

When he told me that he was willing to fly back and forth to continue working in New York while we lived in our new home, I chose to believe him.

Once I was engaged to Quar, I told myself, *Now that we're a legitimate couple and soon to be married, everything's going to be totally different.* It was as if being in that jewelry store and picking out my ring had erased every issue we had had, including the fact that thirty minutes earlier I'd been lining up his plants in the street like targets. Once again, I was normalizing a situation that was anything but. My justifications played out like a checklist: *I have money; I'm not being beaten; Quar isn't in prison; he's better than any of the other men I've been with.* And, of course, I was still married to Robert—but that was about to change.

In October 1997, a few months after Quar and I got engaged and two years after Robert had first noticed the hickey on my neck, he got word from someone in the prison that I was still cheating on him with Quar. When I showed up for our first trailer visit since Jamie's death in July, I had no idea what I was walking into.

He said, "Let's have a romantic night together. Why don't you let me run a nice bubble bath for you?"

"That sounds nice," I said. Once the tub was full, I eased in and closed my eyes.

The next thing I knew, Robert was standing over me, holding a portable radio. "You're still fucking cheating on me?" he yelled. "You've got me in here looking like a freakin' chump!" With that, he threw the radio into the water, trying to electrocute me.

"You've lost your damn mind!" I screamed. I managed to jump out of the bath before I was burned to a crisp, but Robert gave my naked body a beating I will never forget.

For two days, he tortured me. I tried screaming for help, yet no one heard me, because, under the premise of marital privacy, none of the COs were allowed to check on us the entire weekend. Robert was so deranged that he kept doing push-ups to keep himself pumped up for another round of attacking me. He would do one hundred push-ups, then stand up and say, "You fucking bitch," and start in on me again. I had never even heard him curse before.

I was trapped in the trailer with Robert until Sunday. He was two hundred and forty pounds of solid muscle, too big for me to physically overpower, and I knew that if I tried to escape, he would kill me. Eventually, I decided to act as calm as possible and tell him what I knew he wanted to hear.

"I promise I only want to be with you," I said. "I'm not going to be with anybody else." I kept telling myself, *I am not dying. I'm not letting another dude try to murder me. I'm going to get out of here alive, and when I do, I'm never coming back here again.*

When the weekend was over, I hugged and kissed Robert and told him I would see him again the following weekend. He said, "You promise?"

"I promise."

"This is a new beginning for us, right?"

"It sure is," I said, and as I exited the trailer, my aching body covered in bruises, I thought, *I'm out of here.*

I filed for divorce as soon as I got home. When Robert tried to call me, I told him to fuck off. But when he refused to sign the papers, my divorce filing stagnated.

I turned my focus to furnishing the house Quar and I had bought in Florida. Quar joined me sometimes and paid for everything. But I had built a house with a fiancé before and knew how it was supposed to feel, and I quickly realized that the process was dragging. Before long, I was sure that all of it—the ring, the house, Quar's talk of marriage—was just a ploy to keep me hooked on him. *This man is not actually trying to build a life with me*, I realized. *He's just trying to make up for all the bullshit he's put me through—and for all the bullshit he's going to put me through in the future.*

I sometimes ask myself now whether I would have put up with so much mistreatment if Quar had been broke. I wish I could say I wouldn't have, but like many other victimized women, I had convinced myself that the emotional abuse and disrespect I endured from him didn't matter as long as all my bills were paid and I had cash to burn.

In the meantime, I continued to delude myself. Quar's business had become so lucrative by the time he bought us the house in Florida that he was stashing money in all of his buildings and giving me more than I could possibly spend—despite my best efforts. Every morning when I stuffed cash in my bra and went shopping, I turned a blind eye to the fact that I was complicit in my partner's criminal behavior. He knew I could be bought, and I let him buy me. It was the price both of us had to pay to play.

CHAPTER 15

A New Direction

After Jamie's death, things began to change for me. I looked at myself in the mirror one day and thought, *Enough is enough. God spared your life, Katrina. He didn't have to do it, but He did. He gave you a gift that almost no one else receives. When are you actually going to stop wasting it and actually do something with it?*

It might have been a conversation I should have had with myself years earlier, but I knew it still wasn't too late to turn myself around. I was twenty-seven, and I had been with a string of men who had kept me down since I was thirteen. *Maybe if I get a legitimate job*, I thought, *that will put me on the right track.*

I had taken a test to become a traffic agent on a whim when I was eighteen. Since I had never graduated from high school, I didn't think I could get a city job and was surprised when I received a letter stating that I had passed. Now, nearly a decade later, I decided to enroll in a sixteen-week course at the NYPD traffic academy, in Long Island City. I had always been taught that having a city job was a way to come up out of poverty, so I wanted to give myself that opportunity. Being a traffic agent didn't come with a high salary, but the long-term benefits were valuable. Besides, I didn't need money—I needed self-respect and a sense of purpose.

I was told to wear business attire for my first day. Since I didn't own any clothes that fit that description, I wore one of my church dresses. When I arrived, I entered a room filled with mostly Black women who were all waiting to be interviewed. When my turn came, a Black woman in her midforties, who was polite enough but not overly friendly, asked me to fill out a stack of paperwork. I had been expecting her to ask me some questions, but after I verified my identity, she simply made a copy of my credentials and told me to wait for a letter in the mail that would provide me with my start date.

I received the letter a few weeks later. When I opened it, I thought, *I'm finally doing something good for myself and my daughters, writing a new chapter of my life story.*

Quar, on the other hand, could not get his head around my decision. "Why are you going to work for a system that's not even going to give you any real money, especially when you've got money from me? Why would you waste your time like that?" As someone who had created his own business network under an illegal umbrella of drug dealing, he just couldn't relate. He couldn't understand that I needed something of my own.

I didn't try to explain it to him any further, because I knew he would never get it, so I blocked out his noise and took some of his cash to go shopping for new clothes. I knew I could wear civilian clothes for my first four weeks of school, so I made sure to buy myself a wardrobe that would keep me looking fly every time I stepped inside the classroom.

On my first day at the academy, we had orientation. They broke up the students into classrooms by our last names. I was in classroom number 1, along with about thirty other people, almost all of whom were also Black women. However, their average age looked to be about forty-five, nearly twenty years older than I was. As I scanned the room, I found myself wondering,

What have they been doing with their lives this whole time? I would never want to be their age and just starting out in this kind of career. What if some of them have their own men like Quar and have been stuck with them all this time? The fact that I was starting to ask myself these kinds of questions was another clue to me that I was heading in the right direction.

Getting dressed for graduation, reflecting on my life.

Our classes were taught by actual traffic agents and took place Monday through Friday from seven a.m. to three p.m. Despite his opposition to my new vocation, Quar took both of my daughters to school in the mornings and picked them up in the afternoons so that I could be at the academy.

My time there felt like an eternity. I was used to getting up early in the morning because I had been a mother for so long, but I had never had to get up for a job, let alone one with such a rigorous schedule. At the beginning, I had trouble staying awake in class; I kept dozing off because I typically took a nap when my daughters were at school, on the days I wasn't out shopping. Sometimes I thought, *This is too much; I should just drop out and go back to my life of leisure.*

Graduation day.

But that life was controlled by Quar, who kept reminding me how stupid I was for enrolling in the traffic academy in the first place. "Do you have any idea how people are going to look at you once you start being a meter maid? Nobody respects them. They're a joke," he'd say. Instead of internalizing his insults, however, I used them to fuel my motivation. I kept going back to my classes, day after day, and before long I had completed my sixteen-week program.

My graduation took place at 1 Police Plaza in the early spring of 1998. I wore my traffic uniform—a sky-blue shirt, blue pants, and shiny black shoes—and Mommy and my daughters came to support me. I held my shoulders back and my head high when I received my certificate commemorating the first goal I had ever consciously set out to achieve in my life.

I was assigned to work in the Brooklyn South traffic division. The headquarters were in East Flatbush, right next door to one of the stores Quar shopped at nearly every day. It was familiar territory, and I knew I was going to do well. In fact, I was so confident I would excel in my new position that on my first day of traffic command, I arrived fifteen minutes late, wearing a flashy outfit and gold jewelry, carrying my uniform, my pocketbook, and a bad attitude. I still had residue from growing up on the streets all over me. All of that was armor I believed I needed because I didn't want anyone to see that I was a woman with no legitimate job history.

When I arrived at the front desk, I found a Black woman standing there. Rather than greeting her courteously, I said, "Hey, I'm Brownlee. What do I need to do?"

She looked me up and down, as if to convey, *You and your sassy mouth don't fool me*, and said, "Your tour started at seven a.m. It's now seven sixteen." She instructed me to sign my name in a book and then sit at a table with a few other people. "You'll get a locker before the day is over," she added.

When I sat down, I saw some familiar faces from my classes at the traffic academy, but I didn't speak to anyone. A few minutes later, a short Black woman wearing thick glasses and a bad wig came over to the table. She weighed at least two hundred pounds, and her light blue uniform shirt was covered with food stains, as if she had used it as a napkin. She introduced herself as Supervisor Alexander.

If this is my boss, this is gonna be crazy, I thought.

Supervisor Alexander turned out to be my boss's boss. Shortly thereafter, a tall, well-kept Jamaican woman with long dreadlocks appeared. Her name was Lexi, and she announced that she would be our immediate supervisor. Both women let us know that we would be on foot patrol. I immediately wondered how I could get a car, because it was early spring and still cold outside and I didn't want to be walking around Brooklyn freezing all day while I wrote tickets.

Over the next few weeks, as I tromped around in the cold, I became fixated on getting myself a car. One of the other agents, Vivian, had quickly become my friend, and we spent most of our workdays together, writing tickets and talking about our daughters, fashion, and our hustler boyfriends. One day during our shift, I told Vivian that I was going to try to get a car because I was tired of walking. I knew Viv hated walking too, but she had a humbler demeanor than I did.

"You actually think you can get a car?" she asked, raising an eyebrow at me.

"Watch me," I said.

When we came in from our post, I walked into Supervisor Alexander's office and said, "Listen, if you give me a car, I will write as many tickets as you want. But I'm not down with this walking-in-the-cold business."

Supervisor Alexander hesitated, because she knew I had just come out of the academy and she had probably never received such a request from a rookie agent before. But she didn't say no, either. She paused just long enough for me to say, "Give me one day to prove to you how aggressive I can be."

She agreed, and true to my word, I wrote ninety to one hundred parking tickets every day and never walked again. My performance only made me cockier, and I realized that the way to ensure that I kept my privileged status was to keep the big bosses happy. For example, since I knew that Supervisor Alexander liked to eat, I started taking food to her every day—fried chicken, layer cakes, or oversized cookies. Whatever she wanted, she would call me the night before and say, "Here's what I want you to bring me tomorrow morning," and I always obliged. I even started dropping off a full Sunday dinner at her house each weekend. Her eyes lit up whenever she saw me coming, and in return, if any of my coworkers complained to her about my chronic lateness or my holier-than-thou attitude, she ignored them, because in her eyes I could do no wrong.

Supervisor Alexander and I remained close until she had a heart attack. The first thing I thought when I heard the news was *I hope I wasn't her pusher.*

My first paycheck was only five hundred dollars. Quar roared with laughter when he found out. When I boasted that I was writing one hundred tickets every day, he said, "*For the government*, you idiot. What percentage of those ticket fees are you getting for yourself?" When I said, "I'm the only rookie agent with a car," he said, "Yeah, so you can make more money for *other people*, when you could be over here making money for yourself."

The more he ranted and tried to intimidate me, the more his attempts backfired. For the first time, I found myself realizing, *I don't care what he thinks. I'm going to make it in this traffic world. He'll see. I'm going to keep working and working until I have enough money of my own that I never need to depend on a man again.* My paycheck may have been meager, but the self-esteem boost it gave me was priceless. Even after, out of spite, Quar decreased my five-thousand-dollar weekly allowance when I started collecting a salary—"You really want to be a freakin' meter maid? Then let *them* give you five grand"—I didn't care. He was still covering all our bills and giving me cash, but every time I got a check, I left the money in my personal bank account, and every deposit I made got me one step closer to freedom.

I eventually decided to put in for a promotion to become a level-two traffic agent, which meant I would direct traffic and receive a slight pay raise. I would also have to leave the Brooklyn office, which was only fifteen minutes from my house. But I knew I didn't want to write tickets forever, so I decided I would take the supervisor's exam when it became available.

CHAPTER 16

Until We Meet Again

On October 10, 1998, I was still celebrating my birthday two days after it was over. My near-death experience with Larry had made me want to start treating each of my birthdays like a national holiday. Every time I was blessed with another 365 days of life felt like a miracle.

After I came home from dinner out with a friend, I planned to go check on Mommy. Earlier in the week, I had gone to Brevoort to visit her and had found her in bed. She was sixty-eight and had been retired for about five months. She had started showing up drunk to work, and eventually her supervisors at the library had said that either they would have to terminate her or she could retire immediately, keep her pension, and avoid tarnishing her reputation. They had forced her hand out of kindness, but now that she didn't have to get up for work anymore, she had given up. She no longer bothered to dress nicely or put on her signature red lipstick; she just drank and drank all day.

When I'd visited her, she looked gravely ill and could barely sit up. I had never even seen her sick before, so I'd rushed her to the emergency room, where the hospital said she was suffering from cirrhosis of the liver. They'd released her shortly after, but asked me to follow up with her regular physician the next day.

Because I had to work, I'd asked my godmother and one of my aunts to accompany her to her doctor visit. The doctor had told them to take her right back to the ER, and this time the hospital admitted her.

As I entered my apartment after my birthday dinner, I noticed that the light on my answering machine was flashing. I played my messages.

"This message is for Katrina Brownlee. Please contact us immediately."

My heart started pounding, and my intuition reared up. *No, no, no. I can't call the hospital. I know they're going to give me bad news.* Even though I had spoken to Mommy earlier that day and she hadn't sounded sick at all, I knew that was no guarantee of anything.

I decided to call my aunt Dorothy instead so that I could ask her to contact the hospital. When she didn't answer her phone, I hung up, but she called me back moments later.

"Hello?" I said. *Please, please, please let Mommy be okay.*

At first, I heard only her breathing on the other end. Finally, Aunt Dorothy said, "Mommy . . . passed away."

Her words seemed to travel a great distance before they reached me. Then I started screaming. Mommy had always been my touchstone. She might have been an alcoholic for as long as I could remember, yet she had functioned for so long in that state that I had somehow never expected her drinking to kill her. I had hoped that God might have some mercy on her, after all the suffering she'd endured. I had hoped that I would have enough money soon to buy my own house and move her in there so that I could take care of her while she enjoyed her retirement.

My mind was so muddled as I ran to Quar's store that my feet didn't even work properly. I stumbled inside and fell into his arms, sobbing. Quar loved Mommy too; he loved all beautiful women, and he thought she was at the top of that list.

Every time she'd come to our house, he had showered her with affection. When I told him that Mommy was gone, he cried too.

When my family and I went to identify Mommy's body, she looked like she was sleeping peacefully. I knew her difficult life had tired her out, but any solace I got from understanding she no longer had to battle her decades-old demons was outweighed by my feelings of having lost my anchor. No one in my life had done as much for me or cared for me as steadily as Mommy had, from infancy to adulthood.

Before I left, I kissed her gently and told her how much I loved her.

Mommy's funeral was a beautiful homegoing service. Miss Betty from her building gave the eulogy to a large crowd of Mommy's friends, relatives, and other admirers. Aunt Lilly cried harder than anyone, but that was only because she was pregnant again and must have realized that Mommy was no longer going to feed her, house her, protect her, or subsidize her addiction. Maybe if Aunt Lilly hadn't been a crackhead, Mommy wouldn't have hit the bottle so much. Then again, maybe it wouldn't have mattered. Mommy's hard times had started long before that. I could only pray that she was finally at peace and that I would eventually figure out how to survive without her.

I took two weeks off work while I grieved Mommy's death. And as my tears began to dry, good news came my way: I had gotten the level-two promotion I had applied for. I attended a ceremony at 1 Police Plaza, where my graduation from the traffic academy had also taken place. Mommy had been so proud of me that day. But this time, she wasn't in the crowd to witness my accomplishment, and the smile I pasted on my face felt like a grimace. I couldn't stop looking out into the audience, as if her face might somehow magically appear there.

AND THEN CAME THE BLUES

I started my new command at the Brooklyn Navy Yard in December 1998. Not only had my commute increased from fifteen minutes to thirty, but I now had to be at work at five a.m. instead of seven a.m. and had to be on my feet all day. As I stood on the corner, directing traffic during my first shift, I couldn't help but think, *Be careful what you wish for. Is this really what you want to do?* Even though I had just been promoted, I knew I wasn't going to be able to tolerate standing on that corner forever.

Larry's sister had once told me I should set goals for my life every five years. Since I knew I didn't want to direct traffic for the next two decades, I decided to finally get my GED and go to college. I enrolled in a program at the College of New Rochelle and started attending classes three nights per week. After twenty-four months, I would have my GED, as well as some college credits toward a bachelor's degree if I chose to go further. Although Quar continued to show nothing but disdain for my career path, he was delighted about my newfound interest in education—he had put a number of his own children through college—and offered to pay my tuition. I had been managing his books for a number of years by then, and he also believed a college degree would help me develop those skills.

For the past fourteen years, since I had dropped out of ninth grade after having Morgan, I had always thought school wasn't for me. But at twenty-eight, I finally realized that if I wanted to continue to make progress toward my goals, I would need at least some higher education. It helped that college felt entirely different from high school. The course material was easier, and I was more interested in the subject matter, whether it was social work, Spanish, or social science classes.

The greatest challenge for me was juggling work and school. My days now started at four a.m. and ended at nine thirty p.m. I would come home from work, take a nap or sometimes help Quar out at the store, cook dinner, take a shower, get dressed for class, and go to school. But that was when I truly started to see what I was made of. I had learned how physically strong I was when I had healed from being shot, and now my mental strength and stamina were being tested in ways I had never experienced; I promised myself I wouldn't allow anything to stop me from completing what I had set out to do. I set my goals, one at a time, and I began to achieve them.

One day, my manager came to roll call and announced that the department was going to be administering the police officers' exam. Much as I didn't want to admit that Quar was right, I knew traffic agents didn't get much respect, so I thought I should explore the idea of becoming a cop. I had developed a sense of ambition almost overnight, and decided I should take advantage of any advancement opportunities that came my way. As a police officer, I would not only have more power but would also look sexy with a gun on my hip. More than that, I thought, *I've always relied on men to protect me. I need to be able to protect my own self. And if I ever find myself responding to a domestic-violence call, I'm never going to treat the victim the way the police treated me. No, I'm going to be a supercop. I'm going to overhaul the entire NYPD from the inside out.* I had a detailed vision of how the whole thing was going to play out. So I raised my hand for an application.

I aced the police officers' exam. I had never thought of myself as a strong test taker, but these standardized exams came naturally to me. In fact, I passed the traffic agents' supervisor's exam as well, though when I found out I would be starting at the NYPD Academy, I chose not to continue along that path.

Once I opened my mind to the idea of personal expansion, blessings started flowing to me. A growth mindset must start within us. The universe will never expand our world unless we are ready for it. And I was ready.

Some of my friends who were traffic agents told me that

people at the command were saying I would never make it into the police department because I had a big mouth. They thought no one would like me, the same way no one in the traffic division besides my supervisors really liked me. But I was so determined to sustain my momentum that I made it my mission to prove them wrong. To this day, if anyone tells me I can't do something, I think, *Watch me.*

As I started feeling better about myself and my accomplishments, I became less and less dependent on Quar. I decided to move out of my apartment right near his. Not only did I no longer qualify for Section 8 housing now that I was working for the city, but it also didn't feel like a safe place for my daughters and me. Between the police attention on Quar for his illegal activities and the many women he was sleeping with, it all just got to be too much.

I rented a cute two-bedroom apartment in Canarsie. I didn't tell Quar about it right away, but about two months later, we had an argument and I mentioned it to provoke him. "I've got my own place now," I said. "I'm moving and taking my kids with me, and getting away from you and all your drama." It wasn't the first time I had threatened to leave, but this time I actually had a place to go.

Quar just laughed at me. He said, "You'll be back. You know you'll never make it on your own."

But what he didn't know was that I had already started on a whole new career path and was halfway checked out of the relationship. I hadn't even bothered to tell him about my admission to the police academy because I knew if he was mocking me for working for the city as a traffic agent, he was going to be furious if he found out I was trying to become an NYPD officer.

I expected Quar to leave me alone once he found out I had a new apartment, testing me to see how long I could go without running back to him. Instead, he started changing. He stopped seeing all of his other girls. We started spending much more time together as a couple. He was no longer verbally abusive. And he kept taking good care of my daughters. On some level, he must have realized what that apartment in Canarsie symbolized. It represented my need to prove to myself how much strength I really had, my need to find out if I could actually be the woman I wanted to be. Every day, the prospect of that quest gave me the will to persevere.

When Mommy died, my inner light dimmed and my grief took over, but it wasn't permanent. I knew Mommy would have wanted me to continue to shine my light as brightly as I could—she understood all too well how debilitating lifelong heartbreak can be. When my light turned back on, fueled by my new sense of purpose, it was brighter than it had ever been.

CHAPTER 17

What God Has for You Is for You

In January 2001, I began the process of becoming a police officer. The requirements were wide-ranging and rigorous and included physical, medical, and psychological exams. The physical portion consisted of running up the stairs of the police academy, jumping over hurdles and over a wall, and pulling a two-hundred-pound dummy across a finish line.

I completed the course, then literally fainted. When I came to, one of the instructors asked how I'd learned to hurdle so well. I explained that I used to run track when I was younger and that my muscle memory must have kicked in. Little did he know that I had managed to jump those hurdles with six bullets still in my body, after having been told that I would never walk again.

The next day, I would be taking the medical exam in Queens. I was concerned about the vision exam because I knew I had needed glasses since I was eight years old. I hadn't wanted to look like a nerd, so I had never divulged to anyone how poor my vision was. In the meantime, my eyes had only worsened.

When a tall, handsome, brown-skinned man summoned me to the area where the vision test would take place, I decided to keep it real with him: "I don't think I'm going to pass this eye exam."

"Why not?" he asked.

"Because I'm blind."

He had me look into the eye holes and examined me quickly. When he was finished, he said, "You passed."

You've got to be kidding, I thought. Then, as I was about to leave, he pulled me aside and said quietly, "Your eyes are really bad. Go get some glasses or contact lenses as soon as possible."

"Oh, wow, okay," I said. "But why'd you pass me, then?"

"Because we need people who look like you in this department. Good luck to you."

I walked back to my seat, pondering his words. For the rest of that day, I kept noticing that of the ten other women who were also going through the process, not one of them looked like me. Whereas almost everyone in my class at the traffic academy had been Black, at the NYPD police academy I was around more white people than I had ever encountered in my life in a professional setting. I was already anxious about completing the testing process, and being outnumbered only compounded my uneasiness. Although all of my fellow candidates were courteous and some tried to make small talk with me, I kept to myself and focused on what I had to do.

The final test was the medical exam. When I entered the room, several other women were already there, and we were instructed to strip down to our underwear. It had never occurred to me that I would have to show my naked body to the doctor. If I had known, I would never have applied to be a police officer in the first place. *I'm done*, I thought. *There's no way the NYPD is going to give me a gun once they see the gunshot wounds on my body. They'll just assume I'm not emotionally fit to have this job, or that I'm going to use my weapon to take revenge on Larry.* I had disclosed on my application that I had been shot, because I hadn't wanted to perjure myself, but no one had brought it up yet.

As I waited for my turn with the doctor, perspiration formed on my forehead and slid slowly down my spine. I kept fanning myself while the two women ahead of me in line had a long conversation with the doctor. They grilled him for about fifteen minutes, asking him all kinds of inane questions. "Doctor, will we have to do a GYN check too?" one of them said, flipping her hair behind her shoulder and practically winking at him.

What is wrong *with these people?* I wondered. To his credit, the doctor kept a straight face throughout this exchange, looking sternly at the women over the rims of his eyeglasses, until finally, just as I was starting to feel as if my legs might give out, he gestured to the rest of the women in line and said, "Everyone else, get dressed."

I had never put my clothes on more quickly in my life. *I need to get out of here before he changes his mind*, I thought, yanking my shirt over my head. But God must have had other plans for me that day, because He made two things that would have immediately ended my police career fall through the cracks. The investigator assigned to my application might never have allowed me to proceed if he had noticed my written statement about having been shot, and I probably wouldn't have passed my medical exam if the doctor had seen my scars. As I hurried out of the exam area that day, I thought, *Yes! What God has for you is for you.*

On my subway ride home, I still had so much adrenaline in my body that I could hardly sit still, as exhausted as I was. I just wanted to eat dinner and go to bed early. But apparently I had used up all my favors for the day.

I got off the train at Rutland Road to pick up Melissa from Quar's store, and we walked to a nearby Chinese restaurant to order takeout. On our way back to the block, I heard helicopters and police sirens blaring. I reached the corner of Rockaway Parkway and Rutland—where Quar's gift shop, his bodega, and four of the apartment buildings he owned were all located—to find it blocked off with police barricades. Then I saw all of Quar's workers, including his secretary, Ms. Dorothy, handcuffed in a chain as officers ushered them into a black van. The only person I didn't see was Quar.

I had thought I couldn't be any more nervous that day, but I felt like I might actually have a heart attack as I stood outside the barricades with Melissa. Quar always used an apartment in one of his buildings as a stash house. He had another apartment where his workers bagged up weed and prepared it for sale. The cops had raided Quar's spots before, but this time was different. They had never brought in helicopters or Emergency Service Units before; they did that only for major busts. Since the cops had the whole area locked down, I knew they must have found the one million dollars in cash that Quar kept hanging in a huge, round, multicolored cloth bag over our bed. The bag was so big that I sometimes hit my head on it when I sat up in the middle of the night. Quar had always told me that if the cops ever got into his apartment on a bust, I was to take the bag and escape through the fire door that led to the backyard of the building. But I had never even made it inside that day, because I had been gone for hours, going through testing to become a cop myself.

When the officers finally brought Quar out, we made eye contact and he yelled to me, "Come to 67th Precinct and get my things!"

I was used to going to the precinct, but this time when I arrived and gave Quar's name to the woman at the window, she called out, "Narco!"

I didn't realize yet that "Narco" was a reference to the Narcotics division and that charges in that category came with a hefty sentence. Moments later, a tall white man approached me and asked, "How may I help you?"

"I'm Quar's wife," I said.

"Okay. How may I help you?" he repeated, looking intently at me with dark, beady eyes.

"What are you locking him up for?" I asked.

The man shook his head. "Let's not play games, lady. You know what your 'husband' does, and this time we've got him for good. He'll be going away for a long time." He smiled at me, and I got chills all over my body.

I tried to conceal my rising alarm as I asked for Quar's property. With a shrug, the man gave me Quar's cell phone and house keys and told me that Quar would probably be down at Central Booking by the morning.

The other times Quar had gotten busted, his attorney had always gotten him back out on the street the next day. But this time they were holding him on a cash bail of one million dollars. I definitely didn't have anywhere near that amount, now that the bag of money over our bed had been seized.

I ultimately found out that the cops most likely stole a lot of that cash. The paperwork stated that they had recovered $583,000, when I knew for a fact that the bag contained around a million. Fourteen years later, I ended up working with a detective who told me he had worked in Narco in the 67th Precinct unit. We started talking more about where we had worked previously, and I asked him, "Did you ever work on Rockaway Parkway and Rutland? There was a bodega there."

He said, "Oh yeah, there was a dread who worked there. My sergeant and I were part of that big bust, but it was just the two of us who went down into the basement. We didn't let the rest of the team down there." He began to vividly describe that part of Quar's building, including the fish tank and the birds, where I had stayed for so many years.

During that conversation, I noticed a gold Rolex on the

detective's wrist. Quar had had a personal collection of nice watches, and one of them had disappeared during the raid.

"That's a nice watch," I said to the detective.

"Thanks. I've had it for a while now," he said, holding it out to me so I could look at it more closely.

I bet you have, I thought.

This detective and I continued to work together off and on, and two years later we had another conversation where he told me he was closing on a new house. He said the house he was selling was one he had bought for $240,000 in cash.

Well, I knew that police just don't make that kind of money. As I looked the detective up and down, I thought, *The money that you stole was my money. I won't forget this.*

A few days after the bust, I was allowed to visit Quar in jail. Our conversation was all business. No apology, no tenderness—just what had to be done. Quar told me, "Get in touch with my sister and my father. I can't be in here. I need to get out. I've got a business to run. Get everything in order; get on my job."

I had always handled his affairs during his previous arrests, but this time Quar was asking me for too much. I was on a mission to become a police officer. I didn't have the energy or the desire to organize his life for him. I needed to be organizing my *own* life. *When is this going to stop?* I thought. *When is this fifty-year-old man going to get himself together?*

Still, I wasn't quite ready to abandon him altogether, so I kept up my visits to the jail. Every time I saw Quar, all he wanted to talk about was how he couldn't wait to marry me and finally move to our house in Florida. We had been engaged for three years by then, and I had given up on moving to Florida long ago, so I just rolled my eyes. He was acting the way a lot of men do when they get locked up—making promises they'll never keep. However, in case there was even the slightest chance that he was serious, I decided to contact a lawyer and restart the process of getting divorced from Robert, whom I hadn't seen in almost three years.

I sometimes wonder if Robert and I could have lived a normal married life if he hadn't been in jail. Part of the reason I started cheating on him was that I just couldn't do the bid anymore, and now here I was, about to do another one with Quar.

Fortunately, about five months after his arrest, the judge granted bail. Quar's father rounded up $250,000 in cash and offered up his house as collateral, and Quar was scheduled for release.

On the day he got out, I waited for ten hours in the car outside the jail with Quar's bodyguard, Soldier. When Quar exited the building, his dreadlocks were so long that they were dragging on the ground behind him like a bridal veil. He looked filthy and tired, but I didn't care. I ran up to him, kissed him, and told him we were there to take him home.

Quar and I sat in the backseat while Soldier drove us. When we got to our block, it was mobbed with people wanting to welcome him back. After he greeted everyone, he said, "Come with me," and took me to his apartment building. Quar went straight to the boiler room, and when he lifted up the door, I saw stacks of cash piled all over the floor.

"Start counting. When you get to three hundred and fifty thousand, let me know," he said.

I gasped. "I thought the cops took all of it!" When he was in custody, Quar had told me that the million dollars they had confiscated from our bedroom was all he had.

Now, he just smiled. "Never keep all your money in one place."

I began walking back and forth between the boiler room and the bedroom while I counted wads of bills held together with rubber bands. Even as I got up near three hundred thousand, I felt as if the stash in the boiler room wasn't dwindling at all.

Shortly after that, the doorbell rang. When I saw Quar's go-to guy, David, come in, I felt his presence like a sucker punch. Marriage, a house in Florida, a crime-free life—all of the things Quar had assured me I would have as soon as he was released were nothing more than the scams I had taken them for. Quar was always going to go back to doing what he had always done. I simply went into our room and shut the door.

After David left, Quar came into the bedroom. I pointed to the money I had accumulated in there and said, "Here's three fifty."

"Good," he said. "Take fifty thousand and buy us a safe house near here. I'm never going to keep my money in this building again. Take ten thousand apiece for Morgan and Melissa and put it into a college fund for them. And then take another five and get yourself a better engagement ring. You need an upgrade."

I took the money, but I had no intention of using it for yet another attempt at a new life with Quar. He was a criminal, and I was going into law enforcement. How was that ever going to work? I did buy myself a ring, but it was just a decorative diamond band. I used the rest of that five thousand to buy my police uniform and other necessities for the police academy. *Who's the idiot now?* I thought.

The night Quar came home from jail, I washed his dreads and made love to him, but the next morning I knew what I had to do. I was thirty years old, and I was tired of living in fear. I was tired of being paranoid at night when I slept with Quar, thinking the police might come in any second. I was tired of worrying that someone might figure out my connection to him and kill me or my kids. I was tired of everything about that life. And as long as I stayed with Quar, I was never going to stop being afraid. So, while he was my bread and butter and my fiancé, I finally had to accept that he wasn't my forever.

CHAPTER 18

And Then Came the Blues

As I stood on the rooftop deck of the police academy in Manhattan alongside 1,200 other rookie officers, I felt like my entire life was playing at high speed on a movie screen inside my head. The idea that a girl like me—from the projects, abused and abandoned, who was raised by an alcoholic grandmother and lived with a crackhead aunt, who was a recovering drug addict and a high school dropout, who was shot and left for dead, who was homeless and hungry and mistreated every which way—could have actually made it as far as I had just couldn't be real.

At any step along the way, I might have given up and decided, *The world owes me, not the other way around*. But I knew if I could protect even a few people from the pain I had suffered, I would be a better person for it. That objective, combined with my insatiable ambition, had led me here. *Look how far God has brought me*, I said to myself.

It was July 2, 2001, my first day at the police academy. I felt sharp in my impeccably ironed gray uniform and shiny black shoes, but the sweltering heat threatened to blind me as perspiration streamed down my face under my blue military cap.

Instructors walked among the rows of trainees, inspecting us from head to toe, calling some of us out. The woman next to me was sweating so badly that her makeup was running down her face. An instructor stopped in front her and snapped, "You look a mess, PPO. Go clean yourself up!" When he got to me, I felt my knees buckle, but I stood up straight and he passed me by without comment.

I had heard a lot of bad things about the academy: that it was pure torture, that the instructors yelled at the rookies every day, that I would be mentally and physically abused, and that it would break me. But I had already endured so much pain over the years, I wasn't going to stand for any more. On the other hand, I was thirty years old and didn't want to have to return to being a traffic agent, so I knew I had to approach my new role with enough humility to survive the six-month training and achieve full officer status. I also knew that some people were expecting me to fail, and I certainly didn't want to prove them right.

I was placed in Company #7, along with thirty-five other rookies, most of whom were in their early twenties. Everyone in my company was assigned to three academic classes and one physical education class, Monday through Friday, as well as alternating weeks of tours from either seven a.m. to three p.m. or three p.m. to eleven p.m. I was part of the A squad, which usually consisted of rookies with special privileges because of their personal connections. I was nobody and knew nobody, but I ended up there anyway.

Our instructors immediately told us what they expected: "No talking"; "No chewing gum"; "No tardiness"; "No cell phones." It felt like the military. On top of that, we were not permitted to drive to the academy; we had to take public transportation. Just to make sure no one broke that rule, they had people patrolling the blocks near the academy to check. I had heard about several people who had gotten caught and received command disciplines. So, for the first time in my life, I actually obeyed the rules and took the train every morning and evening.

That didn't stop my instructors from laying into me, though. They mocked me relentlessly, even after my main academic instructor appointed me company sergeant. I kept dropping out of the daily mandatory two-mile runs because I couldn't control my breathing without chewing gum, and gum wasn't allowed. "You're a loser, Brownlee," they'd yell. "Everybody look at Brownlee—she's a loser." They eventually dismissed me from the company sergeant post. They wanted to break me. But they had no idea what I had been through. When they got in my face, I would say under my breath, "You don't even know who I am." I didn't care what they said to me. *So what?* I'd think. *I've got money. I'm fly. I'm from the hood. I'm a freakin' savage.* Anytime they called me names, I figured they were just describing themselves while they hid behind their power and their shields.

Despite all the hazing I experienced, the academy taught me about self-discipline in every area of my life. I had never been so accountable to any person or institution before. I learned to be on time for everything. I learned to eat right. I learned that the way you present yourself physically impacts the way other people perceive you—my instructors always said that if I was out of shape, no one would respect me.

The more self-reliant and disciplined I became, the more prepared and eager I felt to finally end my relationship with Quar. I wasn't going to leave him impulsively, the way I had with Larry; now I knew how to be more strategic. We hadn't had a sexual relationship in over a year by then, and my five-thousand-dollar weekly allowance was long gone, but technically we were still together and he was still paying some of my bills while I continued to stockpile my income in my own bank account. All that time, while I was doing my training at the academy, I kept him thinking I was just doing a lot of overtime as a traffic agent. Quar hated cops because they had busted him so many times, so I didn't see any benefit in telling him the truth.

CHAPTER 19

9/11

It was a beautiful September morning in New York, with clear skies and mild weather. I dropped my daughters off at school and headed to my old elementary school, P.S. 21, to cast my vote in the primary election. After I left, I began to hear passersby mentioning that a plane had just hit the World Trade Center, though I didn't think much of it until I got home and turned on the TV.

Although I had spent most of my life in Brooklyn, the events in Manhattan felt as close to home for me—and every other New Yorker—as if they were occurring right next door. Tears welled up in my eyes as I watched image after image of those majestic skyscrapers burning and collapsing.

My immediate concern was for my cousin, who was newly married. He and his wife both worked at the World Trade Center, so I called him. Fortunately, he had been sick that morning and had left for work late, but his wife was unaccounted for. During the hours when he couldn't reach her on the phone, we were forced to consider, like so many others that day, how our family would go on if she did not survive. To our relief, we eventually learned that she survived the attack with only minor injuries.

I was still watching CNN when I noticed on the ticker that

the NYPD was ordering all officers to report to their nearest precinct. I called the police academy, and they told me to appear at the Driver Education and Training Unit at Floyd Bennett Field in Brooklyn. Then I called Quar, told him I needed to go to work, and asked him to look after the girls. I had finally told Quar about my plans, and he had reluctantly accepted the fact that I was not going to give up on being a cop; he had also come to believe my assurances that I would never rat him out.

After Quar agreed to help with Morgan and Melissa for the day, I put on my uniform and headed to Floyd Bennett Field. When I got there, I encountered a sea of rookies and seasoned officers alike. All of us were told we would eventually board a bus that would take us to the police academy.

After a few hours of waiting, we had a break. I snuck back home to check on the girls. They were doing fine, so I returned to the field. My body was so jacked up on adrenaline that I couldn't stop moving. I was only halfway through my training at the academy—how could I possibly handle a major terrorist attack? *I'm not ready for something like this*, I kept thinking, but the truth was that the entire police force was unprepared for a tragedy of this magnitude.

Once we arrived at the academy, each of us was assigned to a specific traffic post near the World Trade Center. I was on a foot post on the West Side Highway most nights, if I wasn't assigned to Ground Zero. Every night for more than two weeks, I was out there from six p.m. to six a.m. Despite my newfound physical fitness, I didn't have the stamina to be on my feet for twelve hours straight. Nighttime in New York in September is cold. I was always freezing and hungry, and I spent most of each shift questioning my choices. All the other struggles I had faced replayed in my head while I stood on that corner, and sometimes I thought I would buckle under the weight of them. I felt as if I had done nothing but run into walls—with my family, my lack of education, my abusive past, my medical trauma—

for my entire life, and I simply couldn't get any relief. And now I was seeing a type of crime that didn't exist on the streets of Bed-Stuy. Friends of mine had been killed, and drug dealing was rampant in my neighborhood, but this was terrorism originating from outside the United States. This was *real* reality, and no one knew exactly how to handle it.

Countless times I thought, *Maybe I'm not cut out for being a cop after all. I should just go back to traffic.* But what motivated me were the other voices I heard in my head—the voices of all the people who didn't believe in me, telling me, *You're never going to make it in the police department.* Every time I wanted to give up, I thought, *I'm not going to give them the satisfaction of seeing me fail at this.*

I was so determined to succeed that when I wasn't on foot patrol, I took on extra assignments that most of the more experienced officers wouldn't touch. Telling myself that I would inevitably encounter death on the job and would need to be prepared for that, I volunteered to go to the morgue. People died in my neighborhood from gunshot and stab wounds, but I never saw their corpses. Niecy and Mommy died of illnesses, not because they had been blown to bits in an explosion. That September, the morgues in New York were overflowing with body parts. Emergency workers were recovering anything they could find in the rubble so that the victims' next of kin could identify them. The first time I went to the morgue, I saw the torso of a female EMS worker, with her uniform still on. I saw the foot of a baby from the day care near the towers. Some of the other officers were throwing up because the whole scene was so gruesome. I just kept wondering why I always seemed to end up in such close proximity to tragedy. When I left, I smelled of ashes and death.

I barely saw my daughters during those first two weeks. Quar took care of them when they weren't in school, and they got home after I had already left for my night shift. I knew

Quar must be anguished over the attacks, but he never spoke about his feelings to me. He didn't want to show any interest in my police work, and I wasn't comfortable initiating a discussion about the topic, so I limited those conversations to my colleagues. We later learned, after we returned to class, that several of our instructors, one of whom I had spoken with many times, had died in the attacks.

Years later, a NY1 reporter interviewed a few of my classmates and me about our initial reactions to 9/11, for a documentary the station was producing. I told him that one of my first thoughts was, *This is what life is going to be like for me as a cop? I'm going to have to defend my city against terrorists?* For a rookie officer, the notion was inconceivable.

Still, I knew the work I was doing was a once-in-a-lifetime experience. In fact, the 9/11 class is likely the most distinctive police academy class in the NYPD's history. It was also the only police academy class to earn overtime pay because of how much work the trainees put in. To be able to say that I was part of it is one of the greatest honors of my life. Once the 9/11 Memorial & Museum opened in 2011, I made a point of going in person each year to pay my respects and relive some of my personal memories.

It took years for New York to recover from the events of 9/11. But that was when I started to understand what I and my fellow New Yorkers were made of. In the aftermath of the attacks, the whole world learned how strong, resilient, and compassionate we are. We witnessed people coming together regardless of their different races, creeds, and backgrounds, bonded simply as human beings who needed one another. We still need one another today, as we continue to pay tribute to all those who lost their lives that day and for all of the families and friends who lost their loved ones, many of whom are still suffering. May we keep them in our prayers forever.

CHAPTER 20

Premonitions

Shortly before Christmas 2001, Quar's trial for his big drug bust started. I never wanted to go into the courtroom in the first place—in fact, I prayed that something would prevent me from having to be there—but I went with him the first day because I knew it was important to him. The next morning, my prayers were answered when I woke up with a bad case of pink eye. I had to seek immediate treatment for it, so I didn't have to go back to the trial, but Quar continued bringing Morgan and Melissa to the courthouse every day.

In the end, Quar was acquitted of all charges because the police botched the entire investigation. The guy their undercover officer was making buys from was another Rasta, one of Quar's primary associates, who looked like Quar and was living in one of the apartments Quar owned, but he wasn't actually Quar. His name was Peter. Peter had met the undercover cop through another one of Quar's associates, Curly, who had been pinched and became a police informant. Curly was still loyal to Quar, so when the police asked him to identify Quar, he introduced them to Peter instead. When the police realized they had arrested the wrong man and had no actual evidence against Quar, the judge was forced to acquit him, while Peter did a ten-year bid. Although Quar and I were both grateful that he didn't have to go back to jail, he didn't have any love left for Curly. Curly might have tricked the cops into thinking Peter was Quar, but he had still turned into a snitch, he had still caused the bust in the first place, and he had still compromised Quar's entire empire. Quar was never going to forgive him for that. But at least he was a free man. Shortly after that, Curly was shot in the back and paralyzed from the waist down. When I asked Quar what had happened, all he would say was "That was his karma."

Once the trial was behind us, I refocused all of my energy on the police academy. I was still having issues academically, but since my training program had been extended because of the 9/11 terrorist attacks, I had some extra time to get things right. I knew that being a police officer was still what I wanted to do, though I sometimes questioned if it was what God wanted me to be doing. When I prayed, I would cry and ask Him why my life always had to be so hard and complicated. I couldn't understand why nothing ever came easily to me. But even when every day seemed harder than the last, I forced myself to keep going, working toward Gun and Shield Day.

Gun and Shield Day is exactly what it sounds like. It's the day police officers get their gun and shield—the day they finally feel official. For me, it was one of the worst days since I had entered the academy, because not only was I failing academically, I also couldn't maintain my composure at the gun range.

For a week, we trained with instructors. I had never fired a gun before, but that wasn't the issue. The issue was that the experience was a severe PTSD trigger for me. Every day I was at the academy's outdoor shooting range, I had flashbacks to when Larry had tried to kill me. The entire scene would play out in vivid detail in my mind. The mere sight, sound, and feel of a gun caused my heart to palpitate and my hands to shake. Each time I fired my weapon, I would start jumping around and miss the target. I was also paranoid that one of the other amateurs I was on the line with would slip up and shoot me by accident. The fact that the range instructors screamed at us all the time only exacerbated the situation; whenever someone yelled at me, I felt like Larry was abusing me all over again. I knew that if I did not manage to qualify during this week of training, my retraining would be one-on-one, just an instructor and me, and I was counting on that scenario to help me pass.

That didn't make Gun and Shield Day any more bearable, though. My fellow trainees and I sat in a classroom while the instructors summoned all the other probationary police officers in Company #7. I was the only person out of thirty-five who would not get a gun or a shield that day. As I watched classmate after classmate return to the room, I had to excuse myself to the restroom. I locked myself in a stall and cried for nearly an hour while I berated myself silently: *No matter how hard I work, I'm a failure. I can't go back in there. I can't face my classmates. Whether they're judging me or pitying me, I don't want any of it.*

The next day, everyone in my company besides me would be going to the precinct to work for a month while I stayed back at the academy with all the trainees from other companies who had failed, whether physically or academically, as well. Those of us who had struggled in the classroom would receive special academic tutoring, and anyone who had failed at the gun range would receive retraining for that.

I spent the next few weeks studying and praying. When my classmates who had been at the precinct for the past month returned to the academy, many of them seemed to have developed a cocky attitude. Others seemed scared all the time, and a few of them resigned. Those who fell into the latter category had most likely never interacted with Black people or Black culture until being forced to do so through police work. Of my classmates, a full two-thirds were white; there were only five Black people and six Latinos among us. Just as I had experienced culture shock from being around more white people than I had ever met in my life, the white rookies in my class were feeling the same thing in the Black communities outside the academy. I knew I would have no trouble policing those communities because I had grown up in them, but the new white officers had no precedent for how to act when they confronted people of color.

Most of the instructors at the academy preyed on any weakness they saw, falsely believing that belittling us would make us tougher cops. Although I certainly had instructors who treated us fairly and equally, the dominant attitude in the law enforcement environment is hostile, demeaning, and divisive—training that perpetuates abuse of power and abuse of others.

Learning how to navigate these dynamics is not easy for anyone, regardless of race. Although the academy offered a sensitivity-training class, its lessons never seemed to resonate. A police department simply can't raise people who are already grown. All people of all races must learn sensitivity, kindness, and compassion at home, when they are children. We must teach our children not to assume that certain people of color are criminals. And if you are a rookie being mistreated during your training, you are then more likely to go out and mistreat others when you become a full-fledged officer yourself.

In January, when I had been with the academy for six months, I was still uneasy nearly every day. I felt like only some kind of miracle would give me the wherewithal I needed to go on. Delving into my spirituality, I decided to go on a fast. For twenty days, I ate only one meal per day. I was hungry and tired all the time, but I asked God to help me through it. Once I prayed on it, however, things only got worse.

One day when I was in my phys ed class, one of my classmates tripped me accidentally. Like a character in a silly cartoon, I flew up into the air and crashed to the ground. I couldn't move, and felt my foot immediately swell up like a balloon. *No!* my mind screamed.

The instructor hurried over, but not to help me. Instead, he stood above me and yelled, "If you weren't a dropout, this wouldn't have happened, Brownlee! Now I have to call an ambulance. What a waste!"

The ambulance arrived and took me across the street to the hospital, where a doctor determined that my ankle was severely sprained. He gave me an ice pack and said I would recover in a week or two. When two weeks turned into a month and my ankle still hadn't healed, I went back to the hospital. This time, they took an X-ray and told me that my ankle was actually broken. I would need to wear a cast for six to eight weeks. I didn't have that kind of time to recover—I was supposed to graduate in ten weeks, and if I didn't, I would have to repeat my entire training at the academy.

"Well," the doctor said, "there's nothing you or I can do about that. But I can tell you that if you don't let your ankle heal correctly, you'll probably never walk the same again."

As soon as I left the hospital, all I could do was cry. My tears brought on a deep depression that lasted for weeks while I stayed home from the academy, lay in my bed, and felt sorry for myself. I was even angry with God—when I prayed, I asked Him, *Why would You let me go so far and get so close to my goal, when You're just going to take it away from me?* In that moment, I had forgotten that God never gives us more than we can handle.

I needed a productive way to distract myself from my physical pain. One of my buddies from another company had formed a small study group with some classmates from the academy, and when I told him what the doctor had said, he suggested that everyone study at my house.

"Maybe they'll let you take the final exam, even if you're not going to classes right now," he said.

"They would never do that," I responded. I wouldn't even be back at the academy until the end of March, when I was supposed to graduate, and I had already failed three of the four exams I was required to take. But I had also forgotten that God works in mysterious ways.

Soon after that, the lieutenant of the police academy's administrative office happened to call me to see how I was doing. *I didn't think anyone there even cared about me enough to check on me*, I thought when I first heard his voice. I reluctantly told him what the doctor had said and explained that I still had to pass one more exam in order to graduate.

The lieutenant paused for an eternity, before he took a deep breath and said, "Here's what I'm going to do for you: I'm going to let you come in and take the exam on testing day, and when you get your cast off, I'm going to send you back to the range so you can qualify for your gun."

For a moment, I couldn't speak. If I hadn't already been sitting down, I would have fallen on the floor. I offered up silent thanks to God and then thanked the lieutenant profusely.

As soon as I hung up, I called my study-group friend and told him about my conversation with the lieutenant.

"You can do this!" my friend said. "We'll all study together every weekend and make sure you pass."

"I have to," I said. "This is my last shot."

The early morning of March 12 was damp and overcast. All I wanted to do was stay in bed, but instead I got up early, left my daughters with Quar, and called a cab at six o'clock. I had to be at the academy by seven, and I was still walking with crutches.

The ride seemed to take forever. I studied from the moment I got into the car until the moment I had to put my books back in my bag. When the driver pulled up in front of the academy, I started shaking. *I can't go through this mental torture again*, I reminded myself. *I have to pass this exam and graduate. If I don't, I don't know what I'm going to do. I have no option but to do well today.*

Most of my classmates hadn't seen me in two months, and I don't think any of them expected to see me hobble in on crutches. I had a small crew of five friends who had kept up with me, and some of the other officers asked how I was doing, but my mind was elsewhere. I didn't want to talk to anyone; I wanted to complete my test and get on with my life.

I took my time. I was focused and diligent and the last one to finish. I didn't care. I had been the outcast the whole time I was in the academy, and today was no different. When I exited the classroom after taking the exam, I didn't know whether I'd passed or failed, but I tried not to think about it, because all the other times I had failed, I thought I had passed.

I had to wait three days for the exam results. The academy would take an average of the scores of all four exams I had taken. I had received scores in the 60s for the first three exams; I needed a high enough score on this last exam to receive an average of 70, the lowest possible passing grade, for all four.

I couldn't eat or sleep during the wait. I even started going back to Tuesday-night prayer at my church, where I asked God to grant me His will—the same prayer I use to this day.

When the third day came and I hadn't heard anything, I was sure I had failed. Not wanting to delay the inevitable, I called the academy to check. One of my instructors happened to answer the phone. She asked me to hold on while she looked up my results. While I waited for her to return, I could hear my heart thundering in my ears.

When the instructor came back to the phone, she said, "Brownlee . . ."

"Yes?"

"Looks like you received a 96. You're on your way."

When I hung up, I was ready to break out into a dance. I

would have, if I hadn't still had my cast on. Instead, I called out, "Thank you, God!"

Two weeks before graduation, when my cast was removed, I went to the shooting range in the police academy's basement and qualified for my gun after only one day of retraining. Away from the chaos of the group training environment, I was able to concentrate on what I had to achieve. The only thing left for me to focus on was going to physical therapy so I could walk better.

After I passed my exam, I bought a thank-you gift for my lieutenant: a glass beer mug with *NYPD* inscribed on it. I went to his office to deliver it to him, and I noticed a picture of his family on his desk. He was a tall, white Irishman; his wife was a Black woman who looked enough like me that I immediately noted the resemblance. They had two adorable children.

"Thank you for everything, Lieutenant," I said as I handed the present to him.

He grinned at me. "I believe in you, Brownlee. Be a good cop. And don't disappoint me."

"I won't," I said. And as I turned to walk out, I added over my shoulder, "And by the way, your wife is beautiful."

Now that I knew I was going to graduate, I started planning a party. I felt like I deserved it after what I had been through. I created a guest list of friends and relatives, and, despite the fact that I had never liked having my picture taken because I never thought I was pretty enough, I decided to hire a photographer to capture the entire ceremony and celebration. After all, I knew one day I would want to look back and remember every moment.

Unlike the day of my exam a few weeks earlier, the morning of my graduation in March was unusually warm, and I felt like the sun was shining just for me. I had finally gotten my GED and completed two years of college, and I had made some true friends along the way. I even dared to ask myself if all the bad times were finally behind me.

My graduation was held at Madison Square Garden in New York City. I had to be there at seven a.m. for rehearsal, so I decided to stay at the Penn Plaza Hotel, directly across the street. My photographer was scheduled to arrive at six thirty a.m.

I rented a white stretch limo for the day to bring my family to the ceremony. I wished Mommy were alive to see what had become of me, but I knew she was watching from heaven, and I could feel how proud of me she was. My aunts, my cousins, my friends, and, of course, my two beautiful daughters were all there to support me, among the thousands of other people filling the arena to honor the legendary 9/11 police academy class. New York City's new mayor, Michael Bloomberg, was there, as well as his predecessor, Rudy Giuliani. Reporters from all the major news outlets covered the event. Even some of the families of the victims of the terrorist attacks turned out.

My ankle was still sore and swollen, and I had to limp down the aisle to collect my certificate, but I held my head high. I wasn't going to let a physical injury or anything else diminish my pride or my gratitude—to my lieutenant for offering me the chance I needed, and to God for touching the lieutenant's heart and allowing him to give me grace. People had been telling me for my whole life that I was worth nothing, yet their words were only distant, meaningless echoes. On that day, while ear-splitting applause surrounded me, all I could hear was a single sentence repeating in my mind: *Look at me now*.

The next thing I knew, it was time to take off our hats and throw them into the air.

I met my family outside Madison Square Garden, and they wrapped me in loving embraces. Then we all jumped into our limo and drove to Central Park with our photographer to take pictures. Once I was confident that my memories would all be preserved, we went to the Upper West Side, where I had reserved a private dining room at one of my favorite restaurants, Carmine's. As I looked around the table at all of my favorite people there to celebrate me, I thought, *I have never accomplished anything that seemed worth talking about—until today. Today is the first day of the rest of my life.*

Never give up on your dreams; your dream is *your* dream.

My graduation party at Carmine's Italian Restaurant in New York City.

CHAPTER 21

The Good Cop

I was hoping to have at least one day off before I had to start working, but I was told to report to the 77th Precinct at nine a.m. the day after my graduation. I arrived thirty minutes early, uniform in hand, hoping that the stories I had heard about the treatment of rookies weren't true. I had been told that the old-timers enjoyed playing cruel pranks, like telling a rookie that the chief needed to see them up on the roof of the building and then locking them up there. Sure enough, only a week later, that was exactly what happened to two rookies in my training class. I, however, wasn't about to become the butt of anyone else's jokes. Hadn't I dealt with enough hazing at the police academy?

Apparently not. When I walked into the precinct, the vibe was dismal. People were milling around everywhere: the admins, the cops who had worked overnight shifts, and a few classmates of mine. When I approached the sergeant's desk, I introduced myself and said, "Good morning."

Instead of responding in kind, he frowned at me and said, "What's so good about it?"

That killed any impulse I'd had to be courteous to him, so I just stood there, waiting for him to tell me what to do next. Eventually, he dismissed me and told me to go into the muster room, which was a lounge-type area with seats and vending machines where the cops always congregated for roll call before we began our tours.

When I entered the room, I recognized two faces from the academy: a girl named Abby from my phys ed block, and my company sergeant. He was a handsome family man from the Dominican Republic, and we had always gotten along well. I sat down next to him, said hello, and made small talk while we waited for someone to come in and tell us what to do. Everyone in that room had the same dumb look on their face that I had, and I'm pretty sure they were thinking the same thing I was: *What the hell are we doing here?*

The whole precinct—the Dirty Seven—had had a bad reputation for years. In 1986, a group of cops from the 77th called the Buddy Boys were investigated for stealing drugs from dealers and reselling them for their own profit. Thirteen officers were indicted, and two hundred had to transfer to other precincts. Ever since then, no one would ever have chosen to end up there—but there I was.

Finally, after an hour, the commanding officer, the administrative lieutenant, and our training sergeant all came in and began telling us basic details—meal breaks, sick leave, our responsibility never to abandon our foot posts—before revealing what tours we would be doing. I was hoping to get the three-to-eleven p.m. tour so I could go to the gym and take Melissa to school in the mornings. Even though my ankle was still healing, I knew I needed to stay in shape. I was working out four times a week at the YMCA, running on the treadmill and lifting weights. I had lost forty pounds at the academy and wanted to keep it that way. I was assigned to the ten a.m.–to–six p.m. tour, but that would still give me time to exercise before work.

After these introductions, I went upstairs to my locker. I decided to wipe it down before I put my belongings inside. I had brought a few cleaning products with me from home, and while I worked, I turned on my little portable radio.

I was playing my music quietly, but within minutes, a big female cop with four stripes—we called them french fries—on the sleeve of her uniform yelled at me, "Yo, Rookie, turn that shit off!"

"Here we go with the bullshit," I mumbled to myself. I tried to ignore her, but she said it again. She even walked over to me and asked, "Yo, didn't you hear what I said?"

"I'm not turning off anything," I replied. As I continued cleaning, the other rookies in the room fell silent.

"You're not even supposed to have that locker, you know," she said. "Old-timers like me are on this side, and the rookies are outside in the hallway."

"Well, this is the locker I saw, and I'm taking it," I countered.

"We'll see about that," she snapped.

That was only the beginning of our problems, which continued for months. The next day, I had gum stuck on my locker. I knew French Fries had done it, but I never said anything. I also never spoke out against her when she left trash in my space, or when she and her crew stayed at the precinct after their night shift just so they could crowd around and harass me. Snitching on another cop at that time was a death sentence. Besides, I still had a lot of street residue on me, so I didn't care what they were doing as long as no one was putting their hands on me. I wasn't afraid to stand up to them—anytime I got tired of their being loud and getting in my space, I would say, "Yo, move out of my way."

It didn't take me long to notice that the other female rookies were doing whatever the older officers told them to do. I couldn't imagine another grown woman who wasn't my mother giving me orders, but most of the rookies just didn't want any trouble. Sometimes the older officers would come up to the locker room and say, "Get out, we don't get dressed with rookies," and all the new cops would vacate. I didn't care. I was still technically with Quar, so I didn't need the income. I would get dressed wherever I pleased. And when I wasn't in uniform, I came to work every day looking like a walking label, wearing Gucci, Louis, or Chanel from my headband down to my shoes and my bags—and, in the winter, one of my long fur coats. No one knew quite what to do with me.

I'd been in training for two weeks. All my friends from my neighborhood had started steering clear of me once they found out I was a cop. Nobody tried to come after me—my status with Quar still gave me protection—but no one wanted to be around me because they all saw me as a snitch. I found myself caught between two worlds: the one I had grown up in, which no longer fully welcomed me, and the one I was just learning to navigate, which didn't seem all that excited about me. I wasn't sure how to handle either environment, and one of the unfortunate ways in which my discomfort manifested itself was my silence when I saw other officers mistreating people of color, sometimes on one of the very same blocks I had hung out on as a teenager. When a cop I was riding with jumped out of the squad car and began frisking a Black person on the street with no probable cause, when they pulled over and ticketed or searched the vehicle of a Brown person who hadn't even committed a traffic infraction, I stayed quiet. I just didn't know how to respond. I didn't want to be seen as a snitch at the precinct, but every time I failed to call out a colleague for corrupt behavior, I would berate myself, thinking, *I can't believe I can't even speak up for my people.*

It wasn't long, however, before I witnessed the "blue family" coming together to protect one of their own. One afternoon, I was patrolling on Franklin Avenue and Lincoln Place and saw a man do a hand-to-hand drug deal right in front of me. I was wearing my uniform, so I could only assume he thought a female cop wouldn't give him any trouble. Of course I tried to apprehend him anyway, but he shoved me and I fell down. When

I called for backup, every police officer in Brooklyn seemed to arrive on the scene within minutes. I felt like I was on a cop show on TV. I had never imagined I would receive such a display of support.

My adrenaline rush didn't last long, though. When the dealer pushed me onto the sidewalk, I hurt the same ankle I had broken in the academy, so EMS had to come. After they put me in the ambulance, my colleagues beat the man mercilessly. He ended up kicking the glass out of the squad car while he was cuffed, and when they were finished with him, they had to put him in an ambulance too.

My ankle was broken again. I had been on the job for only two months, and now I was about to be off duty for several weeks. When my commanding officer found out, he called me to his office and frowned as he said, "I like strong people, not weak people, and you're showing me early on that you're weak."

"I'm not weak," I said. *Who does he think he's talking to? He wouldn't be saying any of this if he knew everything I've been through.*

"I'm done," he said, and waved a hand to dismiss me.

As I hobbled out of his office, I thought, *I just can't catch a break. My CO hates me, my stupid ankle is broken again, the women at work won't leave me alone, and I still haven't managed to get out of my relationship with Quar.* It was one of the only times in my life when I seriously considered committing suicide. I didn't have the tools to cope with so many challenges at once, and I just wanted my pain to end. But there was still a little part of me that said, *Trina, you can't go out like this. Don't blow your brains out just because you're having a hard time. You have too much to live for.* And that voice of reason saved me—that, plus the fact that I didn't want to become a statistic. I already knew that law enforcement had elevated suicide rates, and I wasn't about to add to that body count.

I'm glad I stuck around, because, as always, God and karma were on my side. While I was on sick leave shortly after the CO reprimanded me about my ankle, he got in trouble for taking steroids and was forced to resign. *Good riddance* was all I thought when I heard the news.

Even better, my new commanding officer seemed to like rookies, and he took a special interest in me. The timing was ideal because I had already begun to question my opportunities at the 77th Precinct. After everything I had done to make it through the academy, I knew I couldn't ride around writing tickets and arresting petty criminals for the next twenty years. *What's next?* I kept asking myself. *How can I do more?*

As soon as my ankle was somewhat better, I returned to the precinct but was limited to desk work. That was fine with me, because I wanted to milk my injury through the holidays. A few months later, when the fracture was completely healed, my new CO announced that he was going to transfer me to the Crime unit, where I would be a plainclothes officer and would have weekends off. He sensed how much I wanted to work, how much ambition I had, and he must have decided, *I'm going to see what she's made of.* The old-timers had a fit because they all coveted my new position. They slung insults at me, calling me a snitch, an ass-kisser, but I just ignored them. I was on the way up, and nothing they said could stop my rise.

One of my new colleagues was a Latino sergeant, and right away I could tell he didn't like me. He looked down on rookies and seemed to favor Latino and white cops. He was also rumored to be sleeping with his driver, a pretty but mean Latina. They always rode in the front of the squad car together while two other plainclothes officers and I squeezed into the backseat.

One day while we were patrolling Albany Avenue near the Albany projects, the driver pulled over so that we could stop some young, suspicious-looking Black guys standing on a corner. I noticed one of them hang a black plastic bag from the fence. When they saw us, they quickly walked away and then began running. I got out of the car and looked in the bag, where I found a black handgun. I pulled it out and told the sergeant what I'd found. He told me we would go back to the precinct and voucher it, but when we got there, he gave the gun to his driver so that she could take credit for my discovery.

I immediately told the sergeant and another officer who was present, "That's not what happened. She didn't find the gun. This isn't right."

The sergeant just looked me up and down and said, "That's what happened, Rookie."

I might have stopped there, but I couldn't let it go; I wanted to punch him in his smug face. I pressed him: "That's *not* what happened. You're lying."

I probably would have kept going if Evan, one of my partners in the Crime unit, hadn't said, "Brownlee, come inside." Once we were alone, he told me, "You don't want to make waves—believe me."

"But this isn't right!" I said.

I knew Evan was only trying to protect me, but it didn't work. From that day on, my sergeant took every good arrest I made on his watch and pretended his girlfriend had done it. And each time she benefited from one of his scams, she just smirked at me, like, *What are you gonna do about it?*

I knew at that point that I had to get out of the 77th Precinct. These other cops had no integrity around rookies. They treated all of us terribly, but the Black cops—and especially the Black female cops—got the worst of it. My attitude and my refusal to do what they wanted only made me more of a punching bag. Any task that nobody else wanted to deal with fell in my lap, from sitting with a DOA body for eight hours, waiting for the coroner, to taking sick prisoners to the hospital and guarding them while they awaited treatment.

One time, my administrative lieutenant made my partner

and me write one hundred moving-violation tickets in one tour. Since my partner was white, I couldn't claim that the assignment was racist, but I knew the LT was out to get me personally. It was one hundred degrees outside that day, and, without stopping to eat or even drink any water, we wrote out all one hundred tickets. My partner never complained to me, but I knew he was struggling. Even if I hadn't done anything to deserve such treatment, that was how things were if the bosses didn't like somebody. I knew my new commanding officer liked me, and I knew he wasn't racist, but he couldn't help because I couldn't tell him what I was going through.

CHAPTER 22

This Ain't *New York Undercover*

Before I started working in law enforcement, the only police show I ever watched on TV was *New York Undercover*, which aired from 1994 to 1999. For some of those years, I was at home every day with no job, so I had time to see every episode. I didn't know better than to believe the police work was true to life, and I loved the way the show humanized cops by depicting their personal stories outside their jobs. I would sit there in front of the TV and think, *That's going to be me someday. I'm going to be a good cop, but I'm going to work undercover too.*

After I joined the NYPD Crime unit in 2003, I decided to get in touch with a guy I knew who had been a school cop when I was in junior high. His name was Lewis, and back in the day he used to chase me when I played hooky. Now he was a first-grade investigator in the Narco unit. My godsister's boyfriend, Earl, was a colleague of his and asked him to help me out.

One day, Lewis came by the precinct and brought me the undercover application. He didn't remember me as the little girl who used to run away from him; he just thought he was doing me a favor. I knew I had an advantage because the Undercover unit was where the NYPD encouraged Black women and men to go, since white people couldn't go into Black neighborhoods and buy drugs, but I still needed all the help I could get. I filled out the application and asked my commanding officer to approve it. He told me he thought I would do well and gave me his blessing. He also made the admin LT—the one who had forced me to issue one hundred tickets in one tour—write up a great recommendation for me. That infuriated him, and he made a point of making my last few months at the precinct miserable. Someone even broke into my locker and stole everything out of it. But what God has for you, no one can take from you. Only three months later, I received my call to enroll in the undercover class.

I had to report to training at seven a.m. Winters in New York can be brutal, and this blustery day was no exception. I was instructed to wear clothes that made me look like I was planning to buy drugs, so I threw on blue jeans and a hoodie, a black bandanna, and my Tims.

When I walked into the classroom, there was one seat open in the last row. I was the only female in the class of twenty-five. Most of the other students were Black men; there were also a few Latino guys and two white guys.

Our first instructor gave us all the logistical information we needed. Our second instructor was Black and introduced himself as a former undercover cop who had been on the job for ten years. He said he would teach us how to protect ourselves if we ever got into a harmful situation, and how to avoid blowing our cover. When our third instructor entered the room, he said he wanted to get to know us personally and asked why we wanted to work undercover.

When he got to me, I explained that I was a fan of *New York Undercover*. He looked me dead in the eyes and burst out laughing.

"Sorry to disappoint you," he said, "but this work is nothing like what you see on TV. In this job you will come face-to-face with real criminals who have killed before and who don't care about dying. They will kill a cop, and especially a rat, in a heartbeat. You may have to buy drugs, and you may not have your gun. And there are no cameras or directors who say 'cut' just when you're about to get killed."

It was January, and I was in the middle of my annual month of fasting, so I was already hungry and irritable. I stared right back at the instructor and said to myself, *I'm not trying to die buying drugs, but I'm not going back to the 77th Precinct either, and I'm definitely not going to be a domestic violence officer, so I'm staying right here.*

The police department generally looked down on undercover cops. People respect power, so the chiefs, the lieutenants, the sergeants, and the first-grade detectives got all the admiration, whereas the idea of buying drugs and fraternizing with dealers made officers in other units think they were better than those of us who were out there on the streets, risking our lives in that way. However, I despised drugs because of what they had done to so many of my loved ones, and I wanted to take down as many crack dealers as I could. I was determined to be the best undercover and for everybody to know my name. Once I accomplished that, my goal was to become a community affairs officer—the ultimate "good cop."

My thirty days of training consisted of a lot of talking and a lot of question-and-answer sessions. I expected to learn more than I did; as it turned out, some of the instruction seemed to contradict the instincts I had developed growing up in Bed-Stuy. When the teacher advised us not to make eye contact or speak too much with the drug dealers we would be targeting, I thought, *That doesn't make any sense. Talking to people is what makes them comfortable.* The one lesson that did stick with me was that if I didn't feel nervous every time I was making a buy, I would end up getting hurt. Nerves would be what prevented me from letting my guard down and getting sloppy.

One of my undercover outfits.

When I graduated and was asked what borough I wanted to work in, I picked Staten Island, since I lived in Brooklyn and didn't want to work where I slept. No one else had requested that location, so I was granted the assignment and was quickly sent out on a major case that would require me to live in a housing development and buy drugs regularly from the dealers around there. The NYPD wanted undercovers there because some Staten Island dealers had recently murdered two cops.

Most people would probably have been terrified, but all I could think about was how I was finally going to live out my dream. I also had an ideal support system. Earl, my godsister's boyfriend, was on the case too, and to be working with a seasoned undercover who was like family made me feel invincible.

I had two years of active policing experience at that point, yet working in narcotics was its own world. Once the assignment began, I adopted my friend's name, Fantasia Moore, as an alias and spent my work hours with Earl in an apartment in the housing development, strategizing about how to buy drugs and arrest as many of the local dealers as we could.

The morning of my first bust, a nice spring day in the hood,

I woke up jittery, but I reminded myself that Earl had been assessing the situation for more than a month before I joined him, and then the two of us had spent another six months familiarizing ourselves with the ins and outs, the whos, whats, whens, wheres, and whys. After he scoped out the scene that afternoon, it was time to move in.

I exited the building and zeroed in on the dealer I needed to approach. My heart knocked hard against my chest as I walked toward a dark-skinned guy wearing glasses and a do-rag beneath a navy blue baseball cap, leaning against a fence. For a moment I froze, forgetting everything I was supposed to do. But then I took a deep breath and all my training came back to me. I sized him up inconspicuously before asking him for two vials of crack and handing him a weathered twenty-dollar bill. My attire—a red-and-white-checkered shirt, dingy blue jeans, and first-generation black Gucci sneakers with my heels coming out of the back like I was wearing slippers—must have been the right costume for the job, because the man barely looked at me. Without a moment's hesitation, he placed the tiny plastic containers in my palm, whereupon I hustled back into my building and up to the apartment.

And just like that, the fictional crackhead in me was born. I never could have guessed when I was growing up in Bed-Stuy that my experience observing the crackheads in my neighborhood—and in Mommy's own home—would pay off in such a valuable way.

When you work undercover, you always have at least one ghost—another officer who observes you in action and who can provide backup if anyone threatens you. Earl was my ghost that day and for every subsequent bust we did. When I returned to our apartment, he told me I had done a great job and asked, "How did you feel out there?"

"I thought it would be a lot easier than it was," I said. "But I want to go make another buy. I need to practice."

Earl and I lived in that apartment for six months. We told the other residents we were boyfriend and girlfriend. I often wore a housing department uniform so that the dealers thought I was coming home from work and just picking up some crack for the evening. During that time, we arrested sixty-four subjects. Two of the cases went to trial, and both defendants were found guilty. The other sixty-two cases took plea deals. And the more people we busted, the more I wanted to keep going. I was walking on water in the department; my name was buzzing the way I wanted it to. No more "Brownlee, you're a loser"—now everyone knew me as a superstar undercover, an expert at getting familiar with the dealers until they let their guard down. I was the only Black woman in my command, and no one mistreated me anymore.

I wasn't always the front person on an assignment; I was also a ghost. The NYPD would give me money to buy ice cream or beer at a bodega and then act casual while I watched the other undercover make a buy. I got restless sitting around, eating and drinking all day. But the dealers got so comfortable with me that eventually I was hosting big parties for all of them—with alcohol and strippers—in my apartment in the development. They trusted me so much that some of them fell in love with me; one man's girlfriend was literally in labor with his child, and he left the hospital to come to one of my parties.

Although I never developed a true friendship with any of the dealers, I had lived with a drug dealer myself for so many years that I knew they weren't all bad. Just as no human being is perfect, no one is entirely imperfect either. Some of the men I met during that assignment on Staten Island had potential to be better than they were; they just hadn't been brought up with the right guidance or had any exposure to other ways of living. Some of their mothers had had drug-dealer boyfriends who had forced these young men to start selling drugs. All I could do was pray that someday they would be liberated from the life they were trapped in.

One of my next high-level assignments was to take down a drug spot that was fronting as a barbershop and nail salon. I fit right in with the clientele and quickly became a weekly customer. After months of getting manicures there, I was friendly enough with my nail tech to seem natural mentioning to her that I wished I could cop a dime bag of crack. When she winked at me and said, "I got you," that was the beginning of the end for the salon.

The nail tech introduced me to the owner, who gave me exactly what I wanted. For six months, I bought drugs from him every time I went to get my nails done. I always used marked money so the department could trace the serial numbers back to the criminals who ended up holding the bills. Some dealers got suspicious and tried to wash the money as soon as they had it in hand, but the ghosts were always watching them and notified the department if they saw that happening.

Dirtbag that he was, the owner didn't waste time before he started propositioning me for sex in exchange for the drugs. Of course, he thought I was a real crackhead, so he couldn't understand why I refused his advances, even when he told me he didn't care about using a condom. Fortunately, I managed to keep fending him off and he continued taking cash for my supply. After many months, the business was busted, the operation was dismantled, and I was able to move on to another assignment. I get my nails done on Staten Island to this day—just not at that salon.

Sometimes the takedown was a little more difficult. One dealer, Shawn, had been an NYPD target for years, to no avail—until the department decided to use me as bait. I was still young and sexy and never lacked attention from men. Despite the fact that school was never my thing, I had no problem posing as a full-time Hunter College student who needed money to fund her education. I started hanging out in Shawn's neighborhood, meeting people and hoping our paths would cross. It didn't take long for someone to introduce us, or for Shawn to become smitten with me. All I had to do was wear nice perfume a few times, and he started telling me how good I smelled every time he saw me.

I played the game and led him on, convincing him to sell me product at a discounted price so that I could sling drugs to white people on my campus. But as his attraction to me grew, he urged me to stop and said that if I agreed to be his girl, he would take care of me. I was trying to buy weight from him—a couple thousand dollars per purchase—and he just wanted me out of the game altogether.

"I can't be with you, Shawn. I'm gay," I said.

I thought that would stop him cold, but he persisted: "Why do you have to be like that? I'm starting to fall in love with you."

"I'm sorry, but it's not going to happen. I hope we can be friends, though," I said.

Over the next seven months, I kept Shawn close enough that he continued selling to me. I wore a wire for every one of our conversations, and by the time I told my team, "He's getting too emotionally attached to me; we need to end this now," I had more than enough evidence to put him away. In fact, I bought so much crack from him that by the time he was arrested, his conviction would have garnered a sentence of twenty-five years to life, had he not flipped on his associates and dropped dimes on several homicides. For his cooperation, he received a reduced sentence of seven years.

Even though undercovers are in the trenches, sometimes we need a little help from those elements that are truly about that life. It is at those times that we might enlist a confidential informant (CI)—typically someone facing criminal charges who has agreed to work with law enforcement to have those charges lessened or dismissed.

During my time in Narco, I learned about a notoriously vicious drug lord—a real-life version of Nino Brown, Wesley Snipes's character in the movie *New Jack City*. This Nino was slick as oil. While he was suspected of numerous heinous acts—including beatings, shootings, and siccing his dogs on people—he always evaded the law. But his luck finally ran out when I was given the task of putting him away once and for all.

A female CI for Narco led me to Nino's drug den. At first, when we approached the pleasant-looking colonial house on Staten Island, I thought she must have the wrong address. But as soon as we got inside, I knew we were in the right place. At the end of the long front hall was a solid steel door. Behind that, thick gray crack smoke filled the air in a dimly lit room packed with zombified crackheads leaning against walls and Nino's soldiers manning the floor.

In the center of it all sat Nino, on some sort of throne. Two 140-pound rottweilers on chain leashes lay on either side of him, and on his lap was an AK-47. As the CI and I approached him, I thought I might actually vomit. He was so evil that I could feel his spirit emanating from him, and I realized, *My street knowledge, not my undercover training, is the only thing that's going to save me from this man.*

My energy must have raised a red flag for Nino, too. He immediately revealed that he didn't trust me, even though the CI introduced me as her cousin. He glared at me as he said, "You're gonna sit your Black ass down and you're gonna smoke some crack."

Oh hell no, I thought. I hadn't touched cocaine in any form in fifteen years, ever since I had promised God I wouldn't, and I wasn't about to start now. *C'mon, c'mon, c'mon—think, Trina.*

How are you going to get out of here? You've got to get out. You've got to get back to your kids.

"I can't do that," I told Nino. "My man's standing right outside. He wants to get high right now, and I'm telling you, if he doesn't, he's going to draw cops here. He's on his venge."

While Nino continued to size me up, I said, "If you don't believe me, you can go outside and see him right now." My ghost was out there, so I knew if Nino did look outside, he would see a man. "I can walk out of here now, or he can call 5-0."

"You better not be lying," Nino said.

"I'm not lying—I swear," I responded.

My CI jumped in to help me: "Yo, Nino, she's right—he's that kind of guy. He'll call the cops on you."

Nino didn't seem to care. He pointed his AK right at me.

I thought, *I already lived through one shooting; I'm not surviving this one. This psychopath is going to blow my head right off.*

"Lou's not going to like this," I said. These were the code words for my backup to intervene.

"Who the fuck's not going to like this?" Nino asked, nudging the butt of his gun even closer to my face.

"Lou's not going to like this," I repeated. "Lou" was short for "Lieutenant," but Nino had no way of knowing that. I started saying it again and again, trying to act like something was a little off with me, doing anything I could to get creative. The door to the room was so thick that it was cutting off the reception for my wire. I was sweating so badly and so nauseated from fear and the crack smoke surrounding me that I actually *did* feel off.

I still don't know what happened to change Nino's mind, but finally he said, "I'm going to sell to you this one time. But don't ever come back here again." We made our buy, then he ordered the CI and me to get the fuck out of his den.

As soon as we were outside, I threw up all over my clothes.

I got back to command and said, "Y'all need to go there right now. Demolish that place." Within thirty minutes, a SWAT team and an Emergency Service Unit were swarming Nino's den. It took them a long time to break down that steel door, but they succeeded in forcibly apprehending him, his soldiers, and all the crackheads in the house. At one point Nino said, "I'm going to kill them bitches." Sure enough, my CI later told me that he put a hit out on both of us. I was always in disguise when I was working, but Nino was the reason I took a gold tooth out of my mouth, just to be extra safe. We had to move the CI out of Staten Island and into Brooklyn to protect her, but she had full-blown AIDS and died two months later.

Nino ended up taking a plea, so his case never went to trial, though his reign was finally over. It still feels like a miracle that I got out of there that night with my life, and being able to see the end of a workday was a blessing that I never took for granted again.

I thought I would never have another undercover assignment as terrifying as the incident with Nino, but my last bust on Staten Island was with a woman who suspected me just the way he had. She was edgy because she had just gotten out of prison a month earlier, after serving a ten-year sentence for murder, and although she didn't know I was a cop when I tried to buy crack from her, she looked me up and down and said, "There's something about you I don't like."

Since I knew she had killed before, I didn't want to stick around and find out whether she would do it again. As soon as I had my crack in hand, I hurried out of her apartment and decided to avoid the elevator because I was afraid her crew would trap me in there. Instead, I pushed open the door to the stairwell and started sprinting down the steps. Only moments later, she and two other dealers, one of them holding a knife, came running after me. They chased me all the way down to the ground floor—seventeen flights—but they couldn't quite catch up to me.

By the grace of God, my ghost, who had been trying to reach me while I was upstairs, was trying to get into the building through the same door I needed to escape through. He had just opened it when I reached it, and I flew across the threshold. All I wanted was to collapse in his arms, but I couldn't blow my cover. Even though my pursuers didn't know who my ghost was, they stopped short and retreated inside as soon as they saw him, and that was the only thing that saved me from being stabbed.

My next assignment was to bust a dealer's operation in front of a bodega on Jersey Street. Some undercovers from Queens and I rented an apartment in the neighborhood so that we could be close to the store. Everything was going smoothly until one day I didn't recognize the dealer I was supposed to cop from. I hung back, waiting for an opening, and when I saw a young white man who was obviously a crackhead lurking around, I approached him.

"Yo, you think you can get me something?" I asked him.

"No problem," he said. "I know this dude. I'll introduce you. We're going to act like we've known each other for a long time."

He led me up to the dealer and did as he had promised. But as soon as I made the buy, the crackhead jumped on me and started fighting me to try to get my drugs. In the midst of fending off blows, I looked around for my ghost, but I didn't see him anywhere. Seconds later, the crackhead punched me so hard in my face that I fell to the ground. While I was reeling from the impact, he grabbed his bicycle and rode right over my bad ankle. I knew right away that it was broken again.

In the midst of my screaming pain, I called for backup. Another officer, Bo, who had huge muscles, picked me up off the ground and carried me through the street, holding me in his arms like a baby. He took me to the investigator van, which drove me to Staten Island University Hospital. While I was there, the cops who had helped me told me that they had found my ghost hiding in the undercover car. Apparently, as soon as the crackhead and I started fighting, he had run off. *So much for having my back*, I thought.

My ghost might not have been any help, but my colleagues surprised me by stepping up in a way I never could have anticipated. While I was in the hospital, they brought me a small stack of photos. "We just wanted to deliver your package to you," they said. They had caught the crackhead and beaten his face in. I couldn't even recognize him in the pictures. Their response on my behalf was a good reminder that many of us on the force did look out for each other.

Still, after all that, I decided I'd had enough of Staten Island. "These people are vicious," I told my partner. Besides, I had already bought everything that wasn't nailed down there—more than five hundred busts. I needed to move on to another borough, and I chose Queens.

CHAPTER 23

No Ordinary Love

On a spring day in 2003, I was working overtime with my partner, a childhood friend of mine from Brevoort, near the Albany projects, when I noticed a familiar face driving by in a Hummer. The man's name was Sun. He lived on Long Island, but he was always in Bed-Stuy because the woman who'd raised him lived there and he owned a pizza shop, as well as some real estate, in Brooklyn. I had flirted with him a little bit in the neighborhood, but this was my first chance to get his undivided attention.

I asked my partner to put our lights and sirens on, and I got on the PA system and said, "Pull over." Then I got out of the squad car and walked slowly up to Sun's window.

"License and registration," I said.

He squinted at me for a moment, then said, "You know who I am."

"No, I don't," I responded—although of course I did.

"Yes, you do. I'm Sun."

"Hmm," I said, examining his license. "I'll be back shortly."

I returned to the squad car to let him sweat for a few minutes. I turned to my friend and said, "I know this dude. I like him. But I think he's married." Sun was rumored to have a wife and girlfriends on the side, and one of my ex-homegirls had slept with him back in the day, so I knew he was off-limits. Still, I loved his look—light skin, heavyset, curly hair, nicely dressed—and I couldn't shake the feeling that we had a connection, which I wasn't tempted to explore.

When I walked back to his car, I said, "Okay, I'm going to let you off with a warning this time. But don't do that again."

"You didn't even tell me what I did," Sun said.

"You ran the light back there," I told him. (He hadn't.)

"I didn't run the light."

I raised an eyebrow. "You going back and forth with me?"

"No, I'm not going back and forth with you," he said, although I could tell he was barely restraining himself from rolling his eyes.

"Good," I said. "Now, drive safely and have a nice evening."

The next time I encountered Sun was on a hot weekend that June. I was looking forward to Brevoort projects' annual Father's Day barbecue. Every year, I dressed in a complete head-to-toe designer outfit and saw my old friends. It was a guaranteed good time.

The day before the event, I was coming out of the beauty parlor, looking like a million bucks. My hair was in a perfect ponytail, and I was in the best shape of my life. I hadn't taken more than ten steps before a silver Lexus drop-top screeched up onto the sidewalk and trapped me against the wall of the nearest building. I saw right away that the driver was Sun. *What the hell is he doing?*

Needless to say, after the prank I had pulled on him, Sun wasn't in the mood to be toyed with again. He jumped out of his car, snatched my phone, and said, "I'm not playing with you anymore." He dialed his own number so that my number would ring on his phone, then handed me my phone, jumped back into his car, and drove off.

I stood on the sidewalk, frozen with desire. No man had

ever been so commanding with me without disrespecting me at the same time, and it shook my whole body.

I was back in my car when an unknown number called my phone. I answered, and Sun said, "Yo, when can I take you out?"

"Aren't you married?" I asked.

He said, "Divorced." I could hear through the phone that this was old news for him, and he must have been thinking, *Why are you even asking me about this?* I had no reason not to believe him, so I agreed to go out with him. I knew people would judge me because of his reputation, but he felt like what I had been longing for all my life. I had been in relationships that I thought were meaningful, and that had served very specific purposes for me, but I had never actually been in love with anyone—including and especially myself—and I didn't want to spend the rest of my life not knowing what that felt like.

Later the same day, Sun and I talked on the phone for eight hours. I was at a barbecue at my cousin's, but I had my charger with me so that every time my phone died, I could plug it right back in and continue the conversation. We agreed to go out to dinner on Monday. Sun told me to meet him at the Gateway BJ's Wholesale Club after my tour ended at three p.m., and said we would continue on to the location of our date from there. That was the only information he would give me.

Two days later, I pulled up to the store in my BMW coupe, wearing an all-white outfit. *Why are we at BJ's?* I wondered. *I hope we're not eating here.* I couldn't help but laugh to myself at the visual.

Sun must have read my mind, because he said, "We need to go inside here and get a couple things."

What things? I shook my head and followed him in, where he picked out a towel and some women's flip-flops. *Uh-uh,* I thought. *If he thinks I'm spending the night at his house and he's getting some on our first date, there's no chance.* I hadn't had sex in more than two years.

Sun didn't say anything as he paid for our purchases; he just took the box the checkout person put everything in and escorted me out to his car. He put the top down, and we hit the freeway. My ponytail was blowing in the wind, we were vibing to old-school music, and as he reached across and took my hand, I didn't care at all that we hadn't gotten wherever we were going yet.

Sun eventually pulled up in front of a marina. Nothing looked familiar to me. *Where are we?* I wondered. When a man wearing a white polo shirt and navy-blue chinos stepped to my door and opened it for me, I thought, *What's this white guy doing here?* But Sun only nodded at him as if they saw each other every day.

I grabbed our BJ's box as I got out of the car, and Sun came around to my side to walk with me. Moments later, I saw a line of boats tethered to a long dock. A few people, all white, were coming and going, looking completely natural. I had never even been on a boat before. The closest I had gotten was a crab fest in Maryland.

I had been quiet during the car ride, but now I blurted out, "I thought you said we were going to eat."

Sun smiled. "We are."

"Where?"

"On my boat."

"You have a *boat*?" I almost choked on the word.

Sun chuckled. "Yeah, I have a boat. What's the big deal?"

"I've just never been on one," I said.

"Well, you're about to be. We're going to City Island."

The man who had helped me out of the car turned out to be the captain of Sun's mini-yacht. It had one bedroom, a separate living room, and a spacious, polished wood deck, which we stood on as we started out across the water from Long Island to the Bronx. When we pulled up at Seashore, our waterfront restaurant, no one could have told me I wasn't in Hollywood.

The sun shone down on us as we walked up a long wooden dock and entered the building. We were seated at a window overlooking the yacht and the water.

Right after we sat down, my cell phone rang. When I checked the caller ID, I saw that it was my friend Carter. I picked up the phone, and he immediately started saying, "Yo, where you get them jeans from that you wore at the barbecue?"

I saw Sun frowning at me while I continued talking to Carter. After a few minutes, Sun gestured at me to hang up. When I didn't, he said, "Hang up the phone. You're being rude. You're at dinner. Whoever that is, tell them you'll call them back."

While we ate, I told Sun about the Father's Day barbecue at Brevoort two days prior. Beyoncé had recently been photographed in a pair of custom jeans with her name across her butt, and I had hired a tailor to make me a similar pair, with my zodiac sign in rhinestones on them, for the event. Back then, I derived all of my self-esteem from people telling me I looked fly. Confident that he would fall in line with everyone else, I bragged to Sun about how many people there had noticed my jeans. He just rolled his eyes and said, "Hold on. You're a grown woman—a *police officer*—and you're running around wearing jeans with a Libra symbol on the ass? Do you know how ridiculous that is? Don't wear clothes to get attention; wear them because they're nice. Wear them because *you* like them."

I screwed up my face, getting ready to spout some sass—*Do you know who you're talking to?*—but I couldn't get the words out before Sun said, "You're too pretty to do that with your face. Stop having an attitude. Learn how to be a lady and calm down."

Calm down. Those last two words echoed in my head. Had I ever been calm? My childhood, my adolescence, my twenties, and now my early thirties all skittered across my mind's eye in that moment, and all I observed was one frantic, desperate struggle after another. I wasn't sure I even knew what it felt like to be truly calm. But maybe, I thought, with Sun's guidance, I could.

That dinner was the first of countless revelatory experiences I would have with Sun. I had made so many great strides in my career by then that I had neglected to evolve in other areas, though I didn't realize this until Sun began to enlighten me.

When our server appeared, I ordered a cocktail. I asked Sun why he wasn't having a drink, and he said, "I don't drink and I don't smoke. I don't put that poison in my body, and neither should you."

My immediate response was, "Well, listen, I've been drinking all my life, and I'm going to have a cocktail."

He said, "It's your choice, but you don't need it."

Part of me thought, *I wish this man would just shut up.* Another part of me—a part I hadn't heard from before—said, *Wow, this is different.*

He ordered king crab legs, a baked potato, and corn. I ordered lobster tail and fried shrimp. Sun said, "Listen, king crab is the Rolls-Royce of crab, and I want you to try it. If you like it, we can order some more." When I tasted it, I was hooked instantly. To this day, I eat king crab legs often.

As we finished eating, Sun said, "I know you'll go back and tell all your friends, 'I had my first date with Sun, and it was on a yacht.'"

I swatted his words away. "Please. You really think I'm going to go blab about this to my girls?" Meanwhile, I was thinking, *You best believe that's the very first thing I'm going to do.*

We walked back down the dock, boarded the boat, lay on the bed, and talked for the whole ride back to Long Island. He drove me back to the Gateway BJ's. I got in my car, went home, and took a shower. I stood in a trance for an eternity, letting the hot water rain down on my body. When I got into bed, I did not sleep for a single minute the whole night—all I could think about was what an unreal human being I had just met.

* * *

We began spending every day together. We took carefree drives up the Long Island Expressway in his Lexus, dined at five-star restaurants, and went on all-day excursions on his boat. One afternoon, he took me with him to buy a Bourget motorcycle. I was used to dudes with dirt bikes. I was used to Quar and his chronic weed smoking and cheating. Sometimes I caught myself wondering who had more money, Sun or Quar, but it didn't matter. Sun was a completely legitimate businessman and a grown-up. Quar was still dealing drugs and running around with different women. Once I met Sun, I believed I might finally have the strength to leave Quar for good. He was my past; Sun felt like my future.

Sun and I weren't even physically intimate until two months after our first date. He kept saying, "It's not about sex with you and me." He taught me what love was supposed to look and feel like. He was the first person who ever told me, "You are absolutely beautiful. You are one badass chick."

The first time he said it, I almost laughed in his face. "Are you crazy? No, I'm not." All my life, I had been called fat, ugly, and stupid. The things he was saying to me were so foreign that I couldn't receive them. Even after all my professional accomplishments, I had not yet undergone any therapy, and I was too broken to process his compliments.

One day, he bought me two dozen long-stemmed red roses. I started crying when he handed them to me, because I had never received flowers from anyone. From that day on, I cried every time he gave me a bouquet. More than that, though, it was that Sun was investing in me as a person. Any hustler could have gotten me roses, but Sun saw in me what I couldn't see in myself.

Sun and I opened up to each other more and more about our personal struggles over the next few months. He had plenty of his own stuff going on. I learned that his mother had been a drug addict who abandoned him, that he had never known his father, and that he had been married to a woman who was the mother of his daughter but had divorced her years earlier.

One summer night, we were at my house. Morgan and Melissa were at Quar's. Sun and I were in bed. He was reclining against the headboard, and my head was on his chest. I glanced up at him and said, "I want to tell you something."

Rubbing my shoulder, he said, "Tell me what it is."

I said, "I got shot before. I got shot ten times."

He sat up all the way in bed. "What?"

I lifted up my T-shirt, pointed at my abdomen, and said, "Look." I began to tell him the whole story of Larry—the story that I hadn't shared with anyone else since it happened. And after I told him, he leaned down and kissed every one of my scars while I cried.

He was quiet for a long time. When he finally spoke, he asked, "Have you ever thought about writing a book?"

I swiped my hand through the air and said, "No. Why would I do that? I'm not telling people my business."

He shook his head. "Look at you—you became a cop after all this. I just think if you told people your story, it could help them. You're going to be huge someday. I swear."

I kept protesting: "No I won't. I'm stupid." But over the next twenty years, that conversation never left me. Sun made me feel safe enough to confess my most private pain to him, and he deserved that trust, because he was the only person who ever held up a mirror to me and showed me the woman I had the potential to become.

After a few months of dating Sun, I was ready to marry him. I couldn't imagine a better man for me. But the feeling wasn't mutual. Instead, I noticed he was beginning to distance himself from me in small ways. Although we had been seeing each other daily, he started making excuses to spend less time with me. I couldn't understand it then, but in hindsight I realize that he had a difficult decision to make. I imagine he thought, *This relationship is too much work for me. I love Katrina, she's a good girl, and I can trust her, but I'm not willing to put in the energy to fix her. I don't want to hurt her, but I'm going to slow things down until they taper off completely.*

I also know now that I wasn't ready for Sun—for what he had and who he was. Back then, though, his behavior reopened all my old wounds and resurrected my abandonment issues, and my emotions started running wild. You could have torn my heart out of my body and baked it in an oven. I would call him and cry. I would show up at his pizza shop or at his mother's house. I would accuse him of lying and cheating. And, for the second time in my life, I started having suicidal thoughts; I told him I couldn't live without him and begged him not to leave me.

My pleas had the opposite of the desired effect. Although Sun was always patient with me and never spoke harshly to me, he let me know indirectly that we weren't going to be together. The only way I could think to move on from my broken heart and fill the void that Sun had left was to start dating my Jamaican neighbor CJ, who had been chasing me for years. I didn't know yet how to go through a breakup on my own, without having somebody else already waiting for me in the wings. I thought getting into a relationship with another guy was what I needed. But that didn't mean that every time I found myself driving somewhere with CJ, I didn't wish I were on one of my long convertible rides with Sun instead.

I was thirty-four, and I wasn't young enough to bounce back from my devastation by hanging with my friends. I did do some retail therapy, but I had to put everything on my credit cards because I didn't have Quar's money behind me, so I maxed out my Visa. I sought additional solace in my aunt Crystal, and we started having crab dinners together on Mondays, my day off.

Years later, she said to me, "Trina, you've always been able to find men who love you deeply. I've never had that kind of love. You should embrace it." But back then, she just kept me close and gave me the gift of her companionship.

As I slowly healed from both my breakup and my even deeper trauma, I was able to see all the good that Sun had done for me. He was the one who taught me how to kiss. He taught me not just to have sex but to make love.

He also told me, "Never be a come-up for a man. You're a bad bitch, and men are going to want you to be that for them, but they need to be successful on their own." On the other hand, he also always said, "I need you to love me." When I asked why, he said, "Because if you love me, I'll be able to trust you and you'll always be loyal to me." I've never forgotten that when someone genuinely loves you, they'll show it by being loyal to you.

In the midst of the demise of my relationship with Sun, the NYPD promoted me to detective. Sun was the only guest I invited to the small ceremony. He was a private person, and I wanted it to be just the two of us. Also, because I was undercover, it wouldn't have been appropriate to ask a large group to attend.

I had just moved as well, into a brand-new home that Quar had given me money to build in Brooklyn. When I signed the closing paperwork on the three-family brick house, I thanked God for beginning to give me some of the things I had wanted for so long. I had my health. I had a job I loved. My oldest daughter was in college. And my relationship with Quar was finally coming to an end. Although he was excited about my new house, which he had gladly agreed to pay for when I approached him about it, he did have one condition: "Whatever you do, don't bring a man in there." He went on to say, "I know that we're at the end of our road together. I'm hoping you'll have a change of heart. But if you don't, don't put another man in that house. If you get a man, let him put you in a house—not the house that I bought you."

A year after that, Quar and I were officially no longer a couple. I would always have love for him, and we remained very close friends, but I wasn't anything like the twenty-four-year-old woman he had met outside the bodega. Now, twelve years later, I wanted to avoid ever allowing the past to drag me down again.

Eventually, though, I realized that Sun was in my life for a reason. The wisdom he imparted to me—wisdom that continues to grow within me—was an everlasting gift. He gave me the blueprint, and I used it to build the life I wanted.

CHAPTER 24

Movin' On Up

Unlike the Staten Island undercover unit, which had been a smaller and more intimate department, Queens Narco, where I'd transferred to, was large and more diverse; crack was also harder to buy in that borough because drug deals were more about who you knew. Fortunately, I was teamed up with two legends in the undercover world, one man and one woman, who helped ease the transition for me. Every time we made a buy, we would play the Chamillionaire song "Ridin' (Dirty)" afterward.

I was now also in the same department as Lewis, the renowned first-grade detective who had chased me down for playing hooky from school decades earlier. That we had started out facing off and ended up as peers was an honor I had never expected. Still, none of those advantages was enough to keep me in Queens. In fact, I was starting to doubt whether I wanted to pursue a long-term career at all, when I got a phone call asking if I was interested in doing a sting for Brooklyn South, in the Cypress Hills projects. The investigation had been underway for a while, but they felt like they needed another Black female undercover to succeed.

I went to Brooklyn, got an apartment there, and did my thing. I bought drugs all over that place. My living situation was similar to what I had had with Earl, but my partner this time was a Black Jamaican woman. People in that project thought we were lovers because I stayed in the gay character I had used for other busts.

The most dangerous undercover situation I had ever been in was when Nino Brown pointed his AK at my face and tried to force me to smoke crack, but in Brooklyn I found myself in the middle of another nearly fatal encounter. Two crack dealers I had been buying from didn't want to compete for my business, so one day they both pulled their guns out and were fixing to shoot each other until I stood right in the line of fire and pushed one of them backward. "Nah, we ain't gonna do this," I said to him. Both he and the other dealer were young, so I began speaking to them like a mother figure. I pulled two twenties out of my pocket and gave one bill to each of them. "Let's all walk away now," I said.

We arrested 167 suspects during the year I worked on the Brooklyn investigation. The NYPD had to charter MTA buses to take all the dealers away. But that year also made me certain that I wanted to end my time in Narcotics for good. I was exhausted mentally and emotionally. I feared for my safety. I knew it was in my best interest to transfer to a safer unit, so I requested a position in Queens Vice, which was granted a few months later.

Soon, I was back inside a precinct for the first time in years. The space was cramped and felt restrictive after my years of roaming around the New York boroughs for work, and I was the only Black female undercover on my team, though I eventually became close with some of my coworkers. My lieutenant was a young, slim Black man who sounded like Lenny Green from the New York radio station WBLS. He was standoffish when I started the job, but when he saw my work ethic and my sassy personality, he relaxed and we became good friends. My commanding officer was also young, a classy Italian man who became close with all of us.

The squad had two teams. I called them the Chocolate Team and the Vanilla Team because my team went to all the Black neighborhoods and the Vanilla Team went to the more ethnically diverse neighborhoods. One day I went out on a tour with the Vanilla Team, and the sergeant and two of his guys went inside a series of illegal gambling dens and searched them without a warrant. They also suggested that we open the registers and take all the cash. When I returned to my command, I told my LT that the Vanilla Team was doing illegal searches. "I'm not going to sacrifice my pension or my reputation because of these corrupt cops," I said. After that, he told them he wanted to make more overtime pay and started going out with them on their assignments a couple of times every week, and naturally they were all on their best behavior.

Their conduct was so reckless that I knew it was only a matter of time before they got punished for it. Sure enough, one of the officers on the Vanilla Team later got arrested for robbing houses on Long Island and ended up getting fifteen years in prison. Of course, I had always known there were plenty of dirty cops out there, because the ones who did the big bust at Quar's house had probably stolen a huge amount of money from us—but there's a difference between being a victim of police corruption and actually working in the midst of it. During that time, I began to believe that no police should spend more than five years in any unit that involves direct contact with drugs and money. The temptation to break the rules was just too great.

I naively thought things might improve if I left Queens and its bad reputation behind, so I requested a transfer to Brooklyn South Vice within a year, but it was the same story there. That was when I decided I didn't want to be in the organized crime bureau anymore. Having done more than seven hundred narcotics buys already, and now having transitioned to vice buys—which consisted of breaking up prostitution rings, illegal gambling, and strip clubs—I didn't think another hundred or two hundred arrests were going to make a difference. I also wanted to pursue a long-standing career objective of mine: to work in Community Affairs. People said that was where the friendly cops were, the ones who wore light blue shirts.

When I applied for Community Affairs, the chief, who seemed like a perfectly nice man at first, was the head of that department. Then his assistant, a friend of mine, confided in me that the chief had said I was "too ghetto" for that division. Yet he was also flirting with me all the time, saying, "Let me take you out to dinner." I kept wondering, *If I'm so ghetto, why are you trying to sex me?*

I wanted to tell him that I knew what he had said to his assistant about me behind my back, but I couldn't betray her confidence, so I kept my mouth shut, even when the chief made sure my Community Affairs application was rejected. Once he crushed that dream, I asked to be made an investigator, but the NYPD was always reluctant to switch talented undercovers over to investigative roles when it still needed to do as many drug and vice busts as possible.

When I was denied that option too, I decided to study for the sergeant's exam. Sergeant is the lowest-ranking supervisory position. I wanted to continue to ascend in this police force so that I could have more of a voice, and I knew I couldn't do that being only a detective or a cop, though I could if I became a sergeant—or so I believed.

I took classes once a week, yet my poor test-taking abilities kicked in again and I failed the qualifying exam. I felt like I was going through the academy all over again, but I wasn't going to let anything get in the way. I couldn't buy drugs for the rest of my life. I was getting older, and I just wanted something different for my professional future. After having zero ambition for the first two and a half decades of my life, I was now addicted to it. I just kept asking myself, *What's next? What's next? I've got to be great.* So I decided I would keep studying and try again.

Class was held every Monday night in Brooklyn. One of my teachers was a young, good-looking Black chief named Davis. I noticed him frequently making eye contact with me and calling on me to answer questions. What he didn't know was that I already knew who he was. When my former friend Benny had shot a man at a barbecue I went to when I was first on the job at the 77th Precinct, it had made the news. He had then told two detectives working his case that he and Davis were brothers. Those detectives had gone and told the press about the relationship between the two men.

Two years earlier, I had had one of my dreams, telling me that Davis and I were destined to get involved somehow. I had always known it was only a matter of time before my premonition came to pass.

One Monday, Davis summoned me after class. *Here we go,* I thought.

He asked me why I was always late. I had no good excuse, but I knew that wasn't why he actually wanted to talk to me anyway. Sure enough, he invited me to have a bite with him at the Applebee's across the street. Although my waking reaction to my dream had been, *I don't really want this man,* now I figured, *What could go wrong? It's just one dinner,* so I agreed to go.

When we sat down, I looked him right in his eyes and said, "I know you, and I know something about you that you don't know."

"You don't know anything about me," he responded.

"Oh, yes I do."

"What do you know?"

"What are you willing to do to get that information?" I asked, smirking.

He smiled. "Buy you a drink?" He called the server right over and ordered me a cocktail.

When it arrived, I pointed at the glass and said, "The more they come, the more I'll tell you."

"You best start now," he countered, settling back in the booth.

I nodded. "Remember when a young man got arrested for shooting a detective's son a couple years ago? It was the 81st Precinct, when you were the commanding officer."

"I think so," Davis said.

"Well, I was hanging out with the shooter at the time. We were friends, and he's your brother."

Davis leaned forward, squinting at me. "My brother? Which brother?"

Davis had two older brothers with the same parents he had, but I wasn't talking about either of them. I said, "The brother that your father had on your mother when he cheated on her with another woman. Benny told me all about that. And the newspapers back then even mentioned a bunch of times that you had this additional sibling." As I was speaking, I was realizing that Davis must not ever have confronted his father when that piece of reporting was in the news cycle. *Maybe I should just stop talking now*, I thought, as I took a sip of my drink.

But Davis wasn't about to end this conversation anytime soon. "What did Benny tell you?"

"Your father only saw him a few times, but he paid child support to Benny's mom and got Benny a job at the water department when he was eighteen."

Davis couldn't even speak at first. He just pressed his fingertips against his temples and stared at the sticky tabletop. After a few minutes, he said, "What else?"

"I'm not in contact with Benny anymore because I cut ties with him after the shooting. But he called me when he was getting booked at the precinct and told me that his brother was a big-time cop boss and that their father was a retired lieutenant. He also said that he called you guys' father for help. I just said to him, 'I hope everything works out for you, take care of yourself,' and left it at that. I was scared that the phone was tapped."

"Tell me more. Tell me more."

We spoke for hours that night; we didn't even notice that Applebee's was closing until our server told us. When we got outside, it was pouring rain; it looked like a storm scene from an old-time movie. Davis walked over to his car to get an umbrella so I wouldn't get wet. When he returned, he was soaked. He said, "I need to make sure you get home safe."

He followed me in his car, and when we arrived at my house, I offered to dry his clothes for him, but I realized he had on a suit, so I hung that up and put his socks and his shirt in the dryer.

When he came inside, he said he was shocked that my house was so clean and inviting. "A lot of women who dress up and wear designer clothes have nasty homes and no furniture."

I just laughed and told him that all women weren't the same.

While his clothes were drying, we went into my room, lay across my bed, and kept talking. We both wound up falling asleep and didn't wake up until morning. When Davis left my house, he asked if he could see me later and I said yes.

Over the next few months, we spent a lot of time together and eventually fell in love. He had a reputation for being with a lot of women on the job. I asked him about it, and he said, "Don't believe everything you hear." He never pressed me for sex, so I thought he must be telling me the truth. The most we ever did was give each other a peck on the lips when we said hello or goodbye. Fearing that he wasn't physically attracted to me, I asked him what was up, and he said he wanted to make sure our relationship went further than his other ones, so he wanted us to take our time. I thought that was noble of him, and took him at his word, and we became intimate in other ways—conversationally and emotionally.

Despite all that, our relationship could never last, because

Davis was married. He never wore a ring, never acted like a married man, and never told me he had a wife, but I did my own investigation and confirmed it.

Then I confronted him: "Don't you think that's something you should have mentioned to me?"

He was immediately defensive: "We talk about a whole lot of things, and you've never asked me about that."

Seriously? I thought, and said, "*I* shouldn't have to ask *you* about this. This changes everything."

But Davis and I were already deep into a friendship. I wanted to keep that alive, though I had to promise myself that I wouldn't compromise my integrity by being romantically involved with a married man. That ended up being one of the hardest but also smartest decisions I ever made, because we are best friends to this day. We are each other's most trusted confidants. He has been my financial advisor for years; he taught me the importance of savings, he taught me about retirement funds, and he taught me how to make wise investments. He was my mentor, and I later filled the same role for him. He is my ride-or-die, and our friendship is unmatched, and I will always love him for that.

The next time I took the sergeant's exam, I failed again. *That's it*, I thought. *I'm giving up. I'm sick of studying for a stupid test I'm never going to pass.* Instead of becoming a sergeant, I decided to focus on trying to become an investigator. I was sure the department was going to deny my request, but now I had a secret weapon: Davis. He got me right on the investigation team.

I thought I was moving in a good direction, but I was miserable on that team. The other investigators made derogatory comments about the fact that I'd had my daughter young: "You had your high school graduation and your baby shower at the same time." They also looked down on me because I lived in

Brooklyn and they considered that the hood—or "Compton," as they insisted on calling it. Their insults were too ridiculous to bother me; I got right up in their faces and said, "Oh yeah? Look at you—you live on Long Island, but you come to work with peanut butter and jelly sandwiches because you can't afford to buy lunch. Meanwhile, over here in 'Compton,' I'm eating freakin' lobster dinners on Tuesdays." Sometimes I wasn't even in the mood to make that much effort, so I'd just say, "Shut up. Get out of my face, you freakin' loser."

All those men got theirs a few years later, when they ended up in jail for running a multimillion-dollar prostitution ring. They never talked about it on the job, but I knew they were doing something corrupt. *I'm a detective, remember?* I would think whenever I sensed they were up to no good. *You're not fooling me.*

Despite Davis's support, all I had really done was move from one crooked team to another. But just when I started to worry that I would never take a real step forward, God intervened again.

CHAPTER 25

Forty, Fabulous, Farrakhan

In 2009, I realized that I needed to make some changes in my life. I couldn't allow myself to keep making the same mistakes. A friend of mine had recommended a therapist, Dr. D, to me, and when I found out that my health insurance would cover my sessions with her, I thought, *Why not at least try?*

The day of my first appointment, I drove my squad car from Queens to Manhattan and parked near her building on 34th Street, down the block from Macy's. Dr. D was waiting for me in her office, a space no larger than an apartment bathroom. The first thing I thought when I saw her sitting in her chair was, *This could be my mother.* She was a heavy, six-foot-tall Black woman in her early sixties, with a beautiful face, a kind smile, and a soft voice. She handed me a questionnaire and invited me to sit on her couch. While I completed it, Dr. D sat quietly, eating Peanut M&M's from a big glass candy dish in front of her. I wanted to reach into the dish myself and pull out a big handful, but I tried to show some self-restraint.

Once I handed the questionnaire back to her, she asked, "How are you? What brings you here?"

The minute she opened that door to me, I walked right

through it. I crumpled on her couch and began sobbing while I tried to tell her my story. My first instinct was to jump right into describing my broken relationships, but she cut me off quickly.

"No, no, no—I want you to start from birth," she said. After that, she remained silent while I unburdened myself.

It took me six months to describe my thirty-nine years of experiences. I had never been so brutally honest with anyone in my entire life, and the fact that I had to keep secret much of what had happened to me, for fear of losing my job, had only weighed me down further.

Dr. D helped me to release some of that heaviness. When I explained to her that the NYPD might fire me if they knew that I had been shot, and stigmatize me for being mentally unstable and manipulating the system to obtain a firearm to kill Larry, she said simply, "I believe you're going to be okay."

It was the first time anyone had ever said anything like that to me—such a simple reassurance, but one that immediately altered my entire perspective. I had felt as if I was out there by myself, one-on-one against the whole wide world. But now I began to believe that I could achieve the personal growth I needed so desperately. And once my therapist started asking me questions about and holding me accountable for certain decisions I had made—"Why do you think you did that?"—I wanted to spend every minute in that office with her. In the midst of the most vulnerable conversations I had ever had in my life, I felt like she had wrapped me in a heated blanket set to its highest temperature. She made me feel so safe that I wished I could just curl up in the pocketbook hanging on her office door and go home with her every evening. The warmth that she exuded was more maternal than any I had ever received from my female relatives.

In the beginning, Dr. D and I met three times per week, on Mondays, Tuesdays, and Thursdays, during my lunch breaks. For the past fourteen years, attending Sunday service every week at Bishop Hezekiah Walker's Love Fellowship Tabernacle had been my therapy. The bishop was a renowned gospel singer, and his music always felt healing. While I was a member of that congregation, my personal relationship with God had grown stronger than ever, and I still wanted to serve Him any way I could, but my time in the church no longer felt as fulfilling as it once had. The sermons started to seem watered down, and the institutional aspect of the services was not nurturing my connection with Him. Once Dr. D came along and opened me up in a different way than the church could, I wanted to focus on doing the kind of personal and spiritual work that I thought would best help me evolve and also be pleasing to God. To this day, however, I still listen to the music of Bishop Walker's Love Fellowship Tabernacle choir while also searching for a Bible-based church that will feed my soul and keep drawing me closer to Him.

In front of Bishop Hezekiah Walker's Love Fellowship Tabernacle with my broken ankle.

* * *

In September 2010, a month before my fortieth birthday, I was ordered to work the New York Labor Day parade as an undercover. Many cops don't like that assignment because it's hot and long and most times some sort of violence jumps off, but I always loved seeing the different Caribbean cultures on display, including the music of Beres Hammond and Bob Marley, my favorite reggae artists; incredible food; opulent costumes; and a wide range of dance styles.

That year, I was working with my sergeant, a Jamaican man. The event went off smoothly, and we managed to get some jerk chicken, rice and peas drenched in brown stew chicken gravy, and sweet plantains. When the parade was over and we were at the end of the route, I saw a few well-groomed African American men dressed in black suits with earpieces in their ears.

I walked over to one enormous guy who stood about six feet six inches tall and must have weighed five hundred pounds. *I've never seen a man this huge in the whole NYPD. I could climb on him*, I thought, looking him up and down and wondering, *Where you been hiding at?*

I asked him, "Are you on the job?"

"Yes," he said.

"Intel?"

"No, Nation of Islam."

"That's not my job," I said, looking at him again.

I was about to walk away, when another, much smaller man, wearing a black suit and a beautiful necktie, came over to where we were standing. The larger man said to him, "Please thank the detective for a job well done."

"Who?" the man in the tie asked. I was dressed in one of my standard undercover outfits—blue jeans, an oversized white T-shirt, Timberland boots, and a black-and-white bandanna— so he didn't understand right away that I was a detective. As he started making small talk, I raised an eyebrow and asked, "Are you one of those Farrakhan people too?"

"Are you talking about the Honorable Minister Louis Farrakhan of the Nation of Islam?" he corrected.

"Yeah," I said, barely resisting the urge to roll my eyes. *This guy is so extra. Why he gotta talk like that?*

"Why do you ask?"

"I always wanted to meet him," I said, remembering all the days I had sat on the stoop of Mommy's landlord's brownstone as a kid and listened to Minister Farrakhan's strong and powerful voice preaching on the radio.

"Well, perhaps that can happen." The man with the beautiful necktie smiled.

I started laughing, thinking, *There's no way he's being serious right now*. But as I began to walk away, he asked for my phone number. I said no, figuring he just wanted to try to convert me to Islam.

"Okay," he said, shrugging. "But how can I introduce you to him if I don't have a way to contact you?"

Although I looked at him sideways, I gave him my work cell phone number just before my sergeant and I walked away laughing.

"This guy's a whole clown," I said. "He don't know no Minister Farrakhan. Dudes will do anything for a phone number, man."

"Yeah, mon," said the sergeant.

Later that night, I was in my bed watching then-governor David Paterson speaking on the eleven o'clock *Eyewitness News*. The smaller man with the tie from the parade was standing behind him. I sat straight up, squinting at the screen.

I quickly dialed my sergeant and told him that I thought the guy we had made fun of earlier might actually be someone important. "I just saw him on eyewitness news," I said. "Turn on Channel 7." But by the time he got to it, the segment was over.

Several days later, I was en route to work and had just stopped at a McDonald's drive-through to buy an apple pie, when my phone rang. It was the man with the tie. This time when he greeted me, I heard my whole voice change as soon as I opened my mouth. I sounded like Michael Jackson, like a humbled little child.

The man said, "Your request to meet Minister Farrakhan is being considered, but you need to be vetted first by the head of the minister's security detail. Where will you be later?"

"I'm on my way to work right now. I'll be at the 71st Precinct all afternoon and evening. You can come by and see me there."

"All right," the man with the tie said. "I'll be in touch later today."

When we hung up, I stared at my phone for a minute. *Did that actually just happen? It has to have been a hoax. This clown is still trying to play me.* But then another voice inside my head said, *Stop calling him a clown, Katrina. You know he's not.*

I spent most of the afternoon trying to put together a search warrant for an illegal gambling operation, yet every few minutes my thoughts returned to the man with the tie. *It's getting late*, I started to think. *Is he ever going to call?*

My phone finally rang at nine thirty p.m. I picked up, and the man with the tie said, "We'll be there in a few minutes. Come outside."

Thanks for the advance notice, I thought as I sprinted into the precinct restroom. I had on my usual work bandanna, and I straightened it in the mirror, rinsed the perspiration off my hands, and put on some lip gloss. The whole time, I rehearsed what I would say to these visitors about why I wanted to meet Minister Farrakhan. It wasn't just about the fact that I had heard him on my neighbor's radio when I was a child; I also had questions about Black people that I had been pondering for a long time. I had a hunch he might be able to answer them.

As I was leaving the restroom, the man with the tie sent me a text: *We're outside but the cops are saying we can't park in front of the precinct.*

I ran outside and saw an entire motorcade of gleaming black SUVs with heavily tinted windows lined up on the curb. "I got this," I told the officers who had gathered out there.

They said, "No problem, Detective," and cleared out.

The man with the tie—a polka-dot bow tie this time—emerged from one of the vehicles, along with an even smaller man in a suit who turned out to be the head of the minister's security detail. He looked up at me with no expression on his face, and said, "I hear that you would like to meet the Honorable Minister Louis Farrakhan."

"Yes, sir, I would," I replied, but as I prepared to explain why, the man cut me off and said, "I must pray about this," and walked back to his SUV without turning back.

I remained rooted to the sidewalk. *Do you know how much time I've spent rehearsing my response?* I thought. *And now you're not even going to let me speak? This is a disaster.*

I finally walked back into the precinct and kicked the door hard to open it. Just before I entered the building, I looked up at the sky and muttered, "God if this is Your will, it will be done." I was too embarrassed to tell my sergeant what had happened, so I lied to him when he asked how my meeting had gone. "They didn't show up," I said.

Around midnight, I was out cold in my bed when my work phone rang. The man with the tie said, "I am pleased to tell you that your meeting with the minister has been granted."

Say what? I almost asked him. *Are you sure you have the right person?* But I didn't want to jinx myself, so instead I just thanked him. He gave me a Brooklyn address, where I was to meet him at five thirty the next morning. I asked him how I should dress, and he told me to wear a black suit.

As he was saying goodbye, I interrupted: "Wait, wait, wait—I don't even know your name. But I noticed you were wearing a nice bow tie today. May I call you Bow Tie?"

He was quiet for a moment, and I thought he might retract his invitation. But then he said, "Yes. I like that."

"Well, then thank you again, Bow Tie."

After I hung up, I ran upstairs to my closet, where my church suits were hanging. All I had was a black pantsuit. The vain part of me wished I had time to get my hair and nails done, but I reminded myself that the only important thing was seeing the minister.

The next morning, I did my best to make myself look presentable. I smoothed down my hair and put a headband on, shaking my head as I looked in the mirror. I showed up a few minutes early at the Fulton Street residence Bow Tie had directed me to. When I called and let him know I was outside, he told me to park my car and said he would be right out. He led me to the corner, where a black SUV was idling. The whole ride, I didn't say a word, but my mind was racing. *My hair is sticking out like a cat's whiskers. I can't believe I'm going to meet the minister looking like this.* For the first time in a long while, I felt powerless. There I was, locked in a car with a group of men I had never met before, and if something had happened to me, no one would even have known. As a detective, I was used to calling the shots and always carrying a weapon, but I wasn't allowed to bring my firearm into this unfamiliar situation. I wanted to meet the minister so badly, however, that I decided I just had to trust in God and the process.

Another man with a suit on was in the passenger seat. He and Bow Tie greeted each other by saying, "*As-Salaam-Alaikum.*" I had heard those words before, but I wasn't sure what they meant, so I made a mental note to ask Bow Tie later.

We drove to a Marriott hotel in New Jersey where Minister Farrakhan was staying. Once we arrived, Bow Tie told me he needed to wait for clearance to escort me to the minister's suite. When he asked me if I wanted breakfast, I knew I wouldn't be able to eat a thing; my stomach was too queasy. Instead, I requested a cup of hot tea.

Bow Tie and I sat down, and he formally introduced himself. But when I asked if I could keep calling him Bow Tie, he agreed.

I also asked him what *As-Salaam-Alaikum* meant.

"It means, 'Peace be unto you,'" he said, adding, "And the proper response is *Wa-Alaikum-Salaam*."

We chatted a little more, and Bow Tie shared that he split his time between Brooklyn and the South, and had once been an A&R rep for Motown Records.

Impressive, I thought, but I didn't disclose any personal information of my own—I was still in detective mode.

After we talked, Bow Tie walked me to the lobby and then went up to the minister's suite alone, while I sat for several hours, hungry and thirsty and wondering if anyone was ever going to come get me. Eventually, I needed to stretch my legs, so I decided to go to the hotel gift shop to buy a T-shirt that the minister might sign. I didn't think anyone would ever believe that I'd met with him unless I had physical proof.

Before I could make my purchase, Bow Tie called. "You better get on the elevator immediately," he said.

I put the T-shirt down and took off running. A few men from the Nation of Islam, who looked to be about my age, were waiting for the elevator. When the doors opened, they gestured for me to get on first. "*As-Salaam-Alaikum*, Queen. How are you today?" one of them asked me.

I don't even have hair on my arms, but I felt it standing up when I heard them call me Queen. I felt like their words were sending me straight to heaven. I managed to reply with some version of *Wa-Alaikum-Salaam*, although I'm sure I butchered it.

While we rode the elevator, I admired them covertly. I had never been in the company of men who were so courteous or well kept. Each one was more handsome than the last. They all had short, nicely groomed hair and wore tailored suits and bow ties. The aromas of the different colognes they wore mingled elegantly in the elevator car.

Bow Tie was waiting for me as we got off the elevator. He asked if I had my weapon with me. When I confirmed that I did not, he walked me into the minister's suite. There were several men inside, and at first I didn't see Minister Farrakhan. But when I turned the corner, there he was, sitting on a couch. He was even more handsome than the men in the elevator had been; although he was nearing his midseventies, he could easily have passed for twenty years younger.

But it wasn't just his looks that mesmerized me; it was his entire aura. I couldn't say a single word. The moment we made eye contact, he peered at me so intently that I found myself sliding down the wall behind me and, without warning, beginning to sob.

Minister Farrakhan got up from the couch and walked right over to me. "Daughter, it's okay," he said. He physically lifted me up off the floor and gathered me in his arms while I cried uncontrollably. His embrace was something I had been needing my entire life—a hug from the father I had never known. It seemed as if he could feel my soul.

When I was finally steady enough to stand on my own two feet again, the minister tapped even further into my energy, telling me my daughters would be okay. *How does he even know I have daughters?* I wondered. But that was just the kind of person he was.

He then said a prayer, asking for God's protection, guidance, spiritual wisdom, and understanding on my behalf, and told me to take care. I was still crying while Bow Tie escorted me out of the suite, into the elevator, and outside.

The same black SUV and driver were waiting to take me back to my car. Bow Tie accompanied me, though we didn't talk, except when he mentioned that the men in Minister Farrakhan's suite thought something was wrong with me because of the way I had reacted to our meeting. *Great—all these people think I'm a straight nut*, I thought. Even the SUV driver seemed like he was trying to drop me off as quickly as possible; it felt like he was doing 120 in a 40 zone on the way back to Brooklyn. But nothing could stop my tears. I cried that whole car ride, and when I got into my car, I cried driving home. I cried in the shower that evening. Then I cried myself to sleep. The only time I didn't cry was when Bow Tie called to check on me and told me that Minister Farrakhan had declared me a "true woman of God."

The next morning, I felt like I always did after a good therapy session with Dr. D—full of light. Anytime we feel extra heavy and we have an opening to cry it out and be vulnerable, we feel the effects of that healing. I carried that light with me all day. I even hand-delivered a long note to Bow Tie, thanking him for the life-changing experience. Over the years, he became my mentor and one of my very best friends.

As my fortieth birthday neared, I thought about what it would mean. One of my aunts had told me that when a woman turns forty, it means she's fully grown and should have her life figured out. I believed she was right. I had already been making big changes, but now I felt like I was ready to set real boundaries—no more crap, no more fake friends, no more fake relationships.

I had been saving up all year so that I could throw myself the bash of a lifetime. For my birthday, I usually hosted a big barbecue in my front yard and invited nearly five hundred people. In the end, though, I decided to have a smaller celebration than usual, with one hundred guests, only my most meaningful family members and friends. I chose a location on Atlantic Avenue in Brooklyn with a beautiful outdoor deck.

When my Hummer limo pulled up in front of the restaurant, I made my grand entrance wearing a custom-made gray romper and black thigh-high boots. With my long ponytail weave and impeccably made-up face, I rolled into forty feeling fabulous.

Everyone partied until dawn, though I had a flight to catch the next day. The best birthday gift I received that year was from the Honorable Minister Louis Farrakhan himself, who had extended an invitation to me to visit his castle in Chicago. Bow Tie called me the day before my party and said the minister had been concerned about me after I collapsed in his hotel room. "When I told him you were about to turn forty, he asked me to invite you to his home for an intimate dinner."

Well, I almost collapsed all over again when I heard that, but I wasn't about to ruin this opportunity. It felt like the culmination of years of learning, and now that I knew about class and quality from Sun, I wanted to be with others who shared those values.

Upon my arrival in Chicago, I was driven from the airport to the minister's castle on the outskirts of the city. There were twelve guests in attendance, including some of the minister's family, friends, and colleagues, along with Bow Tie and me. Throughout our four-course meal of soup, salad, chicken and rice, and dessert, served in the formal dining room on the finest china I had ever seen, Minister Farrakhan sat at the head of the table, captivating all of us while he shared his seemingly infinite knowledge and wisdom. He spoke not about racism or discrimination but about people. He told us that our minds control what we do with our lives, and how we have to be honorable people, people with integrity and morals, how we must never allow our emotions to dictate decisions that will be forever detrimental to us; and how we must always love, be kind to, and forgive everyone, no matter what they've done.

I stayed for several hours. The dinner was over, and the minister was still dropping knowledge, but I had to catch my flight back to New York. He must have noticed me push my chair back slightly, because he asked, "Are you going somewhere, daughter?"

"I'm sorry," I said, "but I have to fly back to New York tonight."

"Oh, that's a shame," he replied. "I was hoping you could stay longer."

God, I wish I could, I thought.

That dinner crystallized for me some of what I had been working toward already. I realized that I had made decisions based on emotions for my entire life, because I had never been taught otherwise, and that now I could do things differently. I could make the right choice or the wrong choice when I found myself at a crossroads. Just as I had with Sun, I was able to take the wisdom Minister Farrakhan shared, bottle it up into a personal concoction just for me, and drink from it when I needed to.

The media has a way of portraying certain people in our culture as racist and evil. Minister Farrakhan is no stranger to such criticism. But during my encounters with him, not one of the negative things I had ever heard about him proved to be true. My experience with him showed me that Minister Farrakhan loves his people and wants to educate not only us but the entire world about who Black people truly are. Knowledge is power, and I will be forever grateful for having spent time in his company.

CHAPTER 26

On to the Next

While I was working at Brooklyn South Vice, I got the call I had been waiting for: My transfer to Community Affairs Youth Services had been approved. My eight and a half years in the Organized Crime Control Bureau were finally up, and even though my Brooklyn South team had come to feel like family, I knew I had to move on.

On my first day in Community Affairs, I was assigned to 1 Police Plaza but reported to the Youth Services office in downtown Brooklyn. I was excited. I believed I would now finally be able to do the kind of work I could be truly proud of. Unfortunately, my excitement didn't last long. I quickly realized that my Caucasian LT wasn't the least bit interested in helping our poverty-stricken community. Every time I approached him with a proposition, he simply said, "We're not going to do that."

I prayed for the LT to embrace my interest and get on board with focusing on the Brownsville/East Brooklyn community. It had a terrible reputation—poverty, murders, teenage pregnancy, food scarcity, drugs, and nearly unlivable housing developments were all rampant there—but it was for these very reasons that I knew I could do a lot of good there. After all, I had firsthand experience in the neighborhood, having lived in Brownsville after leaving the homeless shelter with my daughters.

I decided to go to Brownsville on my own to meet with local community leaders. As a police officer, I expected some resistance to my presence, but they all seemed excited to meet with me. As they spoke to me about their concerns, I realized how many people cared deeply about the area.

Several of them told me that I should meet with a man named Mr. Brooklyn, who was in charge of the Brownsville Recreational Center (BRC) and essentially the neighborhood mayor. "Everything in Brownsville goes through him," I was told. "You want to do anything here, you've got to get permission from Mr. Brooklyn."

When I met with him and his beautiful wife, I explained my hopes for the community. I told them I wanted to build a bridge between the community and law enforcement to improve relations.

After listening intently, Mr. Brooklyn agreed to help me facilitate my goals. However, he also gave me a warning. He looked me right in the eye and said, "This is *my* place. I'll help you, but you ain't comin' here and playin' no games. If you do, I will run you out of here."

I felt my eyes turning into saucers while he stared me down. As a detective, I wasn't used to having anyone speak to me so sternly, without any fear or deference, but I took him seriously. "Sir," I said, "I have no bad intentions; I just want to help. But I understand your concerns and I won't let you down."

I turned around to leave and walked out mechanically, like a robot he had just programmed to do his bidding. I could feel his eyes on my back until I was gone.

I got right to work. The very first thing I wanted to do was schedule a barbecue and resource fair so that I could introduce myself to the Brownsville community. Mr. Brooklyn agreed to help me and said he would allow me to use the BRC space for the event. We accomplished more planning in one week than I ever could have imagined—until something even less conceivable happened. Only seven days after our first meeting, Mr. Brooklyn had a massive heart attack while working and passed away. He was only in his early sixties.

Although I hadn't had enough time to get to know Mr. Brooklyn well, I decided to attend his funeral. Every person who got up and spoke on his behalf had only wonderful things to say. After hearing all of their stories, I felt as if Mr. Brooklyn had been my personal friend too. In honor of who he was to Brownsville, I was more determined than ever to make a difference for his people.

The resource fair moved forward with Mr. Brooklyn's assistant director and replacement's permission. Mr. Brooklyn's wife, Ms. Brooklyn; some of their children; Mr. Tanis, from Shoppers World, who became a major sponsor and still is to this day; and BRC staff all worked diligently with me over the next month to organize and promote the event. We hired a popular deejay, DJ Lance, to create a festive vibe, we planned a carnival with all the bells and whistles, and we invited various resource agencies to participate. Emblem Health, the YMCA, the Parks Department, the Brooklyn Public Library, the Borough President Community Council Office, and many other organizations were all happy to contribute. The NYPD, not so much. I had asked for two specific units, Mounted and Aviation, to join us, but my lieutenant canceled the request behind my back.

Still, the event was a success by any measure, and more than three hundred people attended. But after it was over, my LT asked me, "Why did you give the community our stuff?"

"What is that supposed to mean, *our stuff*?" I asked. Yet I knew what he was referring to. Community Affairs had a sizable budget for event giveaways, and I had used some of that money to benefit the guests at my event.

But my LT had other ideas: "All those resources should be for cops and their families."

"With all due respect, sir, I disagree," I said. "This event is a way for us to introduce ourselves to the community so that people feel comfortable and safe with the police. I can't just go into a neighborhood where people don't know me and tell them, 'I want you to have a better education,' or, 'I want you to have better housing.' No one's going to listen to me. So I wanted to be able to show these people some sort of kindness and give myself some credibility. Plus, cops can take their kids anywhere they want; most of these Brownsville kids don't have that luxury."

The LT responded, "Well, that's not my fault."

Since the resource fair had already happened, the LT couldn't do anything about it, but he was quick to assure me that no more events of that nature would ever happen again while he was on the job. I vowed to keep servicing these areas anyway. I was doing God's work, on a mission to make a difference in people's lives, and neither this man nor anyone else in the police department was going to stop me. And I knew I had new allies because of the commitment I had already demonstrated to Brownsville, including Ms. Brooklyn herself, who became my close friend. For years after that, she attended every event I hosted in her community, because she knew I was upholding my promise to honor her husband's legacy.

In 2003, I had founded a charitable organization, the Katrina Cooke Brownlee Charity, to donate winter coats and boots to children in need. I had gotten the idea from the coat drive the NYPD hosted at each precinct every December. I noticed the sorry condition of the coats people were bringing in, and I thought, *No, these people need new coats, not this dirty, raggedy stuff.* Having been homeless and ashamed, I knew the extra effort would help the beneficiaries hold their heads a little higher during the holiday season.

Now, I wanted to extend that charity work to help the citizens of Brownsville. I saved money from my salary all year to buy enough brand-new coats and boots for anyone who showed up, as well as to give them a nourishing catered meal.

Despite my best efforts to do good, my LT seemed bent on trying to sabotage me. His next scheme was to give me an assignment as a counselor at the NYPD's youth summer camp in Queens. Although he framed it as an altruistic undertaking, I knew it was actually an attempt to prevent me from being hands-on in Brooklyn. It was obvious that he didn't want me out there in the streets, doing the real work of helping people. But what I have learned repeatedly is that what people do for evil, God can turn into good. And that's exactly what He did.

When the camp started, I noticed that it was filled with mostly cops' kids. It was a well-kept secret that, ironically, the people in charge didn't actually want the kids who lived in the community to attend the camp because, as they told me, they didn't want it to become "ghetto." I saw myself in every one of the underprivileged children who were being kept out of the program. I had never had access to certain important life lessons when I was a child, and neither had they. No one at the camp seemed to care that high schoolers were reading at a second-grade level or that generations of families who had never been gainfully employed were living in housing developments on welfare. Some of these kids had never even been out of their own neighborhoods. I just knew that if only somebody would give them an opportunity, they would take off like I had. I said to myself, *If I can help even one or two people this way, I'm going to do it.*

Keeping in line with my mission, I began approving applications for the kids who had been kept out and rejecting applications for the children of cops. Soon enough, I started getting all kinds of phone calls from livid chiefs and inspectors wondering, *Who's this Brownlee person?* But I didn't care if my maneuvering was upsetting them. Besides, I was protected from all the naysayers by my friend Chief Davis. When I talked to him about what I was doing, he said, "Do whatever you want to do, and if anyone questions you, tell them to come talk to me about it."

After I had gotten the kids I thought would benefit most into the camp, my next goal was to implement a curriculum, instead of just letting them play outside all day. I had them do gym in the morning, classroom work in the afternoon, then lunch, followed by free play at the end of each day. Even though the LT had sent me there to punish me and derail my mission, I was still making a positive impact—so much so that I decided that I wanted to continue as a counselor every year. The program went so well that the following summer, my LT transferred me from the Queens camp to one at my former high school, Boys and Girls High School, in Bed-Stuy. I think he finally saw how determined I was to make a change, but the location also suited me perfectly because I could now walk to work and save money on gas and lunch. One beautiful summer morning on my way to the camp, I realized, *Every time this man does something to try to hurt me, it ends up working out in my favor instead.*

It was through this work that I first had the idea to start a program mentoring young girls. I never wanted another girl to endure what I had been through, and I knew I could help. I talked over my idea with the chief and my LT during separate meetings, and they both agreed to back me.

I wanted the program to focus on girls in middle school and high school. I chose two schools that seemed to need my attention most. The middle school I targeted was PS 298 in Brownsville, where a mother of twelve had recently been hit by a stray bullet while she was picking up her kids. And the high school I picked was Bedford Academy in Bed-Stuy. The principal, who was a friend of mine, cared deeply for his students, but since the school had no physical education facilities, the gym teacher brought the kids every day to the YMCA next door, where I worked out. The principal frequently stopped in to check on them. When I saw how dedicated he was to these young people, I knew I wanted to get involved.

I called my organization Young Ladies of Our Future.

The logo for my organization.

Each mentoring cycle lasted for four months. I met with the middle schoolers on Tuesdays and the high schoolers on Thursdays, for two hours apiece. The curriculum explored all the concepts I had never been taught about when I was these girls' age: self-esteem building, confidence, self-love, hygiene, nutrition, spirituality, romantic relationships, and etiquette. I taught many of them myself and brought in specialists as needed. During the holidays, the girls participated in community service events, helping my Community Affairs team deliver gifts to families who were struggling. I even paid out of my own pocket for one family to furnish their entire apartment. I wanted the girls I was mentoring to understand the importance of giving and to learn by my example.

Once the girls completed the program, I arranged a graduation ceremony for them to celebrate their accomplishments. We started with a praise dance to set a tone of appreciation before I called each graduate up to the front of the room. Once she was at the podium, I would shower her with accolades and give her a rose. Even though they were able to invite as many guests as they wanted, most of the girls didn't have anyone show up for them. I hoped that the love their peers and I gave them made up for those absent audience members. I wanted each girl to walk away knowing she had worth and that someone cared about her.

By the end of every graduation, all of us would be crying, including me. While I knew I wouldn't stay in contact with most of the girls as they forged their own futures, I hoped that they would hold on to at least some of the lessons they had learned from my mentorship. If they walked away from the program with even one lifelong lesson, I felt like my job was done. The program didn't just heal the young ladies I mentored; it helped heal me too.

Proudly wearing my organization's T-shirt.

* * *

In July 2013, I received a phone call that I had never expected. Chief Davis contacted me one evening when I was driving home from work and said, "I wanted to be the first to congratulate you."

"On what?"

"You're getting promoted to second-grade detective in two days."

I had to grip my steering wheel tightly to avoid swerving. "What? No, I'm not," I said.

"Yes, you are."

"Are you serious?" I asked, but it was beginning to dawn on me that this man was the boss, so he probably knew what he was talking about.

"You know I am."

In my disbelief, I had to pause for a moment to absorb his words, and then I said, "I can't thank you enough for this, Chief."

"You deserve it for a job well done. I love you."

"I love you too."

"The ceremony's in two days," he added. "Make sure your hat and uniform are up to par when you walk across that stage. I'll be watching."

I laughed so hard that I almost ran myself off the road.

After he hung up, I thought, *Well, I have to add this to my prayers—Chief Davis just promoted me.* Being made third-grade detective had been shocking enough; I never thought I would make it to a higher rank or a higher pay grade than that, nor had I ever fought for a promotion the way many other officers did—but here I was.

After the ceremony, all the detectives who were being promoted had an opportunity to go to the chief's office to take pictures, but I wasn't interested in that—I just wanted to take my family up there for a quick visit and introduce my relatives who hadn't already met him, to thank him for once again being so supportive of my career and to congratulate him on his recent promotion to chief of the department. I couldn't stay long, though, because I wanted to have dinner with my friends and family, and the next morning I had to travel to the South. My daughter Morgan was getting married in a week, and I had promised her I would go in advance to help her prepare.

On my short flight, I reflected on how chaotic my life felt, but how for the first time it was a good kind of chaos. I was finally happy, and so were my kids. I had prayed countless times that my girls' lives would be better and easier than my own, and I believed that was happening. To see my healthy, twenty-seven-year-old daughter walk down the aisle to marry the man she loved would be the fulfillment of one of my lifelong dreams. She had met her fiancé when she was in college and he had just gotten out of the military, and they had been together ever since.

We planned to have the wedding poolside at a beautiful venue, but Mother Nature decided not to cooperate. Clouds moved in and opened up, unleashing a storm that quickly forced the coordinator to move the ceremony inside the Marriott. One hundred people were invited, but somehow even more than that showed up. I even had to give up my plate of food for an unexpected guest.

None of that mattered—Morgan radiated love and joy as she walked down the aisle. I recalled the day a few months earlier when I had visited her to watch her try on wedding gowns. I had sipped leisurely from a flute of champagne as I sat in the bridal shop and she came out of the dressing room again and again, each dress more beautiful than the last. Although she'd looked stunning in every one and had a hard time making her decision, the one she picked was especially gorgeous. And since the cost of the wedding was my responsibility, I drank until my heart was content that day, hoping to forget all about the bill that was ultimately coming. Now, as I sat in the front row of her ceremony, I was certain that every dollar had been worth it.

But I also had to get back to New York to attend to other family matters. My aunt Dorothy, whom I visited several times a year at her house in Florida, was dying of a burst appendix. My cousin recommended that I go to the hospital as soon as possible if I wanted to see her, but by the time I arrived, Aunt Dorothy had already passed away. She was only sixty years old.

While I was in Macy's, buying a dress for Aunt Dorothy's funeral, I received a phone call from Shanice, who told me that Robert's grandmother Gaga had also recently died. Gaga and I had remained close even after Robert and I divorced. We talked on the phone at least once a week, and even though I always worked on Thanksgiving, she would set aside a plate of food for me so I could come eat after my tour.

Some people believe bad things happen in threes. Sure enough, I found out that my aunt Crystal—the one who had brought me home from the hospital with Mommy when I was born; the one who had given me the beautiful name Katrina, after her own daughter; the one I had eaten crab dinners with nearly every Monday since Sun broke up with me; and one of the few close family members I had left—was fighting pancreatic cancer and losing her battle. When she died two weeks later, I cried so much at her funeral that I had to be escorted out of the service, just as I had when Mommy died. These losses were just several more in what felt like an endless parade. Death seemed to surround me like a haze I couldn't swat away or see through.

The only redemption after all these tragedies came from Robert, of all people. He was allowed to attend Gaga's funeral, even though he was still in prison. Two guards brought him in wearing a green jumpsuit, handcuffs, and shackles, just as they had when he'd attended his mother's service. Under the watchful eye of the officers, we spoke briefly. We had communicated once in a while since our divorce, but I hadn't seen him in person in years. He was even finer than he had been when we were together—his muscles were so taut that no one could have pinched an inch of skin on any part of his body. He was now married to a woman he'd started messing with while we were still legally married, but that didn't bother me. I just wanted him to be happy—and he was when, only two months later, he was released from prison. He had finished his twenty-year sentence, and the parole board had accepted his request for release.

I saw him after he got out. He came over to my house, and we had a long talk. He was humble and kind and apologized to me for abusing me in his prison trailer. He also thanked me for ministering to him about God. He hadn't been religious when we got together, but now he understood the power of God's will and the power of prayer. Robert is a living example that people can change for the better. Just as his mother, Jamie, got herself off drugs and turned her life around, he did the same. In fact, he did exactly what the judge who had resentenced him years earlier had predicted: he was released when he was still young, and he made something of himself. He became a man of integrity, a hardworking man employed by the City of New York, and a man who loved God. Who would ever have thought he would end up free and so happy?

CHAPTER 27

The Call

Once I was in a financial position to travel on my own, beach vacations became my happy place. I had five weeks of paid time off per year, and I always went to five different places for one week apiece, and always by myself. Like many people, I used to be unable to imagine being alone because I believed I had to be in a relationship with someone all the time. Now I know that learning to live in our own space is essential for our well-being.

In December 2013, I was on a trip to Jamaica when I received another life-changing call. I had spent several hours at the pool under the hot sun and then returned to my room for a nap before dinner. From the depths of my slumber, I heard my phone ringing. When I answered, it was Chief Davis. "What would you think about being on the mayor's detail?" he asked, as if we had discussed it many times.

Since I was still half asleep, I actually thought I was dreaming. Trying to focus my vision and propping myself up on one elbow, I cleared my throat. "Can you say that again?"

Although the chief repeated his question, I was still foggy. "What mayor?" I asked.

"The one who will be in office in a couple of weeks."

I wasn't particularly into politics, but I certainly knew that

New York had a newly elected mayor, Bill de Blasio. I had voted for him myself. However, the only details I could remember about him were that he was a white man married to a Black woman, that he was a Democrat, and that their daughter and son had been in a lot of his campaign commercials.

"Wait one minute," I said to Chief Davis. "Are you asking me to be a part of the new mayoral detail for Bill de Blasio?" While I spoke, I climbed out of my hotel bed to be 100 percent sure I was awake. As my bare feet hit the room's cool tile floor, I knew I needed to get my head into this conversation.

Despite all the promotions I had received, and despite all my career ambition, it had never occurred to me that the most coveted position in the entire NYPD could be held by a Black woman. I had simply never seen any evidence of it in my twelve years as an officer. But Chief Davis had never led me astray in my career. He had the vision for me that I couldn't have for myself. Ever since I had become an undercover, he had steadfastly believed that I could achieve a higher rank within the NYPD than I ever could have imagined. He just kept putting challenges in front of me, because he knew I could rise to the occasion.

"You would be one of very few Black women to have this job, but I assure you it can happen if you are interested," he told me.

When I asked what I needed to do on my end in order to make it happen, he replied, "Nothing."

Of course I was interested, now that I knew the role was a real possibility for me, but I hesitated when the chief gave me three options to choose from: "You can be on the mayor's detail, his wife's detail, or their children's detail."

"I'll take the kids," I said.

"Nah, you can do more than that. I think you should start with the wife."

In my experience, women could be catty, and I didn't want

my job ever to be in jeopardy in the event that Chirlane McCray had a negative opinion of me.

The chief must have sensed my concern, because he added, "I believe in you. You'll be fine. She's going to love you. Who doesn't?"

And that was that. We said goodbye and agreed to talk again soon.

After I got off the phone with him, I climbed back into bed and stared up at the ceiling, thinking, *Yo, this can't be real. But it's happening anyway.* I smiled as I pictured my new work style: *I'm going to wear designer suits. I'm going to have an earpiece. I'm going to do my hair like this or that. I need to make sure I look fly at all times. I'm going to be looking like a secret service agent every day.* Even though I was happy in Community Affairs, this new opportunity to move from the "friendly suit" to the "secret service suit" was irresistible. With most of the other NYPD positions I had held, I had gotten there by making conscious decisions. I had calculated a lot of steps along my path because I had to. But this was a gift straight from God, rewarding me for all my hard work over more than a decade. I just felt like it was my time.

For the rest of my vacation, I got up early every morning and went straight to the beach, where I prayed and meditated while I gazed out at the ocean. I hung out in a private seaside cabana during the day, enjoying cocktails and resting, then dressed up and treated myself to a nice dinner and live entertainment at the resort every evening. As peaceful as I felt, most of my mind was already back in New York, where my whole life was about to change.

Chief Davis and I stayed in contact over those few days, but he didn't give me much more detail about the job. It wasn't until I returned home and spoke with a female captain that I learned I would have to undergo a week of intel training. She also told me I would have to wear conservative suits and flat shoes. Imagine how unexcited I was about ditching my signature heels and head-to-toe labels. When I explained to her that I would need to purchase the proper clothing, she moved my start date to two weeks later so that I could adequately prepare for the job.

When I hung up with her, I buried my face in my hands and began to weep. My tears were equal parts joy and sadness. I was about to begin the most high-profile phase of my entire career, but I had lost so many people I loved, I wasn't sure whom to talk to about my victory. How I wished Mommy were there to celebrate with me. How I wished that every one of my deceased loved ones could have witnessed in person this next chapter of my incredible life. The only thing that finally got me to stop crying was knowing they were all smiling down proudly on me.

CHAPTER 28

Another New Beginning

When I started on the mayor's detail in January 2014, I was ready to put 2013 behind me. Although it had been a year of many highs and lows and I had lost several important people in my life, I also made sure to thank God for the peace and happiness He had brought me in other areas. My daughters were doing well. I was a second-grade detective and about to start working closely with the wife of the newly elected mayor of New York City. As I moved forward into this new stage, I did my best to focus more on my blessings than on my grief.

My first order of business on the detail was the week of intel training that I had to complete. The class consisted of nearly everyone who would be on de Blasio's detail and others who were going to be working for different politicians. I was pleased to discover that my fellow students were surprisingly diverse; although the majority of them were of course white males, there were also a few other Black people, some Latino people, and some women.

De Blasio's detail was huge because he had a wife and children who needed to be protected. A uniformed segment of the detail typically watches over Gracie Mansion and city hall, and then other members of the detail are considered bodyguards. The bodyguards are always in suits and always rolling with the mayor or one of his family members. That would be my job.

Days before I was to meet Chirlane McCray, I couldn't stop wondering what the First Lady of New York City would be like. I prayed that we would get along well. I kept reminding myself what Chief Davis had said when he first called me about the position: "She's going to love you."

Naturally, I had to google her so I could figure out what I was getting myself into. I knew Chirlane was from Boston and had once identified as a lesbian. She had met her husband while they were both working for David Dinkins, who was the mayor of New York City from 1990 to 1993 and the first African American to hold that office. Chirlane had been a speechwriter for Dinkins, while Bill held the position of a "body man," which is the person responsible for making sure the mayor has everything he needs.

I thought, *Okay, I got this*. The fact that she was also a Black woman and held one of the highest roles in New York City made a deep bond between us seem inevitable.

That optimism sustained me until my first day of official detail. At six a.m. sharp, I entered the mayoral home, Gracie Mansion. I was expecting opulence befitting the head of the largest US city; what I found was neglect. The yellow-painted exterior of the Federal-style building was faded and showed hairline cracks, and the interior featured a hodgepodge of rugs and furniture that I thought could have used some updating. Although de Blasio's predecessor, Michael Bloomberg, had renovated a few of the rooms while he was in office, it still left much to be desired. Worse, no overnight quarters existed for the female guards. Although I knew women had not historically had this job, I thought there was no better time than the present to dismantle this sexist arrangement. But no—on the two consecutive seventeen-hour days per week when I was working for the mayor, I had no place to rest. The men would work their seventeen hours, then go to sleep in the mansion, then wake up and do their next shift. I had to finish my shift, drive an hour home to Brooklyn, sleep for four or five hours, then turn right back around and be in upper Manhattan by six o'clock the next morning. Not until years later did a female captain call out the unequal treatment of male and female guards at Gracie and succeed in making the security room available to both genders. In the meantime, I just sacrificed because I didn't want to make waves so early on in my new role. My saving grace was that I had three to four days off the rest of the week, and I took advantage of that downtime to get out of town and rest at least two long weekends each month. Having that respite to look forward to made the tedious parts of the job—including my new partner—more bearable.

I met Carlton, a middle-aged white man, on my first day at Gracie. He was the designated driver of a black Suburban with dark-tinted windows, which would serve as our office on wheels. I realized quickly that if I was going to have to work with him twice a week for seventeen hours at a stretch, God would definitely need to help me. Carlton never stopped talking, and I often wondered how he had gotten the job on the detail. All he did was complain to me about his toxic home life. He told me how his kids were always taking his money and buying stuff they didn't need, and how his wife yelled at him all the time, and how he never got any rest. *No wonder this man always shows up to work two hours early*, I thought.

Our dynamic almost immediately developed into that of therapist and client; it was as if he was addicted to sharing dysfunctional details with me. Not wanting to rock the boat or complain so early on, I had to learn how to tune him out. I kept thinking, *It's crazy how the NYPD will just stick you in a car with someone you don't know anything about.* He did try to ask about my business early on, but I let him know, "Don't ask me those questions. We ain't cool like that."

Our first assignment was to pick up the First Lady from the airport. The night before, I studied pictures of her online to make sure I would be able to recognize her. In the car on the way to the airport, I mentally rehearsed how I would introduce myself. I wondered if I should hug her, offer a handshake, or just say hello.

Carlton and I pulled up to the terminal two hours early. Our airport liaison signed us in so I could go to the gate. When we finally got word that she had landed, I was a little shaky. Although it had been only a few weeks since I had begun my job, the anticipation had built up to feel much longer than that.

I spotted her immediately when she emerged from the Jetway. She looked like she had in the pictures—dark-skinned, only five feet tall, with long, thin dreadlocks and a friendly face. I had been expecting someone with more glamorous attire, but her sensible outfit made her seem more approachable.

I walked up to her with a warm smile and said, "Good morning, ma'am. I'm Detective Katrina Brownlee."

She was toting two bags, so I couldn't shake her hand, but she returned my smile as she said good morning.

I offered to carry her luggage, and we exited the terminal. Once we were inside the Suburban, we chatted for a few minutes, until Chirlane dozed off.

It would be six months before de Blasio's family moved into Gracie Mansion. Meanwhile, they were still living in their family home in Park Slope, Brooklyn. Although their row house was on a tree-lined block dominated by high-end real estate, it sat behind a chain-link fence and was attached on both sides to other properties. The mustard-yellow paint on the brick-and-clapboard structure was dirty, and what I could see of the small yard looked poorly kept. *I guess there's no accounting for taste,*

I thought, as Chirlane thanked us for the ride and headed to her front door.

As soon as she had disappeared inside, Carlton asked what I thought of Chirlane.

"Well, she looks way younger than what Google said her age is, so whatever she's taking, I want some," I said, and we both laughed.

Initially, Chirlane didn't throw up any red flags. In fact, she was consistently kind, soft-spoken, and humble. But I reminded myself and Carlton that she wasn't our friend and that I just wanted to do my best as a member of her security detail. Mostly, that consisted of sitting outside her house in the Suburban for hours at a time, just waiting in case she needed to go somewhere. As she settled more into her role as First Lady, she began accompanying de Blasio to his engagements more frequently, though initially she rarely went out in public—she was either in the house or needed a ride for personal business only.

Chirlane and I were both adjusting in our own ways. After a few months, I felt as if things were falling into place for me. I was alert and curious and paid close attention to everything that was going on around me politically and professionally—and the fact that I was finally single meant I could focus all my energy on my job. Since I had personally voted for the mayor, I wanted to know all about his plans for New York City and to see him execute them. I wouldn't understand until later that I was being scrutinized too.

CHAPTER 29

Loss After Losses

On the early morning of March 9, 2014, my phone rang and woke me from a deep sleep. To my surprise, it was my friend CJ calling.

"My condolences to you," he said.

"What are you talking about?" I asked, rubbing my eyes.

"Quar dropped off yesterday. I heard he had cancer."

I sat straight up in bed. *Quar is dead? That can't be right. If he had cancer, somebody would have told me.* "No, he didn't. Where did you get that from?"

"That's what I heard."

"Let me call you back," I said to CJ, and hung up without even saying goodbye.

I immediately dialed Quar's number. He didn't answer.

I had been seeing Quar only once or twice a year at that point. I periodically stopped by his bodega to check on him, always very early in the morning or very late at night, and just said, "Hey, you good?" I worried that something bad would happen to him because of his lifestyle. But we had been broken up for years, and now that I had a prominent police job, I could not jeopardize my career because of even a loose involvement with a known drug dealer, so I had been keeping my distance.

Quar was always welcoming and often made unnecessary conversation so that I would stick around a little longer, but every time I left one of those encounters with him, I thought, *I'm so glad I'm not in that place anymore. I'm so glad I did something with my life.*

The last time I had seen Quar in person was the previous summer. I stopped by his store to tell him that Morgan was getting married, and he hadn't seemed physically well. He had lost a lot of weight, and his face looked pinched and tense. I had chalked up the changes in his appearance to stress or aging; I certainly didn't think he was sick. I also thought maybe all his running around had finally caught up with him. In fact, I knew he was dating a girl I had caught him cheating with years earlier.

That December, I spoke to him for the last time. Quar called me at work one day and blindsided me by complaining about how ungrateful Morgan and Melissa were, telling me, "I was a father to them all that time, and they can't even call me now." I spoke quietly to him, yet he was hell-bent on attacking me and began telling me I had never really been a good mother.

I said, "Listen, I can't talk about this. I'm at work. But I will call the girls, I will tell them what you said, and I will have them call you," and ended the call as quickly as I could. I didn't realize at the time that he was already sick and not in his right mind.

After CJ called me, I rushed to the bodega in search of answers. Quar's employee Barry was working the register when I came running in, out of breath, and said, "What's going on?"

Barry shook his head. "Trina, the dread been sick for a few months. You didn't know that?"

"No, I definitely did *not* know that," I said. "Why didn't anyone call me?"

He suggested that I ring Quar's daughter Erica if I wanted more information.

When I spoke with Erica, she told me that Quar had had brain cancer and had been bedridden since January. His cancer was so aggressive that it killed him in only two months.

I'd had more than enough struggles with Quar over the years, but if someone had told me he had a terminal illness, I would never have hesitated to take care of him. I had spent so much of my youth with him, and we had been through so much together, it was the least I could have done. Throughout our lives, certain things happen that outweigh any personal issues we may have going on with someone. And in these situations, we have to rise above. We have to be the better person. We have to be kind to those who are suffering, just as we hope they will be kind to us if our roles are reversed someday.

All this was going through my head when I asked Erica why no one had called to tell me that her father was sick.

"No one had your number," she said.

Well, that's a lie, I thought. Not only had Quar kept in touch with my daughters, but I also knew his eleven biological kids had always resented me because Morgan and Melissa were the only children he had actually raised under his own roof. I wasn't going to let that make me feel guilty, though, because all of his other kids had seen him constantly. They were in his stores every day, and he always took care of them.

I listened as Erica told me how Quar's current girlfriend, Natalie, had mistreated him while he was dying. He wasn't able to walk, and she let him lie in his feces and urine for days. She never even bothered to seek a formal diagnosis for his illness; it wasn't until Erica went over to Quar's house one day and saw how grave her father's condition was that she took him to the hospital. He was dead one week later.

While Erica and I were still on the phone, I told her that we should stay in touch and that I would help with Quar's funeral arrangements. She consented, but before we ended the conversation, she delivered a terrible blow: "You know, Daddy asked for you every day, and his last words were 'I guess Trina isn't coming.'"

As soon as we said goodbye, I collapsed on my floor.

When I told my daughters about Quar's passing, they immediately came to be with me. Within days, the funeral arrangements were made. Since Quar didn't have any insurance, his oldest daughter paid ten thousand dollars in cash for the service and I paid for the repast at a catering hall. We decided to have a private, family-only service, followed by a public service at a funeral parlor in Flatbush. We laid him to rest wearing new, earth-tone clothes from his closet—a vest, a shirt, and some khaki pants, clothes I knew he would like. I wore all white, and my daughters wore Quar's favorite earth colors. For the private service, I let his dreads out of his hat; they reached all the way to the floor. When guests started coming in for the public service, I rewrapped his hair.

I knew Quar wouldn't have wanted a big crowd at his funeral, so I had tried to keep it as quiet as possible, but at least six hundred people showed up to pay their respects. He was essentially the mayor of Flatbush, after all.

The event was mostly smooth, with two hitches. Quar's oldest daughter, who wrote his obituary, disrespected my daughters and me by trying to make it seem as if Quar and her mother—his ex-wife, who had given birth to five of his kids—were still a couple when he died. She also did not print Morgan's and Melissa's names in the obituary, yet she included all of his other eleven children. Fortunately, Melissa made her presence known by reading a beautiful poem that she had written, which had the whole funeral parlor in tears.

Natalie was noticeably absent from the service—apparently, she had told Erica she didn't want to risk an altercation with me—but a few of Quar's exes flocked to the scene, some of whom I had physically fought in the past. *Damn*, I thought, *you can't even let me grieve for the last time without staying in the background?* On the other hand, one of his longtime side chicks—the neighbor whose building I had caught Quar walking out of one early morning—cautiously approached me and told me that I had always been Quar's number one lady. And at the repast, many people told me that no matter what Quar had done in the streets, he had never stopped loving me and my daughters.

Morgan and Melissa went to Quar's burial, but even the thought of watching his body lowered into that grave was too much for me to bear. To distract myself, I decided to go to work instead. I did pay for Quar's headstone, though. Despite everything he had done for our community over the decades, no one else even offered to contribute a cent, and it felt like the right thing to do for him.

After Quar passed away, depression came calling for me again. I didn't want to eat or talk to anyone, and I began to fixate on regret. I wondered obsessively if he would have been able to survive his illness if I hadn't left him. If I had been the one caring for him, maybe he would have beaten cancer, or at least lived longer than he had. The guilt I felt was so consuming that I began to contemplate suicide again. Some days I thought, *I can't catch a break. I'm going to blow my freakin' brains out and be done with all this.* But then I remembered my therapist Dr. D saying to me, "If you ever feel like you want to take your own life, I need you to call me immediately." Instead of picking up my gun, I picked up the phone and made an appointment with her.

It took me a long time to emerge from that dark place, but I managed to do so through therapy, exercise, and prayer. All that took a turn, however, when I walked into work one morning after five months on the First Lady's detail, and the sergeant informed me that the commanding officer had instructed him to remove me from my post. The sergeant also told me that I would need to get a job car because I was no longer permitted to ride with the First Lady.

I called the commanding officer the next day, looking for an explanation. All the CO said was "She doesn't like you. It is what it is. If you don't like it, you can leave."

"Leave and go where?" I asked.

He shrugged. "Pick a command."

Why can't anybody here tell me what's actually happening? I fumed as I walked to my car. *If I did something wrong, I need someone to tell me so that at least I have a chance to correct it.*

Yo, really? This is how you treat a sister? The fact that this high-level public figure, who appeared to be a strong Black woman and who was ideally positioned to use her power for good, didn't actually live in a way that aligned her with the people she claimed to advocate for, was inconceivable to me. In 2015 she would go on to start an $850 million program called ThriveNYC, designed to support Black communities in the area of mental health and wellness, but it was quickly criticized for its financial ambiguity and lack of clear goals. Chirlane was a fraud to her core. She was supposed to be making a positive impact on the psychological stability of Black people in New York, but by 2023 mental health issues were at an all-time high in the city. While on her detail, I had come to realize, through observing her at work and hearing comments from my colleagues on the detail, that the only people she'd wanted around her were those who would respond with a smile and never offer her an opinion. And, ironically, Black people in her camp—not just on her detail but her assistants and her staff—especially Black women, had seemed to disappear quickly. She should have had those dreads cut right off her head for the way she behaved. I was angry for months at myself and at the other New Yorkers who put Bill and Chirlane in office, because I felt like the whole city had been tricked.

* * *

After my removal from the First Lady's detail, I was reassigned to the mayoral detail. Typically, officers in this scenario are pushed out of the detail completely, but Mayor de Blasio seemed to have taken enough of a liking to me to green-light my transfer. Although we didn't have a working relationship when I was on his wife's detail, he had always made an effort at small talk with me when he was around, and he had always shown me kindness and respect.

Since the mayor already had a full detail, I was essentially just an extra body. At first, my workdays were long and lonely. All I did was sit by myself in the security room at Gracie Mansion. But I was happy to still be on the detail, so I didn't complain. My schedule also remained the same—two days per week—and I knew that was better than working forty-plus hours on a regular beat.

I noticed that the detail's CO had a specific team of detectives who were assigned to go on all of the trips. These detectives were able to move around freely, experience exciting job perks, do all the important tasks for the detail, and receive overtime pay. The fact that they were all white males didn't seem like a coincidence, nor did the fact that none of them wanted me to travel with them. They treated me like the "help"—as if the only thing I was good for was driving the staff from place to place. Adding insult to injury, the younger, less experienced administrative staff, which consisted mainly of white twenty- and thirtysomethings, had carte blanche to give me orders. I wasn't sure if my lowly status had anything to do with my being Black, female, or both, but it was made clear to me every day, through micro- and macroaggressions, that my years in the academy, on the force, on the street, and as an undercover and decorated detective meant nothing in this environment.

Still, in my heart I knew I was doing better than most NYPD detectives. Plus, I was breaking barriers, making history, and paving the way for others who looked like me. There had never been a Black woman on any New York mayoral detail, not even when the city had had a Black mayor. Despite the toll that the mistreatment I endured took on me personally, I knew this thing was bigger than I was. I just had to be patient.

CHAPTER 30

The Road to Resolution

On October 31, 2014, nearly one year after Mayor de Blasio was elected for his first term, my best friend, Chief Davis, made the difficult decision to retire after the FBI and the Internal Affairs Bureau opened a widespread investigation into police escorts for certain Orthodox Jews in New York in exchange for cash and other gifts. A wealthy Jewish businessman named JR had gotten pinched for a separate crime and, in order to avoid a prison sentence, had flipped and become an informant for the feds. He infiltrated the department, developed false friendships with Chief Davis and numerous other officers, and tried to take them down.

The experience gutted me. The chief had supported me in countless personal and professional ways, and I never doubted his integrity, though apparently others did. When his name was ultimately cleared and he was tapped for an even more prestigious position with the city, I knew God had made things right for him.

By 2016, after I had spent two years on the mayor's detail, things began to change for me and around me. As coveted as my job was, the turnover was high, and most of the people who left did so because they weren't happy with how the detail was run. Promotions were scarce and the politics were questionable, and the commanding officer was notorious for being a poor leader, playing favorites, and carrying out the mayor's every wish without thinking about anyone besides himself and the people he served.

Now, though, I had a plan. I decided I wasn't willing to tolerate being made to feel less than by my white male counterparts anymore. So when my CO told me that he was promoting me to be Mayor de Blasio's advance one—the person who would go ahead of the mayor to any location he was planning to appear at, make sure the site was secure, and escort him throughout his time there—I jumped at the chance.

I should have known that another heartbreak lay right around the corner. On a beautiful day in May 2016, the sun's warmth hit me in all the right places as I drove home from the gym after a vigorous workout, feeling alive and renewed. But when my phone rang, the caller, a close friend of mine, ripped the smile right off my face when he told me that my boy MA, a forty-four-year-old highway inspector, had gone to a park on Long Island early that morning and shot himself in the head with his own service revolver.

I had known MA since 2005. We met when he was my commanding officer in Vice, and we became friends almost instantly. He was a fine-ass white boy who always dressed well and smelled good, and all he wanted was to be a cop and marry a Black or Brown woman. He was constantly trying to get me to hook him up with my friends. "You got anyone for me yet?" he would ask.

But I just spoke with him a few days ago, I thought, as soon as my friend told me the news. I knew that MA was being investigated in the same corruption probe as Chief Davis; as a commander, he would have had to sign off on the unauthorized lights-and-sirens escorts to the Orthodox Jewish community. I also knew that one day before his death, the Internal Affairs Bureau had raided MA's station house and confiscated two years worth of escort logs. However, MA had already heard from the head of the police union that his job was not in jeopardy, and I reiterated that reassurance when I spoke to him, saying, "I don't think this is enough to get you fired." I knew he was nervous, but he didn't sound nervous enough to take his own life.

My vision was too blurred by tears for me to drive safely through the Brooklyn streets. Perfect weather in New York can feel like a cruel gesture in an instant when a tragedy blots out the sun. When I got home, still crying, I questioned my entire career path. I had gone into law enforcement because I wanted to make a difference for others after all the violence and abuse I had suffered. But had I?

Since 2019, the national suicide rate among police officers has hovered between 140 and 200 fatalities per year, and suicides among New York cops top that list. A study published in the January 2021 issue of *Policing: An International Journal* revealed that law enforcement professional are 54 percent more likely to die by suicide than civilians. The job pressures can be insurmountable. Officers are expected to make arrests and endure workplace bullying from other cops all while making their quotas. Cops put their lives on the line daily for salaries that are often measly at best, and frequently have to depend on overtime pay just to be able to take care of their families, who never get to see them because they're always working. People need to understand that police officers have an identity outside their jobs. We are human beings with real-life issues, yet society treats us like robots.

Alcoholism and depression are rampant—as high as 30 percent of all cops suffer from alcohol addiction, according to American Addiction Centers. There's a bogus hotline that cops can call if they feel especially troubled, but they often don't want to use it because mental illness among law enforcement is so heavily stigmatized, and because they fear their guns will be taken away if they are perceived as too unwell to carry. So they suffer in silence, which often turns deadly. As a July 2023 American Addiction Centers article entitled "Substance Abuse Among Police & Law Enforcement" says:

> The police force is notorious for crafting a culture of repression and omission. Diane Wetendorf, who has written extensively on the issue of violence in the police force, suggests that this culture shift comes with training. When learning to be police officers, trainees lose their individuality. They are no longer people with thoughts, feelings, and opinions. They are all officers, and they are all the same.
>
> That culture could protect an officer in trouble, as peers might be quick to see the officer's side of an argument, but that same culture could also hamstring an officer in need. An expression of worry or fear could be interpreted as weakness. And because weakness could put another officer's life on the line, the culture admits no space for expressing deep or overwhelming emotional concerns.

Those of us in law enforcement simply have to be better about checking in on our people. We have to ask them, "Are you okay? Are you sure you're safe?" Every police department has a budget. They need to allocate a generous portion of it to investing in mental health professionals who specialize in supporting law enforcement—people with whom police officers feel safe and able to heal. If people within police departments were treated more compassionately, it's possible that law enforcement as a whole would attract better people to take on these jobs. If my friend MA had been able to share his deepest fears with a qualified police therapist, he might still be alive today.

Despite all the deaths I had seen in my life, I had never experienced the suicide of anyone close to me. When I went to MA's funeral, I spoke with his sister and told her to call me if she ever needed to talk to someone. But I didn't know what to say to his teenage son; although I could see a long road of trauma stretching out ahead of him, I didn't have the words to comfort him.

Having shot himself in the head, MA didn't look like himself in the casket. I wished I hadn't glimpsed him so that my mental image of his beautiful face could have remained intact. Even more, I wished he had really talked to me about his burdens. After all, I had certainly had many moments of such profound pain that taking my own life had seemed like the best possible option. But I had realized that choosing this side—life—is always the better approach. If you have to crawl to get to a better situation, just crawl. If you have to sit there and wait, sit there and wait—because better days *will* come. I gave credit to God for eliminating those deadly thoughts from my psyche and delivering me from those demons, and I wished He could have done the same for MA.

After Chief Davis's retirement and MA's suicide, I found myself right back in the same impossibly dark place I had been in after Quar's passing. I had been looking for someone to love me for as long as I could remember, but I still hadn't found that person and I just couldn't seem to fill the void that seemed to have taken up permanent residence in my soul. Nothing, not even God's love, was sufficient to deliver me from the loneliness and feelings of inadequacy that plagued me.

Finally, one day, God spoke to me. He told me that I needed to love myself, because that would be the greatest gift I could have. I had heard that before, and I had always wanted to believe it was true, but this particular time it resonated differently. Still, I had no idea how I was supposed to do what God was asking me, because in my mind I thought I already loved myself. I had to dig deeper. I had to sit still. And I had to listen.

"How can you love yourself when the very person who gave birth to you couldn't love you or show you affection?" I heard a voice ask. At first I didn't realize it was God speaking to me. I just knew the voice wasn't my own, because it sounded and felt different.

Once I realized it was indeed God, I tuned in completely. I acknowledged that I had deep-seated issues about the way my mother had treated me, which was why I had sought out so many other maternal figures over the years. I also acknowledged that I had remained for too long in a toxic and dysfunctional relationship with a man twenty years older than I was because I had been looking for a father to replace the one I never knew. The very people who were supposed to teach me about self-worth and confidence had failed me terribly; as a result, everything I did and every way I thought happened through an impaired lens. But I also understood that those people couldn't have given me something they never had themselves.

I needed to do emergency surgery on my soul. I began to pray more deeply and earnestly than I ever had before. Every day, I begged God to deliver me. I started listening to Steve Harvey's six a.m. motivational talks. I read inspiration books about cultivating self-worth. I consumed a daily diet of emotional and spiritual enrichment, filling my mind and heart with only ideas and questions that encouraged my growth and inner peace. I also began to more closely evaluate the people in my life. I decided who mattered and who didn't, and assessed who was making withdrawals in my life bank without making deposits. I had already done so with Quar and Sun; now, I permanently closed the accounts of anyone remaining on that list who had insufficient funds. I even changed the gym workouts I had been doing for years. I began running and controlling my breathing. I became tapped in, turned on, and deliberate in everything I did, because I knew that what I fed my soul would determine my character and ultimately my future. I couldn't get it from my parents. I couldn't get it from my family. I couldn't get it from any of the men I had been involved with. So I had to look deep down inside and say, *Girl, come on, now. Fight, fight, fight.*

After engaging in these daily practices, I felt my mindset begin to change. My confidence increased to a level I didn't know existed. A healer at heart, I started a group text where I would send friends the scriptures God laid in my heart every morning. God also started moving differently in my life. He had always been amazing to me, but now I saw how He was truly building and changing me, readying me for great things to come.

In addition to receiving all of God's wisdom, I realized I also needed to talk to a mental health professional. Although Dr. D had served an invaluable purpose for me, I had stopped seeing her about a year earlier, and I didn't think she was the right person to support me on the journey I wanted to now take. One night while watching mindless TV, I stumbled upon the reality show *Basketball Wives LA*. I paused to watch, hoping to get a laugh or two, but ended up transfixed by a scene in which one of the wives had an intensely emotional session with her therapist.

The therapist, Delena Zimmerman, was warm, insightful, and wise, and when the show ended, God said to me, *Get in touch with her*. I googled her, found her contact information, and sent her an email. I told her who I was, including the fact that I was a detective on the New York mayor's detail, in hopes that she would reply. Sure enough, within a couple of days, she called me and said that she couldn't practice in New York but that if I happened to physically travel to California, she could take me on as a client and continue to be my therapist once I returned to New York. After a fifteen-minute free consult with her, I had such a strong sense that this woman could help me that I agreed to fly to Los Angeles.

The timing was perfect—the mayor was already planning

to visit his family in California over Christmas, and I would be traveling with him. I flew out early and went to see Dr. Zimmerman at her office in Culver City. When I arrived, she sent me a text saying, *Go to room 102. I'll meet you there.*

When I entered the room, it was empty, save for a couple chairs and an aquarium full of vividly colored fish. I felt like a congregant about to confess all my sins to a Catholic priest. I didn't know if I should sit down, so I remained standing.

She was so quiet when she came up behind me that by the time I turned around, she was only about six inches away. She was taller than I was, and she looked down, dead into my eyes, and said, "Have a seat."

When she sat in the chair opposite mine, I took a good look at her. She had long, honey-brown hair and wore stylish glasses, and she looked bigger than she had on TV, though she was slim and as composed as anyone I had ever seen. She crossed her legs and asked, "What brings you to Culver City?"

I said, "I don't know where I should start."

"Where would you like to start?"

"Well, I was in therapy for many years, but I believe I've run my course with her, and when I saw you on TV, God told me to come see you, so here I am."

When I paused to exhale, Dr. Zimmerman asked, "What's currently going on in your life?"

I gave her as much of a summary as I could: about how I was now heavily involved with Mayor de Blasio's detail and was very successful in my career. By then he had launched his presidential campaign and I was traveling all over the United States with him. It had taken me years to detox from my relationships with men, but now I had been single for too long. I was sick of being alone all the time, and I didn't know what my next steps should be.

At that point, I had no idea I'd end up writing this memoir; all I had was a journal I had been keeping for years. I was stuck wondering what I was supposed to be doing, what the larger meaning of my life was, and wanting someone to show me the way. Although I was serving a purpose professionally and had achieved everything I wanted to achieve, my personal life was empty. I had spent all my young-adult years blowing cash like it was play money. Now, I knew there had to be more to life. Now, when I found myself working overtime constantly, getting my hair and nails done, shopping, traveling, and dining at five-star restaurants, I felt as if I were just eating and eating without ever feeling full.

As I shared all this with Dr. Zimmerman, I hoped that she might be the one person on Earth who could help me find the nourishment I craved.

Here I am with Mayor Bill de Blasio and Reverend Jesse Jackson at NY1, launching the mayor's presidential campaign.

CHAPTER 31

The Details of the Detail

It was no secret that a lot of crooked activities went on within the mayor's detail. There had been a lengthy stint where no one was getting promoted because the inspector was taking care of only his own people. Some Black officers in Intel even brought and won a lawsuit against the department because they claimed that they were not being promoted as readily as their white counterparts.

I wasn't one of them. One day in December 2017, I was preparing for a town hall that the mayor was hosting in Fort Greene, Brooklyn. These events were open to the public, and hundreds of community members would attend to air grievances and make requests. The scene was always chaotic.

While I tried to get everything together, my phone rang and I saw my inspector's name on my caller ID. He was always calling me to fact-check everything. I didn't really have time to talk to him, but I had no choice.

I picked up and said, "Hey, Inspector, how you doing?"

"What's going on, KBL?" he asked.

"Nothing much—just getting ready for this town hall."

I thought he was going to ask me for a debriefing on my

preparations. Instead, I heard him say, "I just wanted to congratulate you."

"On what, sir?" What could he possibly have had to tell me?

"I'm congratulating you because you're getting promoted to first-grade detective this Friday."

"What?" I wanted to reach inside my ears and shake out whatever was blocking my hearing.

"First-grade," he repeated.

I looked down at my ragged nails and thought, *How am I going to find time to get my hands done in three days?* I wanted to break out into a dance. In my mind, I was screaming and running through the building with both my arms up, a marathon winner about to break through the tape at the finish line. On the outside, I was just a buttoned-up woman on the phone with her colleague.

I prepared for him to say something like, "I'm going to get somebody to come in and replace you today so you can go home, get your dress uniform ready, and do the rest of your preparations." Instead, he said, "Get back to work, KBL. See you soon."

For the rest of the evening, my mind was a washing machine on spin cycle. I was on my feet for hours, and I kept having to excuse myself to the ladies' room to cry in a stall. *Is this really happening? This cannot be my life.* I tried to muffle the sounds of my weeping; nothing and nobody could ever have convinced me that I would achieve this level of success.

Although I floated through the next three days on a cloud of pride and joy, not everyone was happy about my good fortune. Only five Black women in the entire NYPD at that time had reached the rank of first-grade detective, and I discovered later on that quite a few of my colleagues thought I had been promoted only because of my race.

That Friday, as I walked across the stage at 1 Police Plaza to receive my decoration, I was the only Black woman up there.

So many people over the years had told me I was worthless, and for a long time I had believed them. *And look at me now*, I thought, as I held my head up high. I had gone from being a misunderstood high school dropout and teenage mother growing up in the projects to being one of the most respected officers in the entire NYPD. The only things missing were the people I loved most: my grandmother, my aunts, even Niecy. I was living proof that no matter what you have gone through in life and no matter what your zip code is, none of that determines who you can ultimately be. Whatever God has for you, nobody can take that from you.

When I was transferred to the mayor's detail in 2014, I thought it would be for just four years. I had no idea what I was going to do after that, but, as fate would have it, de Blasio was reelected. That meant my four-year plan instantly turned into an eight-year plan, and after that I would be eligible for retirement. Could my life have been mapped out more perfectly?

Mayor de Blasio was sworn in for his second term on January 1, 2018. It was my day on and it was freezing outside, though I didn't have to stand out in the elements with everyone else. Now that I had advanced, I was allowed to stay inside city hall during the ceremony.

Two weeks had passed since my promotion, and I was still on a high, especially now that I knew it would be only a few more years before I had the option of retiring from the NYPD. Despite how long I had been in the NYPD, I could not support the department's policies and all it stood for. I could not stand for its rampant racism and sexism. Since I had been promoted, however, I thought the mayor might be preparing to make some system-wide changes. The job had always been geared toward keeping white people in power and Black people oppressed, but I hoped a new day was on the horizon—until I realized that the man who was in charge of all of New York City was actually part of the problem.

Black communities in the United States have always been subject to their own set of rules, and white people who engage in the same illicit activities as Black people tend to be punished less severely. Seeing this divide up close as a law enforcement officer, someone in a perceived position of power who was actually helpless, was jarring. I learned more about biases during my eight years on the mayor's detail than I did during the rest of my time on the force.

When de Blasio got a second chance to be mayor, I thought maybe his gratitude would kick in and he'd think, *You know what? These people trusted me enough to vote me in again. Let me do something for them.* Although he never mistreated me personally and never displayed any racist behavior—in fact, I felt as if he liked Black people—it was clear to me that he knew all about biases and very little about how to be a compelling leader. His staff, filled with white millennials, disliked him and were mostly using his name on their résumés to catapult themselves into bigger roles. While they smiled to his face daily, they had only bad things to say about him behind his back. They would talk about him to me, saying, "He's stupid. He doesn't know what he's doing. He's not consistent. He doesn't know how to run this city. He's a disgrace." I had gotten used to cutthroat people and backstabbing and white privilege over the course of my career, but this level of criticism of a public official felt vicious and reckless. I never said a word to them, but they seemed to feel comfortable running their mouths to anyone on the detail who would listen.

As much as I didn't approve of the staffers' nasty comments, I also didn't feel sorry for the mayor. He was incapable of managing his staff in a way that encouraged their growth or advancement and wasn't remotely interested in creating new leaders. This pattern was evident at every level of his administration, and especially at the token holiday party he threw every year as a half-assed gesture of gratitude for the security detail. He would make a speech about how important we were and thank us for all we did for him, but the very next day he wouldn't even say good morning. Countless times, I saw him talk down to staff. The way he treated us the other 364 days of the year made it clear to me that the "gratitude" he displayed at his party was fake, a photo op of sorts, a halfhearted gesture he used to make *himself* think he was a good person. I didn't need him to weigh my importance in the world.

I also sensed that the mayor generally did not like police officers. Although he never disrespected me directly, he was so insecure about his own status that he couldn't stand the thought of anyone else around him having power. Once, when de Blasio was talking on the phone on the grounds of city hall, a uniformed cop posted there briefly took off his hat, and de Blasio, on one of his typical power trips, took it as such a gesture of disrespect that he called the officer's sergeant to complain.

Mayor de Blasio was used to getting booed at city parades, but on Saturday, September 22, 2018, as he walked out onto a massive stage that had been erected in Flushing Meadows Corona Park in Queens for Paul Simon's final concert, almost fifty thousand people joined together to hiss and holler at him, trying to force him out of their sight. He was in his second term and had fully revealed his true colors to a city that wasn't having it. The more he attempted to grab power and assert himself, the less the people rallied behind him. He wasn't playing it cool when he should have—he was giving off a desperate vibe.

My fellow officers and I looked at each other and hung our heads for our commander in chief. If the crowd could have thrown tomatoes at him and gotten away with it, they would have. New Yorkers are tough, man. Either they like you or they don't, and it had never been more evident to me that de Blasio was on the losing side of that equation. Even so, nobody deserves that kind of treatment. If I could have figured out a way to tell all fifty thousand people there, "Hey, knock it off," I would have.

The mayor quickly announced Paul Simon and hustled off the stage. I could tell how flustered he was by the negative reception, but, to his credit, he stayed to listen to the concert for a little while longer—and it was a good thing he did, because the performance was so memorable that it could have uplifted anyone. I had never followed Paul Simon or his music, but that night I became a lifelong fan.

As we were about to leave, one of Paul's staffers handed me the concert playlist and led me to him so that I could shake his hand. As I escorted the mayor back to his car, I was still smiling.

One thing that was always difficult for me to reconcile was de Blasio the man versus de Blasio the mayor. One Christmas Eve, I was working and he wanted to go shopping for his wife and their children. We walked down Sixth Avenue in Manhattan, looking in several different stores. When we got to Macy's, he wanted just the two of us to go into the women's department because the media could put some kind of negative spin on things. He probably thought they would claim he was shopping for a mistress he didn't have.

While we browsed, he and I got to talking—really talking—and he asked me some personal questions: about my daughters and what they did for work, what my favorite places in New York were, and what my family usually did for Christmas. I told him that I hosted a Christmas party every year for my relatives and friends and how I made sure to have a wrapped gift under the tree for everybody who RSVP'd.

From then on, I was able to see some humanity in the mayor. I realized he could be a genuinely caring person, someone I wouldn't mind going out for wine with when I retired.

That evening was also how I got every subsequent Christmas off while I was working for him. He believed in people going home and being with their families during holidays. Even though I knew I would never be exempt from his bad moods and cruel comments, I came to think he wanted authentic people around him, rather than the ones who were always kissing up to him, and I believe he saw me as the former. All people are complicated, but the mayor was extra complicated because his ego sometimes took precedence over his kindheartedness, especially when his public persona was on display and all his insecurities came out.

Despite these brief respites from having to walk on eggshells at work, I could never fully relax because I knew politics and microaggressions would always be part of my job. In 2017, when the mayor was on the campaign trail for his second term, I traveled with him to Maine to attend a women's march.

As my fellow officers and I drove through the town where the march was to be held, we saw a billboard that displayed de Blasio's name and announced his upcoming speaking engagement at a senior citizens' center. We had been under the impression that we were merely accompanying him to the march and to visit a local relative of his.

Once we learned that he was scheduled to speak, I was charged with the task of advancing the location.

When two of my colleagues and I arrived at the center, I spotted some older white women finishing up a dance class. I identified myself and explained why we were there. I experienced racism in real time when one of the women looked me up and down as if she had never seen a Black person before, and especially not one with any authority.

Shortly after that encounter, someone called the director of the center and told him I was there to "case the joint." It felt like the equivalent of asking, "Why did you send a Black woman to rob us?" The same person then called de Blasio himself to complain about my presence, and that prompted the mayor to contact his inspector and demand that he get me out of Maine immediately. Two white officers and one Black female officer went into a community center that was occupied by white people, and because someone didn't like that, the Black woman got penalized. I was kicked off the trip without explanation, while the two white officers continued on to the mayor's next stop, in DC.

The NYPD is too often all about who you know, not about how good your work ethic is. I thought the mayor's detail would be different. It took me eighteen years to move past my denial and accept the fact that I worked for a racist organization that was designed to keep Black people oppressed. As much as I wanted systemic changes to occur, I knew if I tried to challenge the NYPD, they would set me up, say I was crazy, and psych me off the job—or worse.

There were good times mixed in that made the whole experience bittersweet. The most fun I ever had on the detail were the days when we left the city and all of these complicated politics behind. I always liked traveling with de Blasio because when we were out of town, the energy was usually different—lighter, more casual, more hopeful. In New York, he was Mayor de Blasio; on the road, he was Bill, and Bill was cool, the kind of guy you could sit down and really rap with.

On September 20, 2019, the day de Blasio dropped out of the presidential race, I believe he checked out of the rest of his second term as mayor. From there, his lack of morale trickled down to his detail. I certainly wasn't looking forward to heading back to New York; I had been on the detail for seven years by then and had seen many coworkers come and go. But I also needed to secure my pension, so I had to tough it out for a little longer.

CHAPTER 32

Messages from the Messenger

In October 2020, I went to the South to visit Morgan. She had been telling me about a city near where she lived and said I should consider buying a house there. I finally consented to go look around the area with her.

The day we set out, it was raining so hard that I said, "Listen, we don't have to go."

"No, I want to," Morgan replied.

While she drove, all I could see at first were woods. My phone wasn't working. I could barely tell where the road started or ended. Then I noticed a sign near a housing development that said, *If you want to purchase a custom home, call this number.*

"Morgan, look," I said. "Maybe we can call that number and find someone who will give us directions."

As soon as Morgan got cell service, she dialed the number and a sales rep named Chris with a heavy Southern accent answered. The only reason she called was to figure out how to get us out of the area, but she had to pretend we were looking for real estate. Chris said he would meet Morgan and me shortly. We parked in Lot 16 of the development. Fifteen minutes later he arrived and started right in with his sales pitch, telling me that I could buy a custom home in the development for $750,000. That was nowhere near my budget of $350,000 to $400,000. I said, "Whoa, whoa, whoa, I can't afford that much. How do we get out of here?"

He gave us directions, and Morgan and I left. As we drove out, I noticed that there were two sides to the development. We got to the opposite side, where Lot 1 was, and were looking for the exit when I heard God say, "No, I need you to go back to where you were."

"Hold up," I told Morgan.

She drove back to the original side. By now it wasn't raining nearly as hard, though the ground was muddy as far as I could see, and I didn't want to get my designer sneakers dirty, so when I heard God say, "Get out the car," I thought, *Are You serious? My Balenciagas?* But of course I did as He asked.

I realized that I was in exactly the same spot I had just been in with the sales rep: Lot 16. As I looked around, I heard God say to me, "This is where I want you to live."

The rain was becoming heavy again, so I got back in the car. Through the blurry windshield, I squinted at the site. "This is where You want me to live, God? I don't know anything about this place."

"Trust me," God said.

I flew back home the next morning, but I had already put Lot 16 out of my mind. *There's no way that was for real*, I thought. I knew God wanted me to leave New York if I decided to retire, but I still had a year of work to go, so I also figured this matter wasn't urgent.

When I returned to work that week, I was driving my black Ford squad car along Eastern Parkway in Brooklyn when I got a phone call from an unfamiliar number. I picked up and heard a man with a Southern accent introduce himself as a realtor named Chris, so I assumed it was the same sales rep Morgan and I had met a few days earlier. But it wasn't.

This man said, "You called somebody's phone and left your name and number, saying you were looking to buy property. But that wasn't a realtor; it was a personal number. They called me and said I might be interested in speaking with you. That's why I'm calling."

"Yes, I was looking in a development in your area," I said, "but I'm not interested in buying there anymore—I've moved on."

"I understand. But if you change your mind, you'll need to put down a $15,000 deposit, which you'll get back when you close on the property."

"Thank you," I said, "but I'm not changing my mind on this."

We talked for a few more minutes and cordially ended the call. But right after we hung up, I started thinking about Lot 16 all over again. *That was strange. That man made it seem so simple, but I just don't see how this is possible, given that the first Chris quoted me $750,000.*

Right away, I heard God say, "Trust me. Let Me be God."

I drove two more blocks and then called my sergeant. I said, "Sarge, I have to take care of something important. I know I have to be on post, but I need you to hold me down for a little while."

He said, "Do what you have to do; just make sure you're safe."

I called Chris back and almost couldn't believe the words coming out of my mouth when I told him, "I want to buy Lot 16. I want to build a custom house there."

"Okay," he said, "just get me that cashier's check, and we'll take it from there."

I was about to drive across the Brooklyn Bridge to go to city hall. Instead, when I hung up, I put my flashing lights on and drove to the Municipal Credit Union in East New York, thirty minutes away. I removed my work earpiece and stuffed it down the front of my suit before I walked inside. I stood in line and got my cashier's check for $15,000. I followed Chris's instructions to initiate the wire. I checked in with God once I was finished and asked Him, "Are You really about to take me on a journey from homeless to *homes*?"

When I called Chris to confirm that I had wired the check, he said, "Now we just have to get you preapproved for a home loan. I'll have my contact at a mortgage company call you."

By the time the man reached me, I was on post at city hall. I told my partner, "Hold me for a minute," and excused myself to the ladies' room so I could answer.

When I said hello, the man said, "You don't qualify for preapproval." I held the phone away from my ear for a moment and just stared at the screen, thinking, *Then why did you call me in the first place? You could have just told Chris I wasn't preapproved, instead of shaming me.* This man didn't know me from anywhere. All he probably knew from Chris was that I was a Black woman. He never asked for my name or any other relevant information.

I tried to keep calm as I put the phone back to my ear and asked, "How do you know I don't qualify when I have an 850 credit score and you don't have any information about my personal finances? You just don't want me in that neighborhood—is that it?"

I didn't even give him time to answer; I hung up immediately.

This man is racist at best, I told myself. *He's not going to handle me like that.* Any obstacles I thought were in my way were between God and me—nobody else.

A friend of mine owned a mortgage company in Brooklyn, so I called him right away and said, "Listen, Jay, do you do mortgages outside New York?"

"Yeah, in thirty other states. Why?"

I said, "Because I'm trying to get preapproved down South, and the guy I just spoke with denied me without even taking down my information."

"Don't worry about it," Jay reassured me. "You know you're my girl; I got you. I cover a lot of the South. Come see me tomorrow, and I'll get you the preapproval letter."

The next day, I was supposed to work. I had to call my sergeant again and repeat the same request. Once I had his permission, there I went again, lights and sirens on, all the way to the mortgage company. I parked right on the sidewalk, threw my police plaque up on the dash, took out my earpiece again, and went inside. Every desk I passed on my way to Jay seemed to have a candy dish on it. I started taking M&M's, Snickers, Skittles, and anything else I could find. While I sat with Jay, waiting for him to draw up my letter, I just kept popping chocolate and Skittles into my mouth.

My heart racing from all the sugar, I said, "God, if it is in Your will, please find me the rest of the money I need."

After I got my preapproval letter, God just started making it happen, making it happen, making it happen. Chris gave me a choice between eleven builders in the development. I chose a man named Joe because I learned that he was a minister as a well as a builder, and my conversations with him were built on God and shared faith.

The real confirmation that I was on the right path came one day when I was waiting for the elevator in a Manhattan office building. I was standing next to an extraordinarily tall, slim, bearded white man wearing glasses. I don't even remember him saying hello; he simply looked at me and said, "Everybody's going to know your name someday."

"I'm sorry?" I responded.

He persisted: "You're going to be famous." And he shared numerous predictions about how my life would unfold that have since come to pass. But the one that stood out to me most on that day was his comment "You're building a house. You're building a house that's on water and has a fountain."

As I pictured the beautiful fountain that was part of my

construction blueprint, everything I was holding in my hands spilled out through my fingers onto the ground. When the elevator doors opened and the man stepped on, I shook my head. *Nah*, I thought, *I'm not getting on there with you.* But as sure as I live today, I knew that this man was an angel, sent to me by God to tell me I was going to thrive.

On New Year's Eve 2020, I got home around one thirty a.m. after standing onstage with the mayor, watching the ball drop. As the sounds of fireworks and partying reverberated in the distance, I mumbled to myself, "Another year down," then got on my knees and began to pray, giving the Lord all the glory. As difficult as that COVID pandemic year had been for everyone, I was grateful to have survived it when so many others hadn't. I prayed for so long my knees got stiff—a reminder of the fact that I had turned fifty a few months earlier.

Two days later, I began my annual Daniel fast, which always runs from January 2 to January 31. I consume one meal per day after six p.m. I don't eat any carbs or sugar; I stay faithful to a routine of fresh vegetables and water. I abstain from going to the gym, watching television, and using social media or even my phone for anything other than work. During that time, it's just God and me. I've been doing this since 1993.

After such a tumultuous year, I knew my fast for 2021 had to be different. I needed instructions from God about how to proceed. I asked Him to give me the strength to get out of my own way so that he could take full control of my life.

"Stay still, be quiet, and allow Me to take over," I heard Him say.

The first thing He told me to do was to stop dating and take a vow of celibacy. He said, "I need you to be with Me. Just you and Me. And I need you not to have sex. The next person you have sex with will be your husband."

There had been periods when I hadn't had sex for a couple

of years, but this was the first time I was making that choice consciously. I didn't want anything to come between God and me. Still, I couldn't help but ask Him, "Really? Where am I going to find a husband who's not going to touch me until we're married?"

This time, God did not respond.

Soon after that, He led me to Bishop Noel Jones, who quickly became my favorite preacher. One of the first messages I listened to from Bishop Jones was about asking God for things that seem impossible. When I finished watching the sermon, I heard God say to me, "You have never asked Me for anything that was impossible. You must show your faith to everyone."

Yet everything that I was asking for did feel utterly impossible. God had already saved and changed my life. He had already blessed my daughters and me with good health, with a career beyond anything I could have imagined, and with two homes of my own. Why did I deserve more than that? Surely I wasn't qualified to ask Him for anything else. But I still knew I needed to do more, and He kept telling me to trust Him, so I decided to take a leap of faith.

One day, after I had listened to a message from Bishop Jones entitled "I Wasn't Built to Break," I thought, *Maybe I wasn't built to break either. God didn't put me back together so I could fall apart.*

I took a close look at myself in the mirror. "You are a beautiful Black woman. A queen," I said aloud. "God gave you a second chance at life. You have wisdom. You have your right mind. You are intelligent. You have morals. Your life is valuable. You have people who love you, so you must love yourself."

I heard God say, "Go to the Book of Philippians, Chapter 3, verses 13–14."

One of the scriptures said, *Brethren, I count not myself to have apprehended: but this one thing I do, forgetting those things which are behind, and reaching forth unto those things which are before, I press toward the mark for the prize of the high calling of God in Christ Jesus.*

I read the scriptures three times so I could understand their message, and my takeaway was that God didn't want me to worry. He was confirming that I was unbreakable and that He would give me the strength to do whatever I needed to do. He wanted me not to worry about yesterday and to prepare for tomorrow.

I knew at that moment that God was preparing me for a mission. While I listened to a song that He told me to play, by the gospel singer Smokie Norful, called "Still Say Thank You," I heard Him say, "I have blessed you with your own organization for at-risk young ladies. That will be your gift back to this universe."

"Is this really where you want me to go? Is this really what you want me to do?"

"I need you to be official," He said.

Whatever that meant, I decided that my first order of business postretirement should be to enhance Young Ladies of Our Future, the organization I had started in 2012. After I filed the paperwork needed for it to become a nonprofit 501(c)3, I put together a staff of ten volunteers, all police officers. I implemented a twenty-week workshop schedule, established a formal commencement for those who completed the program, and decided to grant a lifetime membership to every young woman who graduated.

I now decided that I wanted to move on from the NYPD as soon as possible. My official end date on the mayor's detail would be June 30, 2021, though I would not have to be physically present at any post, unless I chose to work overtime, after February 14. Most members of the mayor's detail would wait to leave until the final day of his term, but I wanted to give myself the option of having a whole summer both to process the long career I was leaving behind and to get in the right mindset to move forward with courage and conviction. I also promised myself that I would not chase success.

I had met the comedian Tracy Morgan once, at the ribbon-cutting ceremony for a community center in the Marcy projects. I was there, along with a few news reporters and the ceremony organizers, when his driver pulled up outside the facility in a purple Rolls-Royce. We followed him into the building and circled around him, and he just started dropping knowledge. Then he turned to me.

"You're special," he said, his eyes boring into mine.

I teared up instantly. *I can't stay here. There's a live camera right in my face, and this guy's about to make me break down.*

As I made a move to leave, Tracy said something I will never forget: "I don't want you to focus on being successful. I want you to go after your purpose. Success is fake and doesn't last forever. But your purpose will be with you for life."

This is my confirmation, I thought, as I hurried away. *This is all I need to begin again.*

On Valentine's Day 2021, I arrived at work at six a.m., as usual. I signed in for the last time with my team; from then on, I would work only overtime with other teams. I walked around city hall, reminiscing about the past eight years of my life. I thought about how easily I could have become a statistic, and how even though I had all the ingredients for that to happen, God had another plan. All of us have a story, but it was my story's surprise ending that made it so different and powerful.

As my eyes welled up with tears, I tried hard not to blink because I didn't want anyone to notice them falling. It was useless. I had hidden too many tears before. This was a day when it was okay to let them out.

My sergeant delivered the roll call for the daily team assignments. Mine was simple—the mayor had only one move for the day. After that, my time with my team would officially be up.

My final day at city hall: June 30, 2021.

I wandered around city hall for another thirty minutes, before making my way to a restroom stall. Hands shaking, breathing shallow, I told myself, *Get it together, girl. Isn't this what you wanted? Take this energy and put all of it toward your new life, not the past.*

That day, I received a phone call from my sergeant, extending his congratulations and thanking me for a job well done over our years working together. I told him I was happy because I didn't want to share the truth: at that moment, I honestly didn't know what my life would look like after the NYPD. Once I put down my shield, what would happen to me?

Then, as always, God spoke to me: "I told you to build up your faith. Believe in Me. Take your leap. You're not built to break."

As I sat in my work car, I took deep breaths and said, "God, please hold my hand and pull me into my next phase of life. I promise not to let go of Your hand, because I'm focused and resolute. I've got work to do."

Signing out of city hall for the last time.

CHAPTER 33

No More Blues

I had tossed and turned all night until the sun rose on June 30, 2021, a day I thought would never arrive. Twenty years had come and gone, just like that. I stretched my arms and neck, smiling to myself, and got out of bed. I had an eight a.m. appointment to get my face done. I had to get back home by nine to make it to 1 Police Plaza and show the world that I had accomplished my goals in the NYPD and was retiring as a first-grade detective.

I had invited only my family, my close friends, my supervisors, and two other colleagues to join me for this monumental experience. Everyone else I worked with seemed like a backstabber, especially during my last five months on the mayor's detail. Now, I was just ready to leave them and their bad behavior behind. I had a big story to tell, and I was about to release a secret that I had been holding for two decades. It was time to air out the room and laugh out loud.

I hired a young, beautiful Black sister who owned a car service to drive my family and me to the ceremony. Everyone else would meet us afterward at city hall, directly across the street.

I was quiet the whole ride to 1 Police Plaza while my whole career, from day one to this very moment, played on a loop in my mind. My hands were sweating; I kept wiping them with a tissue. I just hoped I didn't sweat off my beautifully made-up face too. I had on an all-white dress—my favorite color—so I could walk out in style.

Outside city hall on June 30, 2021.

Exiting the NYPD requires the same huge amount of paperwork as it takes to join the force. One of my good friends, who had retired from the mayor's detail a few months before me, helped me fill everything out. I don't know if I could have completed all of it on my own. After I finished signing the documents and received my retired police ID card, my family and I headed across the street to city hall for my official walkout.

I had decided against the traditional walkout, which featured NYPD helicopters, squad cars, and horses. I just wanted to keep the procedure as simple as possible—to sign out in the command log and exit city hall for the last time to find my family and friends waiting for me on the other side of the door.

I'm not going to cry. I'm not going to cry, I repeated after I penned my final signature. I took a moment to appreciate the historic building that I had spent so much time in—its grand double marble staircase, its sparkling crystal chandeliers, its Corinthian columns, its repeating interior arches, its ornate domed ceiling. Then I looked straight ahead of me at the exit. I walked through that door to deafening applause and a photographer snapping away. I hugged everyone and made sure the photographer took pictures of me with my family, my friends, and my girls from Young Ladies of Our Future. Each time I put my arm around someone who was there to support me felt like a celebration unto itself.

My reception was across the street in our administrative office because we were still in COVID times and I couldn't find a restaurant close by to accommodate my party for dinner. My supervisors provided a catered Italian meal, my favorite, and I brought my own red velvet cake. While we ate, my supervisors told funny stories about me. My LT couldn't wait to point out that I came in two days before I retired to work overtime. "I couldn't believe my eyes," he said.

When I responded, "I ain't leaving nothing on the table, Lieutenant," we all laughed.

I had a farewell meeting scheduled with the mayor, but it wasn't until four p.m. because it was the last day of city hall budget planning. I wanted to thank him for the opportunity to be a part of the detail, and I wanted to say goodbye to a few nice people I had worked with in city hall over the years. I also wanted the mayor to meet my family. Most of my guests were tired from the long day and elected to go home, but a handful of them said they would wait.

Shortly before four o'clock, I walked the people who were leaving to their cars and then went back into city hall to meet the mayor. As I sat in the lobby, I kept playing out different scenarios in my mind: *What should I say? Should I tell him my plans or just let him talk?* I knew this was my one opportunity to share my secret with him, but I decided to let things play out naturally.

Within a few minutes, the mayor's assistant came out and told me he was ready to see me. My heart pounded along with my high heels as I followed her to de Blasio's office.

He greeted me with a warm hug. As we sat down across from each other, he said, "So, this is it?"

"Yes, sir."

He thanked me for my service, and I thanked him for having allowed me to be a part of his history-making detail. When he asked me what was next for me, I knew what I had to do.

I took a deep breath. "Mr. Mayor, I'm writing a book."

He said, "You are?"

"Yes."

"What is the book about?"

My knee-jerk reaction was almost to laugh, as I realized he might have thought I had written a tell-all about him. I pressed my lips together to keep from smiling as I said, "It's about my life. I was shot ten times."

The mayor sat quietly for a moment, his brow furrowed, looking right into my eyes. "Can you repeat what you just said?"

I felt my palms beginning to sweat. "I was shot ten times by my ex-fiancé, and I was paralyzed."

He didn't speak for a long time. Finally, he asked me, "Why didn't you ever say anything?"

"Because I knew I would be fired. Plus, there are some things you just can't say."

He just nodded. I knew he understood. Mayor Bill de Blasio was a rare politician in my eyes—both a considerate human and a politician who sometimes seemed to care only about what the next race would be or how he could run for office again. But all that mattered in that moment was for me to unburden myself and show my gratitude for the past eight years.

I told the mayor I had some family members who wanted to meet him, and he said, "Sure, go get them." They were waiting in the hallway, the very same hallway I had waited in for the mayor every day during my time on his detail.

I gathered up my people and escorted them into the mayor's office. He asked everyone to be seated. He sat in the middle of us as we went around the room and introduced ourselves. Melissa was there, and she didn't seem a bit impressed. I had to laugh about that.

We talked and shared stories over the next hour, while de Blasio's assistant took a few photos of us. When it was time for us to say our goodbyes, we all began to exit his office. But then I heard the mayor say, "Katrina, come back."

I walked over to him. "Yes, sir?"

From his great height, he leaned down and kissed me on my cheek. "Thanks again for everything, and good luck."

It was a meaningful and kind gesture he had extended to me. I actually felt a little woozy as I left, and once again I had to fight back tears.

While my driver took me home, I was as quiet as I had been on the way to city hall that morning. I knew I needed to cry, yet I wanted to cry in my own space. I had accomplished half of my goals, and now I had to focus on accomplishing the other half, which included turning this story into a book and living in my dream house in a new state that I knew nothing about.

While my mind whirled, people were calling and texting me to wish me a happy retirement. I had posted a few pictures on social media, and the word was getting out. Keri, my ADA bestie, texted me saying she wanted to post something about my story on her social media and asking if I was okay with it. *Sure*, I wrote back. *Just let me know when you post it so I can go to your page and see exactly what you said about me.*

Keri Herzog, who had been ADA for my domestic violence case and became a close friend.

I had been hiding my true identity—the real Katrina Chantel Cooke—for so long. I had kept Robert's last name, Brownlee, all these years because the people from my past knew me as Cooke and I had to protect my secret at all costs. I knew that as soon as I permitted Keri to reveal a glimpse of my story, everyone would know my secret—people I had been friends with for decades, my former coworkers, and even the general public. But I finally realized, now that I had spoken to the mayor, I was okay with all of it.

The next morning, Keri called me and said, "A journalist from the *New York Times* wants to interview you."

"Are you serious?" *Me, a kid from the projects, in the* New York Times? I thought. *Not a chance.*

"I'm dead serious," she said.

"Okay, let me get back to you." I hung up with Keri and immediately called a good friend of mine, who would later become my publicist, to get her advice. "Is this something I should do?"

I could practically see her rolling her eyes as she said, "Um, *hell yeah* you want to do this story." She asked me if I knew who the writer was, and I gave her his name: Michael Wilson. I had already done my own research and knew he was well respected in the media world.

After that, I called Keri back and said I wanted to meet with Mr. Wilson. Shortly thereafter, he called to introduce himself and arrange an interview with me. We set a date and agreed to meet at my house. I was in the midst of moving, but Mr. Wilson said all he needed was a table and a couple of chairs.

I rang my soon-to-be publicist and said, "We're all set."

"I'm so glad," she told me. Then she paused for so long that I thought she might have hung up on me, until I heard her voice again: "But don't tell him everything. You have a book to publish."

The *New York Times* story

CHAPTER 34

The Power of Prayer and Forgiveness

The first thing I do every morning when I open my eyes is pray. I give thanks to God and open my heart to Him. This process starts my day with great energy so that if anything negative comes my way, I have the power to repel it. Prayer is my suit of armor.

When I finally mastered the art of being still and listening to God's voice, it became evident that He was determined to turn my life around. Some of His most profound conversations with me were about forgiveness. He told me that in order to have peace, I had to learn how to forgive.

At first, I thought, *Hold up. How is this even going to be possible? I've been hurt far too deeply for this to work.* Still, I couldn't ignore God's instructions, so I had to pull Him aside and ask Him some questions that I thought were unanswerable.

"Lord, hold on," I began. "Are You saying I should forgive my mother? She's the one who abandoned me at birth and left me in the hospital! Am I also supposed to forgive the man who was my father? He never even recognized that I was alive! How am I supposed to forgive someone I've never even met? Am I supposed to forgive my cousin who molested me for years too?"

Quiet and tuned in, I heard the Lord say, "Yes."

Still reluctant, I asked more questions: "Am I seriously supposed to forgive the man who shot me ten times and left me for dead? How about his evil mother, who threw me out into the street when I had nowhere else to go? Am I supposed to forgive the men who ripped my heart apart when all I was trying to do was love them?"

Again, "Yes."

I kept reminding Him what had happened over the course of my life, as if He didn't already know. "What about all the people in the NYPD who tried to disrespect me and block my career advancement?"

But God just said, "Forgive, forgive, and forgive again."

With that, I tried to outsmart Him. I thought I could strike a compromise. I said, "God, I'll forgive everybody else, but I need you to give me a pass on certain people."

Right away, He said, "Absolutely not. I've forgiven *you*. What if I were to pick and choose the things you've done that I should forgive you for?"

Well, that got to me, but I had to sit on it. When God is moving in me and needs something done, I can't sleep, I can't eat, I can't do anything but hear His voice. And I get clear on what I'm supposed to do; I can feel it in my stomach and my chest, and I know I have to do it.

At that point, I just wanted to surrender. God had already gotten me so far. I was more mature than I had ever been, and solidly on a road to recovery in every area of my life.

The next time I spoke with God, I said, "Okay, but if I have to forgive, You have to show me how to do this."

He said, "I don't have to show you anything. When you come to Me and ask Me for forgiveness, it's already done."

I can't deny that I continued to struggle with forgiveness from time to time after that. No one's life is exempt from betrayal. But today I believe that we must always forgive because forgiveness makes *us* feel better. We don't have to keep certain people in our lives, but we must release any ill feelings toward them that are lingering in our hearts. Those feelings only contaminate our souls and destroy us from the inside out.

Once I created space for new beginnings, I was rewarded with one of the greatest gifts of my lifetime—answers to the decades-long questions I had been harboring about why my life had been filled with so much turmoil.

I had always disliked my stepfather, Leo. I never thought I would speak to him again after Niecy died, but, as with many other things in my life, I turned out to be wrong. In 2005, he had just been released from prison for a drug conviction, and we reconnected for long enough for me to help him find a room for rent, though we soon lost touch again. Fourteen years later, in 2019, I found out he was still living in that same room when my sister, his daughter with Niecy, called me and said, "My father asks about you all the time."

Do I want to speak with this man, or do I want to continue to keep my distance? I had to ask myself. But I was well into my healing process by then, and I didn't want to continue to harbor toxicity, so I told my sister he could call me.

The first time he and I spoke, we were on the phone for four hours. It was a snowy day in Brooklyn, and I sat at my kitchen table while Leo told me things I had never heard before. One aspect of Leo I always appreciated: He was brutally honest, and he knew things about Niecy that no one else ever did. The longer I talked with him, the more I wanted to know.

Leo revealed to me that he, too, was a broken man, and that the hateful behavior, drug use, and rage I had witnessed in him were simply a disguise for the abuse he had suffered in his own life. With no way to heal and no outlet to address his agony and inner turmoil, he became an abuser himself because it was the only channel for his fury.

He told me that his mother had given birth to him at the age of fourteen. I knew firsthand what it was like to become a mother so young—and I certainly hadn't been present for Morgan the way I was when I got older. When Leo's mother's parents kicked her out of their house for having a baby, she had no choice but to give Leo to her older sister, who severely abused him, giving him rotten food to eat and beating him mercilessly. Traumatized, dehumanized, and unwanted, Leo ran away at age eleven. Learning to survive as an adolescent on the streets of New York was no easy feat. Over the years, Leo became a drug dealer, a junkie, a gangster, and a womanizer, and developed a reputation for having a thick layer of ice surrounding his heart. He always carried a gun, ready to put a piece of steel into anyone who dared to cross him, and everyone feared him. And, not surprisingly, because his mother had abandoned him and his aunt had abused him, he also developed a disdain for women that was evident every time he interacted with one.

In one of our conversations in 2019, Leo revealed to me that he was never in love with Niecy. He said she was a terrible drug addict, the type who would do any drug available to her at any time, and that he never even wanted her to be his girlfriend. The only reason he got involved with her in the first place was that he witnessed a previous boyfriend of Niecy's savagely abusing her, and in order to convince the man to stop, Leo intervened and said, "She's my girl now. Leave her alone."

Because the other man knew what Leo was capable of, he backed off. But after that, Leo couldn't get rid of Niecy. She took his comment literally, felt indebted to him, and remained loyal to him until she died. Although he was romantically involved with plenty of other women over the years, he kept Niecy around, even fathering her two other children, my sister and brother.

After revealing these secrets, Leo told me the biggest one of all—one that had me nearly collapse on my kitchen floor. The other reason he kept dealing with Niecy, he said, was that he felt sorry for her. He said she was the most damaged woman he had ever known—because she had been violently raped at sixteen by a much older friend of my uncle Joe's, and because I was conceived through that brutal assault.

I remember looking around my kitchen and wondering if it was even real, feeling my body and wondering if I was even inhabiting it, as Leo's words echoed in my ears. Yet, finally, everything made sense to me.

Niecy got raped, and then she got pregnant. Abortion was still illegal in New York in 1970, so she was forced to have me. Even when she tried to leave me in the hospital, thinking no one would find out, she was unsuccessful. After that, every time she had to see me must have triggered unfathomably painful memories of the attack she had endured.

That was why she could barely look at me.

That was why she could barely talk to me.

That was why she hated me.

That was why she never mentioned who my father was.

My father was a rapist.

I didn't even want to get off the phone with Leo that night. I worried that if I did, the conversation would somehow no longer be real, that the explanation I had been searching for all my life would elude me again. And when we finally did hang up, I cried myself to sleep, thinking, *I am worthless. I have no value. I have no purpose.*

I asked God, "What in the world could I have done in this world, in this lifetime, to deserve this? There's no way I can survive this. This time, I'm killing myself for sure."

"What did *I* do to deserve to be on the cross?" God replied.

That question was what stopped me from blowing my brains out, even on the days when my pain felt unbearable.

Children born of rape face an excruciating legacy. Before I even knew who or what I was, I was the victim and the by-product of a violent crime. Studies have shown that children conceived through rape are more likely to suffer from acute psychological disorders than those who are not. The bond between those children and their mothers is compromised from the moment of conception, and that often results in abusive parenting and neglect—both of which I experienced to the fullest extent. The brownstone I was raised in before Mommy moved to Brevoort was a horror house. My mother was raped there. I was conceived there. I was sexually abused there. Children became addicted to drugs there. My grandmother became an alcoholic there.

For years, I blamed myself for much of the terrible treatment I had received. All I could think about was the pain I had experienced. I kept crying, hoping my tears would wash the pain from my heart. *Why doesn't anyone love me? Why doesn't my mother want me? What is wrong with me?* I asked myself those questions for decades, but I never found answers until I spoke with Leo.

I get it now, I realized. Nothing I had experienced as a child really had anything to do with me. I was not responsible for the pain and abuse that occurred all around me any more than I was responsible for the way I was conceived. For the first time in my life, I felt truly sorry for Niecy, but now I couldn't even tell her that, because she had already been dead for so long. What I *could* do was turn my anger into empathy, and I could start forgiving everybody in my family who had hurt me: my mother, my father, Leo, and Cherry. The generational trauma that had been passed down to me was going to end with me. I could promise myself that.

One day in December 2019, I was watching TV in bed when I received a three-way call from my daughters. They revealed to me that their grandmother—the mother of the man who shot me—was at death's door. She had several different types of cancer and evidently only had a week to live.

At first, I couldn't understand why Morgan and Melissa were calling to tell me about their grandmother's condition. This was a woman who had mistreated me from the first moment her son, Larry, introduced me to her. She had watched him beat me and never once intervened. She had initially denied that Larry was my younger daughter's father and said she wished he had killed me. When he shot me and she knew I had nowhere to go, she had thrown me out of the house because I wouldn't sign a letter saying I'd shot myself, and then she had forged that letter anyway.

All of those times she had hurt me stood on one side of my thinking. My daughters' heartache stood on the other. I got very quiet and said to myself, *Lord, help me.*

Because of my love for my girls, I asked them what they needed from me.

"We need our mother," they said.

I bit my tongue hard as I thought, *They're crazy if they think I'm going to help that woman in any way.* But helping her wasn't about me—it was about being a supportive mother to my daughters. Taking a deep breath, I told them I would catch a flight to see them in the city where both Morgan and the girls' grandmother lived. I continued to ask God for strength as I let my team know that I had a family emergency.

I knew that when I arrived, I would have to see not only the grandmother but also the man who had tried to kill me. I didn't know how I would handle coming face-to-face with him after all those years and all that suffering. The Lord reminded me that I must not have forgiven Larry yet, because if I had, I would not have questioned how to act in the environment I was thrusting myself into.

As fate would have it, two days before I was supposed to travel, Larry's mother passed away. I flew down South anyway to support Morgan and Melissa.

I was in their aunt's kitchen when Larry walked in with his

third wife by his side. I barely looked at her; the man who had tried to murder me, and whom I had thought I would never see again, was standing right in front of me.

I acknowledged him only with my eyes, not with my voice. I took in the shell of a man he had become: worn and weathered and dull skinned. After Larry was released from prison, his life had apparently hit rock bottom, hard. He was unemployable because of his criminal record and had been living off his mother for years. Now that she was dead, he was about to be homeless. And when he saw me that day, I imagined that he was thinking about the last time he had seen me: unconscious, lying in a pool of my own blood in his bathroom, destined for a grave in his backyard. Yet somehow I felt no compulsion to speak to him, to give him even a moment of my time. I was so far past all that, it wouldn't even have been the same Katrina. I was in the kitchen with him for no more than one minute before I excused myself. "I'm leaving," I said to my daughters, and they followed me out.

I found out from my girls the next day that Larry had packed his bags early that morning and left with his wife. The man who had shot *me* ten times and left *me* for dead was unable to be in *my* company. *Well*, I thought, *if that isn't ironic, I don't know what is.*

I decided not to go to Larry's mother's wake or funeral. I stayed at Morgan's house for a few days after the services just to make sure my daughters were both okay. They both returned to work quickly, and I headed back to New York. My job was done. I was at peace.

As I traveled home, I spoke candidly with God: "You said You would never leave or forsake me, Lord. And You didn't. Thank You."

I knew the only way I could have gotten through the entire experience was by the power of God. The peaceful feeling that came over me shortly after my departure was an indication that

AND THEN CAME THE BLUES

I had forgiven Larry and his mother. It was one of the hardest things I have ever had to do. Many people will never understand why I did it at all, yet I have learned that forgiveness allows us to regain our control. Once I let go of all the grudges I had been holding, I was infinitely lighter. I was free from the power my abusers had had over me since my childhood. I finally felt delivered, like a bird that has spread her wings and taken off flying to a place where she can be free.

CHAPTER 35

Thank You, Rats

On July 4, 2021, I woke up in the middle of the night to a message from God that would change my life forever. "I'm going to send you this man," I heard Him say. He showed me a mental image of a handsome gentleman with a nice smile and a salt-and-pepper beard.

Someone I had dated a while earlier fit that description. I asked, "God, did I do wrong by ending things with him? Is he the guy I'm supposed to be with?"

As He always did, God said, "Trust me."

Exactly one year later, on the Fourth of July 2022, that guy FaceTimed me out of the blue. As soon as I saw him on my phone screen, I was wondering if he was the man God had chosen for me. But right away, I heard God say, loud and clear, "Not him."

But it's got to be him, I thought. This guy looked like my vision.

"Not him," God repeated.

Okay, okay. But then who is it?

Three months later, in October 2022, I was flying all over the United States, doing various speaking engagements about domestic violence. Right before Halloween, I was in New York to take my friend to a Beres Hammond concert for her birthday. After that, I planned to return to my house in the South and stay there for two weeks. But before I left, I had a rodent issue to contend with.

It's no secret that New York City has more rats than people. The rats on my block had started tunneling under the building adjacent to mine. The owner of that building lived in Nigeria, so I knew the issue wasn't going to resolve itself. And, rats being rats, I also knew that if my neighbor had a rat problem, it wouldn't be long before I had the same problem.

The morning of October 30, I woke up telling myself, *You gotta deal with the rats*. It was the last thing I wanted to do on a Saturday, but I was flying south the next day, so off I went to the Home Depot to buy some traps for my building.

I found what I needed and was standing in the self-checkout line when I heard a man's voice say something indecipherable to me from one of the nearby registers.

I barely turned around. *He's not talking to me*, I thought. *And even if he is, I don't want him to be. I don't even want him looking at me.* By then I was so entrenched in my work with God that my vow not to date or have sex was stronger than ever.

I walked out of the store after I paid for my rattraps, and as I reached the exit of the Home Depot, I felt something like a wind whispering to me—something that I couldn't understand but that disoriented me so thoroughly that I couldn't remember where I had parked my rental car. My legs felt nearly disconnected from my feet as I began wandering around the parking lot.

Soon, I heard the voice of the man from the checkout line close behind me, and now I could understand every word he was saying to me. "You're not going to give me your phone number?" he asked, in a British-sounding accent.

Without turning around, I said, "Nope." I picked up my

pace as I continued to wonder, *Where did I park that stupid car?*

The man spoke again: "You're really not going to give me your phone number?"

I rolled my eyes. *Is this guy for real?* I shouldn't even have responded, but maybe he was hard of hearing, so I repeated, "No, sir, I'm not going to give you my number."

A minute later, when I could sense that he was still behind me, I stopped walking and put my hand on the car closest to me. This time, I did turn around, but I kept my eyes lowered as I said, "Please stop following me. I'm just trying to find my car."

"You don't know what you did with your car?" he asked, as if he were an old friend of mine.

"No."

"*And* you're not going to give me your phone number?"

"No."

"Pretty pleeease?" he said, in the tone of a whiny child.

At that, we both burst out laughing, and the moment gave me enough of a break from my daze to really look at the car that my hand was on—which was when I realized that it was my very own rental car.

What in God's name is going on right now? I thought, as I unlocked the driver's-side door and slid into the low seat as quickly as I could.

The man was standing over me. I still refused to look at him. When he asked me again, "What's your number?" I knew he wasn't going to give up, so I tried a different approach. I thought, *I'll just give him a fake number.* Seconds later, I realized, *No, that won't work—he's going to call that number right now, and then I'll be busted.* So I decided, *I'm going to give him my real number and just block him as soon as he calls me for the first time.*

After I gave it to him, I practically peeled out of that parking lot, thinking, *What I wouldn't give to have a squad car right now.*

I hadn't even reached the Home Depot exit when my phone rang. I always answer incoming calls, so I said, "Hello?"

"Hello, my dear," I heard a man with a British accent say. "My name is Beau." And I just started laughing.

"What's so funny?" he asked.

After that, we started really talking. We talked about everything we could think of—not anything too personal or serious, but enough to keep us laughing and enough for me to realize that our vibe was different right away. We didn't stop for the next six hours. By the time we hung up that night, I knew it was going to be even harder to get rid of Beau than it would be to get rid of my neighbor's rats. The difference was, I liked him a whole lot more than I liked them.

Two days later, I was back in the South when Beau called me and said, "Would you mind if we FaceTimed?"

"Okay," I replied. *I need to get a good look at this guy anyway.* By that point, I was beginning to feel strange that I hadn't once looked at his face when we had met, and I was growing more and more curious.

"I'll call you right now," he said.

When I saw that man's face on my screen, my phone slipped right out of my hands and fell on the floor. As I scrambled around, trying to grab it, I kept saying, "Hold on, hold on, hold on a minute."

I finally picked the phone back up and held it in front of my face.

"Is everything all right?" Beau asked.

"Everything's okay," I said, but he could tell something was distracting me. "You know what? Matter of fact, I'm going to call you back in a minute."

As soon as I hung up, I started hyperventilating. I was dripping with sweat. Because the man who had just FaceTimed me was the man God had shown me in my dream on the Fourth of July 2021—fifteen months earlier. It wasn't the man I had dated after all—the man about whom God had said, "Not him." No, it was Beau.

After a few minutes, I felt well enough to call him back. This time when he asked if I was okay, I said yes and he believed me. From there, we had a series of beautiful daily conversations, just vibing and vibing. Everything was going so well that I figured something had to go wrong.

That happened after a week, when Beau said, "I looked you up online."

"What do you mean?"

"Yeah, I did. I know who you are."

You know who I am? Great. I knew this was too good to be true. And now Brooklyn came out of me. "Nah," I said, "You did *what?* Why would you do that? That's very creepy, you know. I can't talk to you anymore. I'm going to hang up now."

When I ended the call, I had to take several deep breaths. *Now what?* I thought. *God, I'm going to need another sign, because I don't understand anything about Your plan for me right now.*

Over the next three days, I couldn't stop thinking about Beau, though I wasn't anywhere close to being ready to speak to him again. He called me once, but I didn't respond. Then God stepped in and told me, "You need to call him. Call him today."

I dialed Beau's number, and he picked up on the first ring. "Before you say anything," he said, "I just want to apologize and explain myself."

"You googled me. Why did you have to do that?"

"No, Katrina, I never googled you. All I did was look on your social media accounts."

Oops, I thought. *My bad.*

Beau continued, "I see that you do some really great things: helping women in your community, speaking as an advocate all over the country—"

"Wait," I interrupted. "You're not talking about the fact that I got shot?"

Beau paused for several seconds. "Huh?"

Oh no, I thought, shaking my head. *God, this is all messed up. Now I have to tell him what he wasn't even looking for in the first place!*

I took a deep breath. "Beau, I have a story for you," I said, and I told him everything—everything I had hidden about myself during my entire career with the NYPD; everything I had concealed from even my closest friends and relatives.

Beau just listened. "I'm so sorry that happened to you," he said. "You're the strongest woman I've ever met."

In early November, I had another dream about a man—the same bearded man God had shown me in my dream on July 4, 2021. But in this vision, the man was wearing distinctive glasses with progressive lenses. *Is this even the same person?* I asked myself.

I got my answer shortly after Thanksgiving, when Beau FaceTimed me. This time, he was wearing a distinctive pair of glasses—the very same ones God had shown me. And I just started crying.

"Katrina, my dear, what's wrong?" Beau asked. "Did I do something?"

"You didn't do anything," I said through my tears.

"Then why are you crying?"

I couldn't give him an answer, yet that night when I went to bed, I heard God say to me, "I told you I was going to send you a husband."

Three days after that, Beau lost those glasses. He had had them for years, but it turned out their true purpose was to be a confirmation from God that I was meant to be with their owner.

On Valentine's Day 2023, Beau and I were in the TWA Hotel

at JFK Airport. He had flown me in, booked the room for me, and taken me to dinner. I asked him to stay with me and leave in the morning. He agreed, with one caveat: "God told me not to touch you until you're my wife."

I had already known that Beau, too, was practicing celibacy and had been for some months before he met me. He had decided he wasn't being fulfilled by any of his physical relationships with women, and that he would trust that God gives us the things we want when we request them authentically enough. He gives us the desires of our hearts. If we ask Him to bring us a spouse who can honor a commitment to celibacy, He will deliver that to us eventually. Beau had been listening to God's voice as much as I had.

On April 27, 2023, Beau and I had just returned to Brooklyn from visiting his family in Trinidad and Tobago, where he grew up. I was cooking a healthy dinner for us in my apartment—fish, avocado, and salad—while he sat in the kitchen, keeping me company. I noticed his eyes watering as he began to talk about the past few months he and I had spent together—about how much he had enjoyed our time, about how much he had grown as a person.

Well, that's nice to hear, I thought, keeping one eye on the snapper while I smiled at him.

Then he said, "My friend Danny needs me to take him to get something. Will you come to his house with me?"

I tried not to sigh as I thought about the shower I would have to take to get the smell of fish off my skin. "Okay," I answered. "But first I need to get myself together, change my clothes, and clean the kitchen."

"I'll do that," Beau said, rising from his stool.

I raised an eyebrow at him. *He sure is in a good mood. He's never offered to clean my kitchen before.* I hurried to my bedroom before he could change his mind.

Twenty minutes later, I was dressed in a black velour sweatsuit and sitting on the floor of my closet, putting on my sneakers.

When I came out, I went into my living room and sat on an ottoman. Beau came over to me and said, "I need to talk to you."

I knew he was off his game tonight, I thought, feeling my lower lip begin to tremble. Even though I was already seated, I had to put my hands on the cushion to brace myself for the inevitable. *This guy's about to break up with me. I can't believe this.*

I frowned up at him, thinking about what a fool he was. Then I noticed that his hands were shaking. He kneeled down on the floor next to the ottoman. He started sort of mumbling, but I couldn't understand a word. I finally said, "Dude, what are you doing? Get up. Land the plane."

Beau stood, pulling me up with him. I didn't even notice at first that he had reached into his back pocket and pulled out a small box, because I was still focused on trying to figure out what he was getting at. But the next time he opened his mouth, his words were loud and clear: "Katrina, I know we've been together for only a short time, but I just love you. I love everything about you. And I want to spend the rest of my life with you. Will you marry me?"

I said, "Huh?" I looked down and saw a three-carat, princess-cut diamond. *What is happening right now? Is this even real?*

Then I looked at his face, and that was all the reassurance I needed that he wasn't playing around. And then I said yes and gave him a kiss. "Wait." I held up my right hand. "So, are we not going to Danny's?"

Beau laughed. "No. That was all a setup."

My whole head was buzzing. I needed air. "Okay, Beau. I'll be right back. I need to go outside."

I left the house as quickly as I could and just started walking and crying, walking and crying. At first, I didn't even know where I was going. I just said, "God, no. This is not happening. For real, God? I can't believe this. You're really giving me a husband?" I stopped in my tracks, thinking of another question. "And why would You have let me build this house by myself if a man was going to end up living in it with me?"

"Because I had to train you," God said. "I had to train you not to depend on a man but to depend on Me."

"Well, then the joke's on me, isn't it?" I chuckled. I also realized exactly where I needed to go: the liquor store. I walked in, spotted a drink that I liked—a premixed cosmopolitan cocktail made by 50 Cent and Effen Vodka—and grabbed a small bottle off the shelf.

I was gone for half an hour. I didn't even have my phone with me; I had left it on my kitchen counter. By the time I got home, Beau was pacing. "What happened? Where did you go? Why didn't you take your phone?"

I just said, "I had to go talk to God. But in the process, I also stopped at the liquor store. I need to make me a cocktail, because this is too crazy. Want one?"

We each had a drink and then went to bed. But after Beau fell asleep, I was still awake. I kept holding up my left hand in our dark bedroom. I had the TV on, and it gave off just enough light for me to see my diamond gleaming.

Oh my God, I practically screamed to myself, *I'm going to be somebody's wife! And it ain't a jail wife—this is for real!*

Had I been engaged several other times? I had, but to men I wasn't meant to be with.

Had I been married before? I had, but to an inmate who could never show me what wedded life outside bars would look like.

Would Beau and I have to learn to adjust to each other? Of course we would, but I knew we could do it.

I remembered having once talked with God about this book. I had been trying to preserve what I thought was my dignity by not including every dirty, heart-crushing detail of my life to date. But God wouldn't let me get away with that. "Nah," He kept saying, "that's not how I want you to tell it. I need you to tell the whole story." And eventually I did as He asked.

Even though I knew I had a success story, however, something was still missing. The conclusion didn't feel right to me. I couldn't just end by saying, "I'm happy and healthy now, but I never did find the right man, even after years of becoming whole and healed on my own." So I had to ask: "God, why can't my book have a happily ever after ending? Wouldn't it be more powerful if I got married in the end?"

Some dreams do come true.

EPILOGUE

When It's All Said and Done

For many years, the agony of having been rejected and abandoned by my mother and father was something I didn't have the words to explain. I used to watch all my friends with their parents and wish I had a mom or a dad too. It took me a long time to accept that I would never know what that kind of love felt like, and that a part of me would always be missing. In arriving at that point of acceptance, however, I also realized I had the ability to use my past experiences as tools to create a better future for myself and my family.

I began to understand that being sexually abused by Cherry had taken away much of my innocence and self-esteem. Since I didn't know who my father was, I was also extremely distrustful of men. And the fact that the person who took my virginity—and took advantage of a thirteen-year-old girl who had no maturity or wisdom—was a grown man didn't help matters.

Once I was old enough to start making some of these connections, I could pull myself slightly out from under the dark cloud that had overshadowed me for so long. I had to teach myself how to value my body and soul so that I could forge ahead and create some kind of success in my life. However, because of the depths of my suffering, I was still constantly looking for love and validation. That led me to marry a convicted murderer, just to feel wanted and protected. But that still wasn't enough. Before I even filed for divorce from Robert, I had started a relationship with a drug dealer who emotionally abused me in exchange for giving me material things that I falsely hoped would fill the void inside me. I had not yet begun to do the real work on myself.

I finally realized that I had become a mother at fourteen because no one cared enough about me to pay any attention to what I was doing with my life. Raised by an alcoholic with no rules or structure, in an apartment where homework was never checked and curfews never implemented, I was not held accountable for anything I did. So when I became a mother myself, I lacked the wisdom, maturity, and experience necessary to parent in a positive and effective way. Unable to give what I didn't have and saddled by my own toxic upbringing, I brought my daughter into this world not loving myself and not capable of loving her. I just couldn't seem to break the cycle I had been born into. The only thing I could really give to Morgan was the brokenness I had inside me.

In an effort to break free from my horrible living conditions, my loneliness, my purposeless, and my boredom, I got into a relationship with Larry, a man I wasn't attracted to and didn't even like, and ended up giving birth to another child, his child, in a broken state. Feeling even more trapped, I accepted the mental, emotional, and physical abuse he bestowed upon me because I had virtually no family support and even less of a sense of self-worth. My glaring lack of self-love, coupled with my desire to escape, almost cost me my life.

Today, we live in a world where a lot of people operate within a broken space. We normalize this circumstance and operate out of a damaged mindset that prevents us from identifying with anything normal that comes into our abnormal zone.

We need to look into the mirror and appreciate our discomfort as human beings. We need to think about our wants, our needs, our rights, and our wrongs. The only way to free ourselves and receive fullness is to pass solitary time and look within ourselves to the core of what has made us who we are.

It took decades for me to learn that having self-esteem is not an automatic personality trait. We are not born with it; it is learned behavior. If we are shown violence and rejection at an early age, low self-esteem inevitably follows. It was not until I turned my life over to God that I realized I had value. It was not until I let Him take control that I found peace. I live knowing that six bullets will remain inside my body forever. They can never be removed and will remain with me until the day the Lord calls me home. That is my proof that only through His grace am I able to tell my story. And it is only because of God that I have been able to share, heal, thrive, and be an inspiration to others.

If you are still struggling to find your way, give it to God. There is nothing He can't fix or do. He always makes a way out of no way. I am living proof that God's plans are the only plans that matter.

Today, I live according to seven core principles, which I want to share with you, in the hope that you will find meaning and joy in applying them to your own life.

Body: Your body is a gift. It should be cared for and used for positive purposes—eating healthy foods, exercising, resting, sleeping, doing things in moderation, and not sexing it away.

Mind: Your mind is the starting point of every thought—what you process, what you focus on, what you allow people to tell you, and what you believe.

Heart: Protect your precious heart with everything you have. Not everyone you meet or even bond with deserves your heart—it is something that must be earned. When you give your heart away freely, it can get torn into little bitty pieces, depriving you of the opportunity to give it to the one who truly deserves it. It should be kept in a locked box until you are ready to share it.

Success: Achievements are only temporary. They can be taken away. They will know your name today but not tomorrow.

Purpose: Your purpose is who you are internally—your value, your meaning. Your reasons for living last forever. No one can take them away from you.

Kindness: Be selfless and compassionate toward others, especially those who are not inclined to be nice themselves, for they need kindness the most. Most importantly, be kind to yourself. Create and hold boundaries to make room for what your soul needs.

Spirituality: Know that there is something greater than you that allows you to keep going every day. Find peace, joy, and lasting happiness through faith, prayer, and anything else that moves you deeply—not through material possessions.

As of 2025, I still do charity work during Thanksgiving and Christmas. I am also still working with Young Ladies of Our Future, though the organization has become a stepping stone for me to expand my role as a public speaker, life coach, and ongoing inspiration to others. I have broadened my reach beyond young women growing up in low-income neighborhoods. Today, I am ready to speak to the whole world—and not exclusively about domestic violence but also about self-esteem, self-awareness, positive policing, personal growth, and the power of forgiveness.

I am also finally the wife I always dreamed of being. On May 18, 2024, I married Beau, the man God chose for me, in a beautiful sunset beach ceremony on the island of Antigua. I wore a white crystal wedding gown with a matching veil and exchanged vows with Beau in front of my biological family, my chosen family and friends, and my NYPD family.

Our wedding was not just a celebration of our union; it was a celebration of where I come from and where I've gotten to, and of the love I share with many people—not just my husband, but all those who have supported me in countless ways throughout my decades-long journey to find wholeness, strengthen my faith, and step into my own power. My efforts are ongoing, but my path is clearer to me than it has ever been before. I can finally say I am healed and free.

Wedding day!

Psalm 23

The Lord is my shepherd; I shall not want.
² He maketh me to lie down in green pastures:
he leadeth me beside the still waters.
³ He restoreth my soul: he leadeth me
in the paths of righteousness for his name's sake.
⁴ Yea, though I walk through the valley
of the shadow of death, I will fear no evil:
for thou art with me;
thy rod and thy staff they comfort me.
⁵ Thou preparest a table before me in the presence
of mine enemies: thou anointest my head with oil;
my cup runneth over.
⁶ Surely goodness and mercy shall follow me
all the days of my life: and I will dwell
in the house of the Lord forever

Here I am in my reception dress after the wedding.

Acknowledgments

Thank You, God. With all my heart and soul, I love You. You turned my life from test to testimony, and I will never stop giving thanks.

To my amazing daughters: I love you. You are the reasons I never gave up. There is power in the truth, and I pray that this truth heals you. I hope that, at last, it all makes sense

Mommy, I love you. You could have left me in the hospital, but you didn't. Despite your own pain and struggles, you gave me all the love you had, and for that, I am eternally grateful. Your strength, even in your brokenness, shaped me in ways words can't capture.

To my mother, Larniece Cooke: Thank you for giving birth to me. I now understand the limitations you faced, and I've grown in ways I never expected. I've become a powerful source of love, and I wish you were here so I could share it with you. May you rest in peace.

To Apostle Wilbur Jones and the Beulah Church of God in Christ Jesus, where my spiritual life began—thank you for laying my foundation.

To Bishop Hezekiah Walker and the Love Fellowship Tabernacle in Brooklyn—I appreciate the continued fellowship and spiritual nourishment.

To Steve Harvey—your six a.m. motivational talks have been a source of inspiration, reminding me of the power of prayer.

To Assistant District Attorney Keri Herzog (retired)—thank you for fighting for me when I couldn't fight for myself. Your consistent backing, both then and now, has been a true testament to our connection. You've always been a steady source in my life.

To Attorney Kendall Minter—thank you for you legal mind and deal making. May your soul rest in peace.

Gratitude to Dr. Pritchard and the dedicated staff at Brookville Memorial Hospital for your care and support.

To Dr. Montaque in New York City—your years of therapy were a blessing. You allowed God to work through you, guiding me toward healing.

To my current therapist, Delena Zimmerman of Culver City, California—from the moment I stepped into your office, I felt God had guided me to you. Thank you for helping me unpack my struggles and take accountability for my growth.

To Phillip Banks III—your unwavering belief in me, your encouragement, and the opportunities you've provided mean more than words can express. Your love and support embody the true essence of friendship.

To Rachel Noerdlinger—you stepped in, offering your expertise and guidance, helping me navigate the press with a steady hand. Without being asked, you became my publicist, my advocate, and my champion. Thank you for seeing me, for amplifying my voice, and for reminding me that my story matters.

Brother Don "Bow Tie" Muhammad—you were more than a friend, more than a mentor. You were my anchor in an unpredictable world, guiding me with wisdom, loyalty. You understood the struggles and the hurdles of the entertainment business, yet you never wavered. You had my back as my manager, my ride-or-die, and my family. I am forever grateful for you.

To my never-give-up literary agent, Regina Brooks, and her assistant, Emma Loy-Santelli, at Serendipity Literary Agency—thank you for recognizing what it would take to make this book exceptional. I'm grateful for your editorial guidance, for connecting me with a powerful collaborator, and for building a remarkable team around my story. Most of all, thank you for relentlessly fighting to make it happen.

To my first editor, Michelle Valentine—your support at the start of my writing process set the foundation for everything that followed. Thank you for making it such a positive experience.

To the Honorable Minister Louis Farrakhan—thank you for the wisdom and knowledge you have shared with me, and for your unwavering love for our people.

And to my dearest friends—you know who you are. Your presence in my life is a blessing beyond measure. Thank you for the community of love, it's a powerful uplift.

To Sid—thank you for everything you taught me, especially the importance of maintaining a peaceful space. Even though it was only for a season, your blueprint is enduring.

To Sharod Griffin—thank you for getting me to the hospital that day. You didn't just show up; you saved my life. I will forever be grateful, and know that I will always be there for you, just as you were for me.

To Halley and Linda Carter—thank you for introducing me to God, for nursing me back to health, and for welcoming me into your home when I had nowhere else to go. You not only cared for me, but you also brought your prayer warriors to the hospital to fight for my life. Your love and devotion left an imprint on my soul.

To my cowriter, Annie Tucker—thank you from the bottom of my heart. Sharing my story with you has been an incredible experience, made even more special by your judgment-free listening. Through this journey, we've built a friendship that means the world to me. I love you, and I'm excited for all that the future holds for us.

Thank you to the team at Open Lens—Regina Brooks,

Marie Brown, and Marva Allen—as well as Johnny Temple and the team at Akashic Books. I am profoundly thankful for the many hours spent in developing my book and for the dedication you've poured into every step of this process.

Thank you to all my readers. I pray that my story will inspire, empower, and educate you. Above all, I hope it leaves you whole—nothing missing, nothing broken, nothing damaged.

Thank you to all my family and friends who have received their wings. I love you.

Finally, to my husband—thank you for listening to God when He told you to choose me. You are my copilot, my rock, and a true blessing. (And thank you for following me that day in the Home Depot parking lot—LOL.) I love you forever and always.